The Last Great Mountain

About the Author

Mick Conefrey is an internationally recognised film-maker and author; he has produced several BBC documentaries on exploration and mountaineering including the award winning series Icemen and Mountain Men. He lives in Oxford.

For further details please visit his website mickconefrey.co.uk

Previous books

Icemen (with Tim Jordan)

Mountain Men (with Tim Jordan)

A Teacup in a Storm (The Adventurer's Handbook)

How to Climb Mont Blanc in a Skirt

Everest 1953

The Ghosts of K2

The Last Great Mountain

The First Ascent of Kangchenjunga

Mick Conefrey

A Mick Conefrey Book

First published 2020

Copyright © Mick Conefrey

All maps © Mick Conefrey

1955 Colour Photographs © The Streather Collection

1990 Reunion Photograph © Gowron, GNU Free Documentation License.

The moral right of Mick Conefrey to be identified as the Author of this work has been asserted by him in accordance with the Copyright, Designs and Patents Act 1988

Hardback ISBN: 978-1-8380396-2-2
Paperback ISBN: 978-1-8380396-0-8
eBook ISBN: 978-1-8380396-1-5

Typeset by Chris Jennings using Chaparral Pro

All rights reserved Copyright under Berne Convention A CIP record for this title is available from the British Library

Cover design by Chris Jennings
Photograph © The Streather Collection

*To
Phyllis Charlotte Conefrey*

CONTENTS

Prologue 1
The First Attempts 11
    A Himalayan Beast 13
    The Struggle for Kangchenjunga................................... 47
    A Mountain God 77
    Monsoon Story...117
The First Ascent 143
    The Sport of Imbeciles.. 145
    Valley Boy 157
    Dogged as Done It 177
    The Great Shelf 197
    The Big Carry 217
    High Achievers.. 233
    The Long Journey Home..263
    And Then 283
Afterword 301
Bibliography... 303
Principle Sources 307
Index.. 311

ILLUSTRATIONS

Aleister Crowley	15
Map: Kangchenjunga lies on the border of Nepal and Sikkm	25
Aleister Crowley, centre, with Panama hat	28
Porters bringing down Alexis Pache's body	39
Paul Bauer	49
Map: The North East Spur and the glaciers of Kangchenjunga	61
Bauer's team on the North East Spur	65
Günter and Hettie Dyhrenfurth	82
Frank Smythe	84
The 1930 Team:	88
Map: The Route to Base Camp 1930	93
The 1931 Team:	120
The 1955 Team	168
Setting out from Rungneet, Jill Henderson on left	177
Camps on the Yalung Glacier	187
The Sherpa Team, Dawa Tenzing on far right	191
Base Camp 2, near the site of Pache's grave	197
The Great Shelf	217
Map: Camps on the South West Face	219
The Summit Cone	233
Map: The Final Camps on Kangchenjunga	236
Charles Evans	263
Dawa Tenzing, Charles Evans, Changjup at the RGS	278
The Kangchenjunga Reunion 1990	293
En route to Kangchenjunga 2017	301

Prologue

At around two in the afternoon on Wednesday May 25th 1955, a pair of young British climbers, George Band and Joe Brown, found themselves sitting on an icy ledge at the top of a steep slope. Back home, George was a geology student who had recently graduated from Cambridge; Joe a general builder who had left school at fourteen. If it hadn't been for climbing, they might never have met but right now, they were partners, the spearhead of the British Kangchenjunga Reconnaissance Expedition.

While they gobbled down toffees and swigged back lemon squash, the wind blew flurries of snow over their heads as it broke on the ridge behind them. At around 27,800 ft they were undoubtedly the highest men in the world who weren't encased within a jet-plane but they were still some 350 vertical feet short of their goal. And that was a big problem because they were way beyond their turnaround time.

If everything had gone according to plan, they would have been on their way down. Time was running out and so was their oxygen. They had just two hours left, enough to reach the summit, if that were possible, but not enough to descend safely. If they went on, there was no guarantee of success and they risked being benighted, of having to sleep out in the open with nothing but the clothes they were wearing to protect them from the freezing cold.

So what should they do – stick or twist? Carry on up or retreat and hand on the baton to their teammates in the second summit party? Over the last five decades there had been four previous expeditions to Kangchenjunga. Nine men had died, trying to achieve what Everest leader Sir John Hunt called "the greatest feat in world mountaineering". Were they willing to risk everything for fame and glory or was it finally time to turn back?

What happened next is both an extraordinary story in its own right and the final chapter of a much longer saga which goes back to the end of the nineteenth century. It is a tale whose cast includes some of the most talented, most driven and occasionally most eccentric characters in the history of mountaineering: men like Aleister Crowley, the occultist nicknamed the 'Great Beast 666', Paul Bauer, the fanatical German climber and Nazi official, and Günter Oscar Dyhrenfurth, the mountaineer known to his friends as GOD.

Today Kangchenjunga has been all but eclipsed by Everest, but in the early nineteen thirties, it was briefly the most famous mountain in the world. Even in the nineteen fifties Kangchenjunga was well known enough to generate hundreds of column inches in the world's press. After the British expedition of 1955 there was a flurry of books. Since then very little has been written but many documents, diaries and letters have emerged which make it possible to give a richer and more complete account of that expedition and the attempts that preceded it. This book is based on those documents as well as interviews with surviving members of the 1955 team.

It is easy to see why so many climbers became so obsessed with Kangchenjunga. It lies on the border of Sikkim in Northern India and Nepal but unlike most of the high mountains of the Himalayas and Karakoram, Kangchenjunga is relatively accessible and is visible from the hill towns of Northern India. It is a huge landmass, technically a massif, with five summits and numerous satellite peaks.

Long before anyone attempted to reach its summit, it was an object of awe and veneration for the indigenous population of Sikkim. They revered it as their holiest mountain, whose summit was home to one of their most important deities. The name 'Kangchenjunga' means 'the five treasuries of the snow', a reference to the huge glaciers that emanate from its main faces.

It wasn't until the nineteenth century when Britain colonised India and eventually invaded Sikkim, that Kangchenjunga's fame spread further. This was an era when in Europe the cultural meaning of mountains was undergoing a dramatic transformation. What previously had been seen as ugly and terrifying topographical features were hailed as "the great cathedrals of the earth...the beginning and end of all natural scenery" in the words of John Ruskin, the Victorian art critic. The Himalayas epitomised mountain landscape at its grandest and most sublime and with no images of Everest or K2 available, the most well-known Himalayan peak was Kangchenjunga. The Victorian artist, Edward Lear, painted it several times and photographs of the mountain were widely reproduced.

Initially Kangchenjunga was assumed to be the highest mountain in the world and even when it was discovered that Everest was about nine hundred feet higher and K2 about eighty feet its superior, Kangchenjunga was still regarded as a great, if not *the* greatest, challenge in Himalayan mountaineering. Its combination of extreme altitude, treacherous terrain and appalling weather made its ascent a virtually impossible task.

Unlike Everest and K2 which lie farther to the north, in the heart of the Himalayas and the Karakoram, Kangchenjunga sits just a few hundred miles above the Bay of Bengal, the watery cauldron which every year spews forth the monsoon. With no significant mountain ranges in between, Kangchenjunga bears the brunt of the bad weather, with hundreds of tonnes of snow falling on it every summer. Higher up, its ridges are pulverised by hurricane force winds, powerful enough to rip a tent to shreds. Lower down, its slopes are raked by huge avalanches. For any climber, Kangchenjunga is immensely daunting.

The first European forays into the Himalayas were made by soldiers and explorers on intelligence gathering missions but by the late nineteenth century, bona fide mountaineers were arriving, aiming to test their skills against the world's biggest mountains. Would-be challengers to Kangchenjunga were able to train their telescopes and binoculars on its South West Face from Tiger Hill in Darjeeling, the famous hill resort of British India. Few saw any chinks in its armour. It remained to be seen whether it might be easier to climb from one of its other sides.

The first European to try to get an all-round view was not a climber, but one of Victorian Britain's most well-known naturalists, Joseph Hooker, a future director of Kew Gardens. In 1848 Hooker made two extended treks through the region. He was amazed by the Himalayas, describing them as being so sublimely beautiful that it was impossible to convey their impact in words. The first time around, he stuck to the western side of Kangchenjunga, travelling through Nepal to Tibet. On his second expedition he attempted to explore the eastern side but his journey was dramatically cut short when he was arrested by Sikkimese border guards.

After a tense diplomatic stand-off, Hooker eventually returned to Britain and wrote a classic account of his travels, *Himalayan Journals*, one of the earliest books to capture the scale and uniqueness of the region. A few years later, a trio of German scientist explorers, the Schlagintweit brothers, made further incursions into the Kangchenjunga region and in 1883, a young British traveller, William Woodman Graham enjoyed what some consider to be the first purely mountaineering expedition to the Himalayas, climbing for "sport and adventure", rather than any serious "scientific" purpose. He made a disputed ascent of Kabru, one of Kangchenjunga's neighbouring peaks, and contemplated doing a circuit of the whole massif but couldn't complete his mission.

The honours for that achievement, the first circuit of Kangchenjunga, went to a rather more eminent Victorian, Douglas Freshfield, a man whose combination of wealth, erudition and steely determination made him the ideal candidate for the job. His mother Jane Quinton Crawford was a passionate hill-walker and the author of two books on the Alps; his wealthy father, Henry Freshfield, was a scion of one of the oldest legal firms in Europe. Douglas looked set to follow in his footsteps but instead of practising law, he devoted most of his life to travelling, writing and doing good works at the Royal Geographical Society and the Alpine Club.

At the age of 18, during his final year at Eton, he became the first schoolboy to climb Mont Blanc, reaching the summit with a handkerchief wrapped around his ears and his hands firmly buried in his pockets to protect himself against the bitter cold. In the years that followed he climbed many other peaks in the Alps but it wasn't long before his wanderlust took him much further afield.

In 1868, he visited the Caucasus mountains of Russia, becoming the first Western European to climb the lower peak of Mt Elbrus. Later in life, he made a world tour including Scandinavia, the United States, Japan and Africa, and even at the age of 60 was intrepid enough to tackle the remote Ruwenzori mountains of modern-day Uganda. His greatest and most influential legacy however is undoubtedly his expedition to the Himalayas in 1899.

Freshfield had been inspired by a "stimulating sentence" in Joseph Hooker's book on the Himalayas, two lines of text which covered a large blank on Hooker's map of the northern side of Kangchenjunga:

> This country is said to present a very elevated, rugged tract of lofty mountains sparingly snowed, uninhabitable by man or domestic animals.

Could this un-surveyed region provide the key to climbing Kangchenjunga? There was only one way to find out.

Freshfield recruited Europe's most celebrated mountain photographer, Vittorio Sella, and a small team of geologists and mountain guides and set off from Darjeeling in late September, vowing to make the first complete tour of

Prologue

Kangchenjunga. Sikkim had by then become a British protectorate so there was no problem gaining official permission to visit the southern side but Freshfield was unable to obtain official clearance to enter Nepal. He refused to change his plans though, hoping that if his party moved quickly enough and stuck close to the mountain, they might just avoid the attentions of Nepali border guards. In case of any difficulties, with officials or bandits, Freshfield took a detachment of well-armed Gurkha policemen.

Initially, the unpredictable weather was Freshfield's main worry. When he and his party reached the Zemu glacier on the eastern side of Kangchenjunga, they were pinned down by a storm which dumped over three feet of snow on their tent in a single night and caused landslides and floods all over northern India. The storm lasted for so long that rumours began circulating in Darjeeling that Freshfield and his men had perished in a huge avalanche. When those reports were telegraphed to London, Freshfield's friends wrote letters to the *Times* insisting that he was "far too prudent and experienced a mountaineer" to take unnecessary risks but after the death of the famous climber A.F. Mummery four years earlier on Nanga Parbat, no-one was under any illusions about the risks of Himalayan climbing.

In fact, to paraphrase Mark Twain, reports of Douglas Freshfield's recent death were greatly exaggerated. After forty-eight hours trapped on the Zemu glacier he had given the order to break camp and retreat. Freshfield refused to give up on his main mission though. After two more days of "shin bruising, ankle twisting, break knee work" he and his men retraced their boot-prints and came up with a different route, which would not make such a tight circle of the mountain but still allow them to complete their tour and survey Kangchenjunga from all sides.

Within a week they had crossed the border into Nepal and come face to face with Kangchenjunga's huge North West face. It was incredibly vast and intimidating, with a partial terrace running across it at around 27,000 ft, which was blanketed by snow and ice and fringed with the biggest and most fragile looking hanging glaciers Freshfield had ever seen.

The view was immortalised in one of Vittorio Sella's most famous photographs, a huge panorama which stretched for several miles with Kangchenjunga at its centre. Equally memorable was Freshfield's description:

> The whole face of the mountain might be imagined to have been constructed by the Demon of Kangchenjunga for the express purpose of defence against human assault, so skilfully is each comparatively weak spot raked by the ice and rock batteries.

The more he looked, the more Freshfield became convinced that the North West face was just as, if not even more, dangerous than the South West Face. There was one possibility though. On the far left hand side at around 22,000 ft there was a low saddle connecting Kangchenjunga to another mountain to the north known as The Twins. From this saddle the Kangchenjunga's north ridge rose up to the summit, 6000 ft higher. Freshfield didn't actually get close enough to make a full assessment but, as he later wrote, the photographic evidence suggested that though the ridge might be difficult at first "it would not be impracticable and towards the summit would grow relatively easy."

Freshfield had no plans, however, to try the north ridge himself. Aged 44, he accepted that climbing Kangchenjunga was beyond him and as they now turned south to make a rapid march through Nepali territory, he was acutely aware of the risks he was taking on his clandestine expedition. After a very tense encounter with a Nepali official at the village of Ghunsa, he hurried his men back towards the border through the most striking landscape that any of them had ever seen. One day from the top of a small peak they spotted Everest and Makalu in the far distance, but Kangchenjunga never ceased to amaze. As the stormy weather gave way to clear nights and moonlit skies, Freshfield gazed on its slopes "illuminated as by a heavenly searchlight" and found himself surrendering completely to the mountain. "The worship of Kangchenjunga," he later wrote, "at that moment seemed very reasonable service."

Freshfield stopped briefly to visit two of the most famous monasteries in Sikkim at Pamionchi and Dubdi before he finally arrived back at Darjeeling in the last week of October, only to find that some local people were blaming his expedition for the recent bad weather. Fortunately, he did not have to fear their retribution. A long religious ceremony had already taken place to appease the 'Demon of Kangchenjunga' and for the last week the mountain had been gloriously cloud free, both at dawn and dusk, a welcome sign that he had been placated.

Back in Europe, Freshfield immediately began work on what would become his magnum opus, *Round Kangchenjunga*. Three years later it was published to great acclaim. As Freshfield freely acknowledged, he hadn't actually set foot on the mountain but he was convinced that his detailed maps, route descriptions and photographs would inspire future mountaineers to make a full blown attempt. If he had known who would be the first climber to take up the challenge, he might have thought twice. For that man was his polar opposite, an Englishman whose lifestyle and approach to mountaineering was anathema to everything Douglas Freshfield stood for: the gun-toting, sensation-seeking, drug dabbling, devil worshipping, poly-sexual poet... Aleister Crowley.

Part I
The First Attempts

CHAPTER ONE
A Himalayan Beast

On the morning of April 29th 1905, a strange procession set out from Boleskine Manor near Loch Ness in Scotland. In the lead was Hugh Gillies, the aptly named housekeeper and hunting ghillie, followed by Jules Jacot-Guillarmod, a bearded Swiss doctor, armed with a very large elephant gun. He was followed by Rose Crowley and last but not least, her husband Aleister, the owner of Boleskine for the last six years.

Even in the murky weather, Aleister Crowley cut a striking figure: thin but athletically built, he had piercing greenish brown eyes, a mop of lank hair and strangely feminine, heavily bejewelled hands. Although he was born in Leamington Spa to solidly English parents, he claimed Irish ancestry and liked to dress like a Scottish laird.

His visitor, Jules Jacot-Guillarmod, was a doctor from Neuchâtel. This was his first visit to Scotland and he was very keen to return home with two things: a hunting trophy and, more importantly, a commitment from Aleister Crowley to join him on an expedition to Kangchenjunga.

In the six years since Douglas Freshfield's grand Himalayan tour, his book had published to great acclaim but no-one had taken up the challenge to actually climb Kangchenjunga. There were very few climbers who had his private resources or his passion. If there was any hope that the mountain would be ascended anytime soon then, strange as it might have sounded, the two men out hunting that day represented the best bet.

In temperament and style, they were utterly different. Aged thirty seven, Jacot-Guillarmod was a solid member of the Swiss bourgeoisie. The son of a successful landscape painter, he had spent most of his twenties studying medicine, first in Lausanne, then Paris. He was a calm, measured individual who was as regular and reliable in his habits as a Swiss watch. Six days after his eighteenth birthday he had begun a daily journal which he steadfastly maintained for the next thirty nine years, barely missing an entry.

Aleister Crowley came from a wealthier but far more unorthodox background. His father inherited a huge fortune built on brewing but had spent much of his time as an itinerant preacher, spreading the word for the Plymouth Brethren, a fundamentalist Christian sect. He died young, leaving his 11-year-old son, Edward Alexander, to be brought up by his equally religious wife Emily, and her brother Thomas, an uncle Edward Alexander quickly came to hate. The death of his beloved father upended Crowley's life. He never bonded with his mother, who nicknamed him 'The Beast' because he was so hard to handle. She sent him to a series of boarding schools but he couldn't settle. It was a boyhood, Crowley later wrote, "that was so horrible that its result was that my will was wholly summed up in hatred of all restraint".

Aged 20, Edward Alexander went to Cambridge to study Moral Science, emerging three years later without a degree but with a new name, 'Aleister' (the Gaelic version of Alexander), and the fervent conviction that one day he would be recognised as a great poet. Throughout his life, Crowley never held down a regular job but, for a few decades at least, his father's money enabled him to live the life of a wealthy Bohemian and to indulge his passions and vices, which ranged from chess to travel to sex, both paid for and free. Most recently he had developed an interest in esoteric religion and had been initiated into the Golden Dawn, Europe's best-known occult society whose members included WB Yeats and Arthur Conan Doyle.

Aleister Crowley

Though so different in background and outlook, Crowley and Jacot-Guillarmod were united by one thing: the shared love of mountaineering. For Crowley it was the only sport that he had ever really liked or excelled in, for Jacot-Guillarmod it represented an escape from his much more controlled professional life. Jacot-Guillarmod had followed a very conventional path into the sport, starting with small expeditions to the Alps with student friends and then going on to join both the Swiss and French Alpine Clubs. He loved to attend lectures and was particularly proud to have recently begun corresponding with Vittorio Sella, the famous mountaineering photographer who had accompanied Douglas Freshfield on his circuit of Kangchenjunga.

Crowley by contrast had begun as teenager and had done much of his early mountaineering solo. He learned to climb in the Lake District but his favourite stomping grounds were the dangerous chalk cliffs of Beachy Head. Though he once wrote that his climbing style "could hardly be described as human", in his early twenties he had been proposed for membership of London's Alpine Club, the world's oldest and most prestigious mountaineering society. Though he was not formally blackballed, Crowley's unconventional reputation preceded him. His nomination was withdrawn before a vote took place, engendering within him a life-long and vocal hatred of Britain's climbing establishment.

In the 1890s Crowley had joined forces with Oscar Eckenstein, a Jewish engineer and fellow maverick, for expeditions to the Alps and the volcanoes of Mexico and then, in 1902, for a pioneering expedition to K2 in the Karakoram range. It was an audacious attempt to climb the world's second highest mountain, by a team of climbers from Britain, Austria and Switzerland which included Jacot-Guillarmod as expedition doctor. Ultimately it was not a happy experience for anyone.

Crowley suffered repeated attacks of malaria, which left him so delirious that at one stage he had threatened a fellow team member with a pistol. Eckenstein was ill throughout and Jacot-Guillarmod spent much of his time ministering to his sick comrades. Though they had spent several weeks on the glacier in front of K2, they barely set foot on the mountain that would not be climbed for another fifty two years.

Back in Switzerland, Jacot-Guillarmod had been amazed to find himself in demand as a lecturer. It didn't matter that the K2 expedition had achieved so little, everyone wanted to hear about his trip to one of the most remote regions of the world. He went back to work as a doctor but was soon dreaming of a return to high altitude. Jacot-Guillarmod didn't want to revisit K2 though; instead he fancied a crack at Kangchenjunga, after being impressed by the photographs that Vittorio Sella had taken on Freshfield's expedition. Who though would go with him?

Jacot-Guillarmod had a few Swiss friends who he thought might be interested but taking on Kangchenjunga would mean a significant commitment of time and money so only the keenest climbers were worth approaching. Oscar Eckenstein declined his offer; the ill health that had plagued him on K2 had not gone away and the other British member of the 1902 team, Guy Knowles, had never really been that keen a climber anyway. That left Aleister Crowley as his only hope. But would he agree to come?

Crowley certainly had the money and the inclination, but he was recently married and his first child had just been born. The walls of Boleskine Manor were decorated with erotic prints and Crowley's most recent publication, *Snowdrops from a Curate's Garden*, was a volume of pornographic poetry dedicated to his beautiful wife. Would the author of *Juggling with Joy Jelly* and *A Family Fuck* want to swap his wine cellar and sumptuous bed for a freezing cold tent in the Himalayas?

There was no way of telling but for the moment at least, Jacot-Guillarmod had his mind fixed on a different target: a mysterious local creature called a haggis. Jacot-Guillarmod had never heard of such a thing and his grasp of English was not good enough to get the joke, but Aleister Crowley had told him that a wild haggis was much prized among hunters. Why everyone else was smiling, Jacot-Guillarmod couldn't quite understand.

Then suddenly Hugh Gillies, pointed towards a dark shape in the mist. Jacot-Guillarmod cocked his gun, fired both barrels and down went the haggis – or to be more precise, a local farmer's prize sheep. Amongst much general merriment, they decapitated the unfortunate creature and returned home carrying its head as a trophy.

As to the more important matter of Kangchenjunga, Jacot-Guillarmod eventually got a commitment from Crowley that he would indeed join him. Though many saw him as the archetypal outsider, Crowley craved fame and recognition and wanted desperately to prove his detractors in the mountaineering establishment wrong. He had one caveat though: he would only go if he could be the climbing leader. Jacot-Guillarmod could select the rest of the team and be in overall charge of the expedition, but Crowley insisted that he should be responsible for all of the route finding and all of the climbing decisions once they reached the mountain. It was a hard bargain but Jacot-Guillarmod needed Crowley's experience as well as 5000 Francs to invest in expedition funds.

Unlike K2, where the expedition leader Oscar Eckenstein spent months planning every detail, there was no time for complicated pre-organisation. Jacot-Guillarmod would procure equipment and confirm the remaining team members, while Crowley would head out to Darjeeling to hire porters and purchase supplies. It was not ideal, they both acknowledged, to embark without any formal permission from either the Sikkimese or the Nepali governments, but Jacot-Guillarmod was confident that everything would work out.

After their meeting in Scotland, everything moved swiftly. Jacot-Guillarmod returned to Switzerland and Crowley left Boleskine on May 6th, after arranging for Rose and his daughter Lillith to come out and meet him in India at the end of the expedition. He was looking forward to the challenge and typically confident of success but he did take the precaution of recording a will and entrusting his friend and fellow occultist, George Cecil Jones, with the responsibility, should there be an accident, of embalming his corpse and burying it with a cache of magical jewels in a secret vault, along with hermetically sealed editions of his literary works.

In London, Crowley reluctantly consulted *Round Kangchenjunga* by "some man called Freshfield". Even though it contained the only detailed account of the mountain's topography, he was never going to pay it much respect. As an Alpine Club stalwart and pillar of the establishment, Douglas Freshfield was the kind of person Crowley loved to hate. In spite of its 300 odd pages, six appendices and numerous illustrations and maps, Crowley summarily dismissed *Round Kangchenjunga* as a book, which "omits with wonderful ingenuity any practical detail likely to be of service to a subsequent party".

He was much more respectful of Freshfield's collaborator, Vittorio Sella and studied the Italian's photographs in detail. Freshfield had thought the best possible route up Kangchenjunga was probably from the north west but having studied Sella's work and all the photographs he could lay his hands on, Crowley decided that it could be climbed via the South-West Face, the side of the mountain visible from Darjeeling. It looked easier to him and anyway the idea that he might succeed by ignoring the great Douglas Freshfield would make his inevitable triumph even sweeter. Kangchenjunga, Crowley reckoned, would be harder than K2, but it had the significant advantage of lying just twelve to fifteen day-marches from the nearest town, so there would not be the same logistical challenges – or so he thought.

On May 12th, Crowley embarked for the Middle East on the *SS Marmora*. While later mountaineers would use their voyages out as opportunities to get fit, Crowley took a different approach. As he wrote in his memoirs, "I fed up and lounged about, and told stories until the ship arrived in Cairo on the 23rd".

After another two weeks of travelling by ship and train he finally pitched up at the Woodlands Hotel in Darjeeling. He was not impressed. When twenty-five years later, Crowley wrote his memoir, or self-styled 'auto-hagiography', he reserved some of his most scathing prose for Darjeeling:

> ...being the last hope of the unmarriageable shabby-genteel, Darjeeling is lousy with young ladies whose only idea of getting a husband is to practice the piano. In such a climate it is of course impossible to keep a piano in tune for five minutes, even if one could get it into that condition. The food itself is a mildewed as the maidens..... Do I like Darjeeling? I do not.

Crowley's main task was to buy provisions and hire porters to "carry civilisation to the snows". He and Jacot-Guillarmod would be away for several months and though there were a number of villages en route to the mountain, there was no guarantee that their inhabitants would be able to supply food or manpower. The government of India had agreed to provide them with 130 porters who would set off in advance of the main party with four tonnes of food but Crowley hired a further 80 men and bought another 4000 lbs of lentils and rice.

In 1905 there weren't the trained high-altitude porters that exist today. Local labourers, or 'coolies', were used to carrying heavy loads but very few of them, if any, had any climbing experience and even fewer had been to high altitude. Crowley and Jacot-Guillarmod took the precaution of engaging three Kashmiris who had served them well on the K2 expedition, Salama, Ramzana and Subhana, but the other men they hired were all local, mainly from Sikkim's Lepcha community.

In addition to the porters, Crowley enlisted a quartermaster and interpreter: a young Italian called Alcesti Rigo de Righi. Boyish looking and handsome, De Righi was well known in Darjeeling as the manager of the Drum Druid Hotel and was fluent in Tibetan and Hindi as well as English. For the moment Crowley was very glad to have De Righi on board, calling him in a letter to Jacot-Guillarmod "a prince in disguise" who would be "very useful for getting the coolies to march and keeping their price down, even if he never does any heroic exploits". They were words he would come to regret.

In theory Kangchenjunga was close enough to Darjeeling to be visible on the horizon but initially Crowley saw nothing of the mountain, just endless banks of cloud and mist. The weather proved so bad that it took twenty-six days before it cleared sufficiently for Crowley to get out his binoculars to have a closer look. It was a great moment though. Crowley was pleased to see that there appeared to be very little new snow on the South West Face and that the route he had plotted back in London using Vittorio Sella's photographs seemed to be feasible.

His pleasure at the state of the mountain contrasted with his annoyance at Jacot-Guillarmod's late appearance. Eventually Crowley grew so bored of waiting that to pass the time and make a little money, he wrote several newspaper articles for the *Daily Mail* and the Indian newspaper, the *Pioneer*. His first dispatch nobly informed readers of the miseries of the local climate, which varied from "hard and persistent rain" to "heavier and more persistent rain" and "rain so heavy and so persistent that I prefer to leave the necessary epithets to the imagination of my readers".

As ever Crowley took the opportunity to pour further insult on his pet hates: the climbers of the Alpine Club and Swiss guides, who he derided as lazy and incompetent. This prompted a rebuttal in the *Pioneer* from an anonymous correspondent who denounced Crowley as "a disappointed candidate for membership of the Alpine Club, to which I add I have not the privilege of belonging. The sport of mountaineering," the writer continued, "will suffer no loss if *Kinchinjunga (sic)* permanently effaces this polished individual".

Crowley would not be cowed. In further articles he continued to insult Alpine Club members, describing them as the "pusillanimous braggarts of Saville Row" while continuing to complain about the tedium and toil of his organisational duties. Eventually however he became so depressed and ground down by Darjeeling's incessant rain that he retreated to Calcutta for a fortnight.

Jacot-Guillarmod, meanwhile was enduring a much slower and more difficult voyage to India than Crowley, his ship at one stage running aground in the Red Sea. He was able to telegraph some good news though, announcing that their climbing party had two new members: Charles Adolphe Reymond, a former mountain guide and soldier then working for the Swiss telegraph agency and Alexis Pache, a dashing 31-year-old cavalry officer with a thirst for adventure. Pache had fought with the Boers against the British in the recent war in the Transvaal and though he had not done any mountaineering, he joined the team confident that he would get very high.

The Swiss climbers finally reached Darjeeling at the end of July and spent a week with Crowley, unpacking and re-ordering the equipment brought from Switzerland and hiring yet more porters for the long march to Kangchenjunga. Jacot-Guillarmod was no more impressed by Darjeeling than Crowley, repeatedly complaining about its expensive hotels and miserable weather. After enduring such a difficult journey, he was not quite so excited at the prospect of his second major expedition, but had no desire to stay any longer than was absolutely necessary at the Woodlands.

At 10.16 on Tuesday August 8th 1905, as he precisely recorded in his diary, barely three months after the two men had met in Scotland, Crowley and Jacot-Guillarmod set off for Kangchenjunga, after an official goodbye from the local deputy commissioner. They still lacked formal permission to enter Nepal but had been told that they would meet a court official at the border. Before they left Darjeeling, Crowley took the precaution of getting Pache and Reymond to sign the expedition contract that he and Jacot-Guillarmod had drafted, in which they acknowledged that Crowley would be the "only and supreme judge on all matters to do with climbing" and in case they were ever tempted, required them to avoid all contact with women, native or foreign.

The rain continued to torment them, and to add to their discomfort, they were beset by legions of leeches, some "big enough to kill a pony" as Crowley noted. Their first four nights were spent in Dak bungalows, the government controlled rest-houses used by postmen and travelling officials, but after that they slept in tents and improvised shelters, vainly battling the continuing rain. In an article for the *Journal de Lausanne*, published months later, Jacot-Guillarmod gave a vivid description of the miseries of life on the trail:

> In the Himalayas, once you've left Darjeeling and its sumptuous, uncomfortable and expensive hotels, once you've gone past the four Dak bungalows that mark the frontier ridge between Sikkim and Nepal, once you've got the 200 coolies going who you have to feed and pay 1.5 fr. per day, there's nothing more to do than go up, do down, wade through puddles, without a dry thread on your body, singing or yodelling just to keep you going when your soul is dead and your joints are all rheumatic.

Unlike the unworldly terrain they experienced on the approach march to K2 three years earlier, the endless forests of Sikkim and Nepal felt strangely familiar, reminding Crowley of Wales and Jacot-Guillarmod of Switzerland. The woodlands were, however, considerably more difficult to cross than anything found in Europe: dense labyrinths of ferns, lianas, and endless twisted rhododendron bushes, which yielded only to their porters' razor-sharp kukris.

A Himalayan Beast

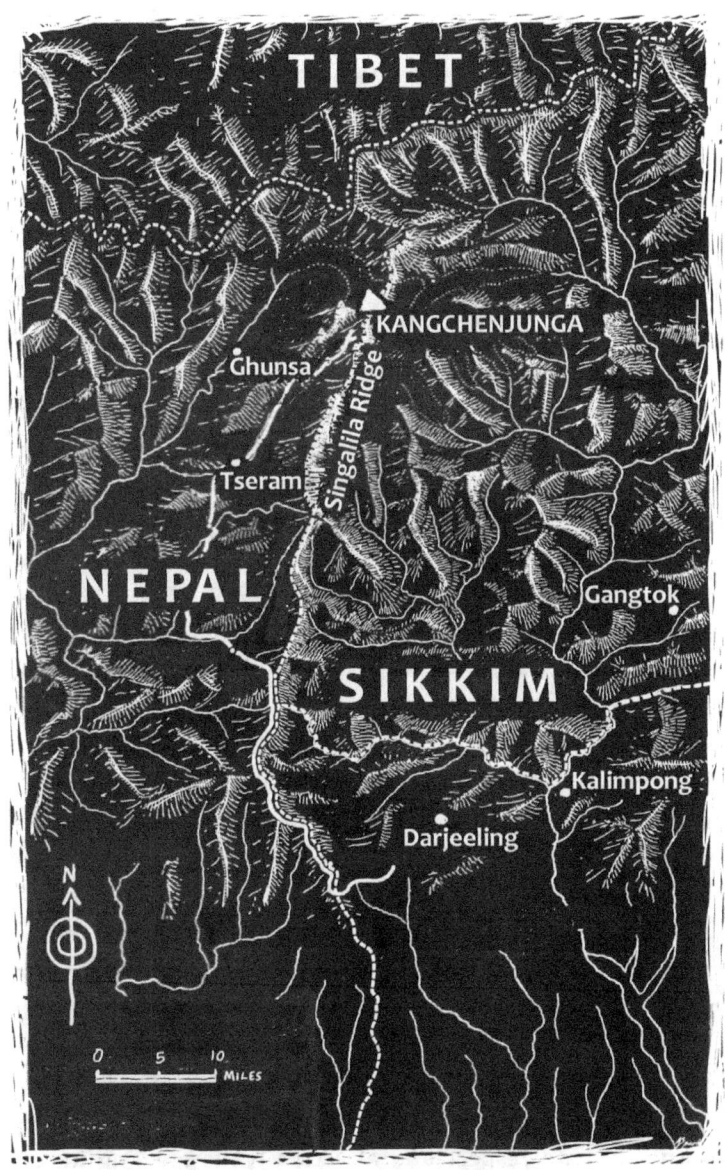

Kangchenjunga lies on the border of Nepal and Sikkm

In between the forests there were roaring glacial rivers, ice-cold and foamy white, and rickety bridges, which needed a strong stomach to negotiate. Just after they crossed the border into Nepal, Jacot-Guillarmod slipped while attempting to ford one particularly turbulent river. He would have been carried away if it had not been for the prompt intervention of his Kashmiri man-servant.

Their Lepcha porters were not quite so helpful. Just two days in, Jacot-Guillarmod had to send one man back because he was permanently drunk. A few mornings later the Darjeeling police arrived to arrest another porter for an unspecified misdemeanour. The remaining men grumbled and complained, and frequently threatened to leave.

Jacot-Guillarmod was shocked by their behaviour, comparing them unfavourably with the tough Balti porters they had hired in 1902 for the K2 expedition. The Lepchas, Jacot-Guillarmod wrote, with no trace of sympathy, needed rice, lentils, butter and spice whereas the hardy Baltis had survived on "little more than bread and water". De Righi, the expedition's transport manager, was given the task of keeping the supply train moving, but in spite of his language skills, he couldn't cope with the daily desertions and repeated bouts of drunkenness.

Crowley stepped in, trying to bring the porters on side by offering bonuses to the fastest carriers and higher wages to anyone who consistently came in ahead of the main body. In his auto-hagiography, he claimed that by instinct he was the porters' friend, declaring, with no hint of irony, that they were best treated like dogs and women – that is to say with "absolute respect and affection while ....being unconscious of my superiority". As for the 130 men provided by the government and supposedly sent out in advance, they were even less disciplined and more elusive than the porters hired by Crowley and frequently had to be chased down by the hapless De Righi.

Twelve distinctly damp and testing days after leaving Darjeeling, they finally arrived at Tseram in Nepal on August 20th. It was the last settlement before Kangchenjunga, a small collection of Yak-herders' huts and rough shelters. They set up Base Camp just beyond the huts and were gifted with a brief glimpse of the summit of Kangchenjunga when the curtain of clouds, which had hidden the mountain for the last fortnight, parted briefly.

"It is covered in fresh snow and looks very hard to get up, at the moment at least," confided Jacot-Guillarmod to his journal gloomily. A day later their first mail runner arrived from Darjeeling, carrying letters from friends in Switzerland and a telegram from the Maharajah of Nepal informing them that they would shortly be given official permission to enter his territory, but after the gruelling approach march Jacot-Guillarmod's dark mood refused to lift.

Crowley, by contrast, felt so optimistic that he could see "not a single dark speck on the horizon". He had spotted a couloir, or narrow channel, which began at what he called a snow basin high up the South West Face and led up to a col to the west of the main summit. "Jacob's Rake", as he christened it, would provide a feasible route to the top. The only question in his mind was whether the snow basin itself was attainable.

Most of the Lepchas were paid off but Jacot-Guillarmod retained roughly 80 men to act as high-altitude porters. As agreed in Darjeeling, Crowley would go ahead with an advance contingent to scout and set up camps. Then Jacot-Guillarmod and the others would move up gradually, carrying all the equipment and supplies needed to conquer the mountain. It seemed like a sensible strategy, but already tensions were beginning to show.

Aleister Crowley, centre, with Panama hat

On K2, Oscar Eckenstein had kept Aleister Crowley's racing instincts in check, insisting that he wait at Base Camp until the whole team had assembled, but this time Crowley was climbing leader and was in no mood to hang around. He'd arrived in Darjeeling over a month ahead of the others and had always been at the front during the approach march. Jacot-Guillarmod was clearly nervous and increasingly wary of the mountain, but Crowley felt in top physical shape and was full of confidence. So he forged ahead, leaving the others to follow in his wake and paying no regard to acclimatisation or the need to reorganise their supplies.

Crowley set up the second camp on the edge of the vast Yalung glacier and then crossed over to the other side to establish Advance Base at around 18,000 ft. It was a good site, a small but flat plateau with a huge rock in the middle, large enough to pitch several tents and improvised shelters. A day later, Jacot-Guillarmod tried to follow with a team of porters but got lost in a maze of dangerous crevasses and eventually pitched camp in the middle of the glacier. Crowley watched in disbelief before descending to angrily demand that he carry on to the higher site. Jacot-Guillarmod refused. It was too late in the day, he claimed, and his men were tired and breathless and besides, it was Crowley's fault for not having put up enough route markers.

The next day both the climbers and the porter team moved on up to Advance Base, but the arguments resumed on the following morning. Crowley wanted to get away early while the snow was still frozen so they could cut any steps before the sun came up fully. Once the snow began to melt, he insisted, it would increase the avalanche risk significantly. But Jacot-Guillarmod disagreed. He wanted to wait until late morning to give the porters a chance to warm up. He'd noticed how poorly they were clothed and shod, and complained that Crowley had not purchased enough equipment for them. Ultimately, Crowley won the day but the delayed start and the onset of bad weather meant that the next camp, Camp 4, was set lower than originally envisaged.

It was nevertheless according to Jacot-Guillarmod 'the most grandiose site you could imagine', a thin rocky ridge which had to be cleared of snow before they could create platforms for their tents. Up above towered the west ridge of Kangchenjunga, occasionally visible when the clouds parted. Jacot-Guillarmod was thrilled to be able to see the summit more clearly but staring at the steep precipices above he became even more pessimistic about their chances and was increasingly unnerved by the avalanches that endlessly tore down the mountain. Declaring himself exhausted by the climb up to Camp 4, he spent the next two days resolutely ensconced in his tent.

Crowley had no choice but to play the reluctant nursemaid, tending to Jacot-Guillarmod and his compatriot Reymond, who was also suffering with altitude sickness. It was just a few days into their attempt but Crowley was already frustrated by what he saw as the slow progress of the expedition. According to his philosophy, the only way to succeed on a big mountain was to rush the summit, so any delay was a torment.

To add to Crowley's exasperation, the porters continued to desert on a regular basis. When he spoke to Jacot-Guillarmod and the other two Swiss climbers about this, they were unwilling to take the strong disciplinary measures he advocated. Instead they sympathised with the Lepcha porters agreeing with them that Crowley's choice of route was frequently just too dangerous.

When Charles Reymond wrote an article about the expedition six months later, he recalled a confrontation with Crowley over a particularly steep section. When he had complained to Crowley, the Englishman's retort had been unequivocal:

> I can see well the avalanche danger, but this is not Switzerland. The obstacles and the dangers are three times greater. Therefore you need to be three times as audacious.

It was a sentiment that would be echoed several decades later by the New Zealander Ed Hillary on the 1953 Everest expedition. He too recognised that any climber who wanted to succeed in the Himalayas had to up their game – and accept a greatly increased level of risk. As he wrote in his diary on the day he reached the summit:

> Whenever I felt feelings of fear regarding it, I'd say to myself: Forget it! This is Everest and you've got to take a few risks.

There was one crucial difference though: whereas in 1953 the British team was able to draw upon a cadre of battle-tested Sherpas, in 1905 there was no such thing as an experienced high-altitude porter. The same men who had carried their supplies from Darjeeling to the foot of Kangchenjunga were now carrying those loads up one of the most dangerous mountains in the world. Many of them were barefoot and those who had shoes sported not tough leather boots but thin cloth bindings and improvised footwear. None of them had crampons. The only way up the steep frozen slopes above them was for the Europeans to laboriously chop steps in the ice and hope they would be good enough for the porters to follow safely .

It didn't take long for the expedition to incur its first casualty when on August 28th, a week into the climb, one of the Lepcha porters fell to his death. When Jacot-Guillarmod descended to find out more, he discovered that the man had slipped at a point where Crowley had been responsible for the step cutting. He was even more convinced that Crowley was moving too quickly, taking too many risks.

Jacot-Guillarmod was equally struck by the stoical reaction of the other Lepcha porters: they said prayers over the dead man's body but seemed strangely unaffected by his passing. Further down the mountain, Jacot-Guillarmod met another group of Lepchas who claimed to be suffering from headaches and snow-blindness but this time even he was not convinced and dismissed them as malingerers.

(left to right) Jacot-Guillarmod, Reymond, De Righi

While Jacot-Guillarmod stayed low for a few days, Crowley had established Camp 5 at around 20,500 ft and was getting ready to move higher up the mountain. Reymond had remained with him and they had been joined by Alexis Pache, the Swiss cavalryman, but Crowley was not happy. The expedition's head porter or sirdar, Nanga, was no-where to be seen and the supply train up the mountain was irregular and ineffective.

Crowley sent a note down to Jacot-Guillarmod, criticising De Righi, the expedition quartermaster, and demanding that he send up more food and fuel. The climbing was going well and they were now making good progress up the mountain but they would not be able to mount a proper attack on the summit unless the logistics improved. "The next three days will be the crisis of the expedition," he warned.

Crowley didn't wait for an answer. Instead, next day he pressed on at full speed. Reymond and Pache were sent ahead with one of their Kashmiri servants, Salama, while Crowley stayed at the back to escort a group of six carefully roped up porters whose job was to enlarge the steps cut by the advance party. For the first few hundred feet, they climbed slowly and steadily. Then Crowley heard a gentle hissing sound – the men above had started a small avalanche.

Almost immediately, the lead porter, Gali, threw himself down in panic. He was helped to his feet by Crowley and the other Lepchas but was so shaken that he tried to untie from the rope and rush back down. This was exactly the wrong thing to do. Crowley ordered him to stay put but Gali just wouldn't listen so Crowley hit him with his ice axe in order, as he later wrote, "to make him more afraid of me, than he was of the mountain".

This rough medicine worked but the terrain in front became steeper and more dangerous, so after climbing a few hundred feet they were forced to retreat back to Camp 5. The incident with Gali was a the final straw for the porters. None of them had any mountaineering experience yet they were being asked to climb higher and higher with nothing but a rope to protect them. If that wasn't enough, the lead climber, "Crowley Sahib", was showing himself to be just as cruel as the Demon of Kangchenjunga. That night several fled down the mountain only to meet Jacot-Guillarmod at Advance Base. They told him they had been maltreated and abused and warned that Crowley's route was ever more dangerous.

The young Italian transport manager, Rigo De Righi was equally disenchanted with Crowley's behaviour. Back in Darjeeling, he had been very excited at the prospect of the expedition but Crowley's continual criticisms had made him feel unappreciated and unfairly treated. As De Righi later wrote, "Crowley might have been a good climber but he was not a good general". Jacot-Guillarmod agreed. It was time, he decided, to stage a coup.

Though De Righi had never been high on any mountain and had had no alpine training, he agreed to accompany Jacot-Guillarmod to Camp 5 to confront Crowley with the porters' complaints. After all the humiliations of the last few weeks, the contract that Crowley had demanded he sign and the arguments over where to place camps, Jacot-Guillarmod was going to take back control of the expedition that he had initiated. He would call a vote to remove Crowley as expedition leader and if necessary call a halt to their attempt.

At 10.00 a.m. Jacot-Guillarmod and De Righi broke camp accompanied by fourteen Lepcha porters. It was a big challenge to get all the way up to Camp 5 in a single day but fuelled by righteous indignation they moved quickly and reached their goal in mid-afternoon – only to find the top camp deserted.

Then through the clouds they spotted Crowley about 300 ft above them surrounded by porters. When Jacot-Guillarmod called up he discovered that his two Swiss comrades, Pache and Reymond, had gone ahead leaving Crowley's party marooned in the middle of a tricky slope without even a rope. This was not what he expected to find, but Jacot-Guillarmod climbed up to help Crowley and his porters down.

Half an hour later Pache and Reymond also descended, very proud to have got about 1000ft higher and to have found a site for their next camp. However, their sterling progress was not enough to deter Jacot-Guillarmod from confronting Crowley. In the argument that followed he called for a vote on Crowley's competence as climbing leader but unsurprisingly his co-leader refused to countenance it. Instead Crowley reminded them of the contract that they had signed and denied mistreating anyone. The porters had to be dealt with firmly for their own safety, Crowley insisted; without discipline the expedition would get nowhere.

Jacot-Guillarmod and De Righi disagreed. They countered that the porters should be treated with "persuasion and kindness", and denounced Crowley as "le Petit Rajah" who too frequently employed "the business end of his ice-axe or the toe of his well shod boot". Crowley steadfastly refused to accept their criticism. For him the whole thing was really about "the feeling of foreigners against being bossed by an Englishman".

Whoever was in the right, it certainly was a crisis moment for the expedition, though not the exciting prelude to a first ascent that Crowley had hoped for a few days earlier. Ultimately, however, Jacot-Guillarmod's High Noon moment fizzled out inconclusively. The more experienced climber, Charles Reymond, elected to stay high with Crowley and two of their Kashmiri servants, while Alexis Pache chose to descend with Jacot-Guillarmod. He had no particular argument with his climbing leader but having reached 21,500 ft on his first ever expedition, just 1300 ft short of the world altitude record, Pache was more than pleased with his performance and ready to call it quits.

Even if they had wanted to stay, there was no room at Camp 5 for all the porters who had come up with Jacot-Guillarmod, so most went down leaving him and Pache to rope up the remaining men. They said their frosty goodbyes and prepared to depart. Jacot-Guillarmod was in the lead followed by De Righi, then two Lepcha porters and finally Alexis Pache and Ramzana, the third of their Kashmiri servants. He was equipped with crampons and an ice-axe.

It was 5.00 p.m., just enough time to reach Camp 4 before the sun set. The Lepcha porters were nervous but Jacot-Guillarmod arranged everyone carefully and though they lost their footing a few times, Pache and Ramzana were able to hold them. The main group of porters seemed to have made their own way down without any assistance so there was no reason why anyone on the second rope should be unduly worried.

Then suddenly, after Jacot-Guillarmod and De Righi had safely descended a particularly steep section, the first porter slipped, dragging down the man behind him. This time Pache couldn't hold their combined weight. He too was pulled off, followed seconds later by Ramzana and then De Righi. Realising the danger, Jacot-Guillarmod tried to take a firm stance but the falling men had set off an avalanche that was growing rapidly. In a confused mass of arms and legs, they hurtled past him, losing their ice axes as they fell towards a large crevasse below. In less than five seconds, the descent had gone from steady progress into utter chaos.

Up at Camp 5, the others couldn't see the disaster taking place below. Crowley had not eaten all day and was feeling very aggrieved at what he saw as Jacot-Guillarmod's mutinous behaviour. He took off his climbing boots and retired to his tent.

Jacot-Guillarmod meanwhile, was battling for his life, desperately trying to stay afloat on top of the huge avalanche of snow. For a split second, time stood still as he was thrown violently on to his back, before his manic descent recommenced. Then just as suddenly as it had all started, Jacot-Guillarmod found himself stopped in his tracks, lying on his back breathless, still tangled up in the rope.

After a few seconds, he followed the rope down to De Righi, who was lying on the snow, seemingly unable to move. The young Italian was alive but so winded that he could barely get up. Jacot-Guillarmod frantically hauled on the rope that connected him to Pache and the porters who had fallen into the crevasse but though he succeeded in digging a funnel into the snow with his bare hands, he reached no-one.

The two survivors desperately called for help but Crowley could not make out what they were saying and had no inclination to find out. Reymond still had his boots on so he descended, gathering the scattered ice axes as he went. For the next hour he helped Jacot-Guillarmod and De Righi dig into the snow but they were unable to rescue any of their comrades.

With night falling and Jacot-Guillarmod's fingers feeling more and more frost-bitten, they reluctantly left the accident site and headed down to the camp below. In the morning they would return but they held out no hope that anyone had survived. De Righi slipped several times on the descent, but Reymond and Jacot-Guillarmod managed to hold him. When they arrived at the tents below, tragically the first person to greet them was the son of one of the porters who had disappeared in the avalanche.

Back at Camp 5, Crowley was still unsure what exactly had happened. He opened his tent flap and marvelled at the view. It was, he later wrote in the *Pioneer,* "the finest and loveliest sunset I had ever seen in these parts…. the clouds lying over the low highlands of Nepal while the mighty masses of ice and rock behind me, lit by the last reflection of the day, stood up reproachfully, like lovers detached, as if they knew that I could do no more."

Next day Crowley descended, leaving his Kashmiri servants and his climbing gear to follow. He passed the accident site and saw the disturbed snow but could not tell exactly what had happened. Then at Camp 4 he met the others and heard their terrible news. None of the subsequent accounts precisely state what was said, but there doesn't seem to have been a second confrontation. As far as Crowley was concerned, responsibility for the accident lay with Jacot-Guillarmod for trying to usurp his role as climbing leader. Once Crowley's belongings had been brought down, he set off for Darjeeling on the following morning, leaving the others to retrieve and bury the corpses of the men caught up in the accident.

It took three long days to complete the grim work of digging them out. They found Alexis Pache upside down, buried under ten feet of snow. Jacot-Guillarmod photographed the porters, lowering his body down the mountain to Camp 3, wrapped in a tarpaulin. As for their comrades, the Lepchas elected to return their corpses to the crevasse where they had died, crossing their arms and saying prayers above them. "The God of Kangchenjunga has taken them," they told Jacot-Guillarmod, "They will be close to him for eternity." Once again Jacot-Guillarmod marvelled at what he called their "Buddhist fatalism".

Porters bringing down Alexis Pache's body

There was no question of taking Alexis Pache's body back to Europe, so they buried him at Camp 3, under a large pile of rocks. Reymond carved his name on a piece of granite along with the date of his death. A pair of crossed skis marked the site of his grave.

Remarkably, as Jacot-Guillarmod later admitted, they briefly considered returning to the fray. Reymond after all had found a site for their sixth camp and with Crowley no longer in charge, the porters said they were willing to climb back up. It didn't take long though to decide against another attempt. Instead, they returned to Base Camp at Tseram only to meet a representative of the Maharajah of Nepal, who had finally arrived to give their expedition official permission.

After a few days to regroup, Jacot-Guillarmod and the others began the march back to Darjeeling. They took a much longer route than Crowley had, in order to visit a number of monasteries and as Jacot-Guillarmod later wrote, turn their sporting expedition into a scientific and ethnographic one. Reymond collected beetles and plants, Jacot-Guillarmod took photographs and De Righi made notes on the different ethnic groups they met along the trail.

After all the strains of the previous two weeks, the return trip was relaxed and light-hearted. The porters celebrated by procuring as much home-made beer as they could find while the Europeans collected flora and fauna and local artefacts. At the Pemionchi monastery, De Righi bought what he thought was an ancient prayer wheel, only to discover that it was made from a worn-out umbrella, labelled "made in Germany". Three weeks later they arrived back at the Woodlands hotel, looking forward to a comfortable bed and a warm bath. But it was not to be. Instead, they found themselves embroiled in a bitter controversy.

Aleister Crowley had reached Darjeeling on September 8 and got his retaliation in first, giving interviews and writing reports for British and Indian newspapers in which he laid the blame for the accident directly at the foot of Jacot-Guillarmod. In the final instalment of a series of articles for the *Pioneer* newspaper, Crowley referred to the deaths on Kangchenjunga as the result of "stupidity, obstinacy and ignorance". He criticised Jacot-Guillarmod for not leaving him with enough men at Camp 5 to render effective help when the accident occurred and lambasted De Righi as an incompetent transport manager, before finishing up by asserting "mountain accidents are always the result of incompetence".

In a rather garbled version of events published in the *Daily Mail* on September 11th, it was reported that four men had been killed on Kangchenjunga after ignoring Aleister Crowley's warning not to go down over "avalanchy" snow. Echoing the sensational reporting of the famous Matterhorn accident of 1865, the article insinuated that either Jacot-Guillarmod or De Righi had cut the rope connecting them to others, in order to save their own skin. The article finished with a supposed quotation from Crowley:

> I am not altogether disappointed with the present results. I know enough to make certain of success another year with a properly equipped and disciplined expedition.

When Jacot-Guillarmod and De Righi read the reports, they were livid. De Righi immediately wrote a rebuttal for the *Pioneer*, denying that there had been any logistical problems and utterly refuting the accusations of incompetence and cowardice. He portrayed Crowley as a tyrant who had alienated the porters, lost the support of the team and made completely unreasonable demands. "If gentlemen are of his stamp," De Righi wrote, "I am glad I am not one."

With no possibility of a reconciliation, Crowley and Jacot-Guillarmod began to argue about expedition funds. The two men had joint charge of the team bank account, but from the moment Jacot-Guillarmod arrived in Darjeeling back in July, they had been divided over how to spend the money. Their disagreements now grew so heated that in order to get back some 300 rupees owed by Crowley to Reymond, Jacot-Guillarmod threatened to show the authorities one of Crowley's pornographic poems from *Snowdrops in a Curate's Garden*.

Crowley consulted a Darjeeling lawyer and only settled after a few more rounds of haggling. Not to be outdone by De Righi's rebuttal, he hit back with an even longer and more critical article in the *Pioneer*, in which he claimed that after the accident he had not gone to their rescue because he was so exhausted after twelve hours with no food. And besides, he added, Jacot-Guillarmod "is old enough to rescue himself and nobody would want to rescue De Righi".

The press controversy continued for months with more articles in Swiss newspapers by Reymond and Jacot-Guillarmod in which they rounded on Crowley. Years later, when they came to write longer accounts of the expedition, Crowley and Jacot-Guillarmod were slightly less harsh in their mutual recriminations, but neither man ever forgave the other.

It was an unseemly end to what had started off as a great adventure but in hindsight, perhaps it was not really surprising. Though Jacot-Guillarmod and Crowley were two of the only Europeans with any high-altitude experience, neither seemed to have learned anything from their previous expedition to K2. They consistently underestimated Kangchenjunga, behaving as if it would be a relatively easy climb for a small team and paying no regard to acclimatisation.

Ultimately the controversy backfired on Crowley. Future historians either underplayed his role on "Jacot-Guillarmod's expedition" or denounced him as a charlatan. Even if he had been undermined by the Swiss climbers and even if the accident was not strictly speaking his fault, Crowley had behaved thoughtlessly at best, callously at worst. If he had gone down to help with the rescue attempt or even just stayed behind to help the others dig out the corpses, then history might have recorded the first Kangchenjunga expedition as a serious but flawed attempt on a very difficult mountain. Instead it was dismissed as a model of poor leadership and selfish behaviour.

It would be a mistake though to think that Crowley didn't take climbing and this expedition seriously. When years later he was compiling his archives, he tried to sum up his life and career in a series of roles:

> Aleister Crowley: Magus, poet, mountaineer, explorer, big game hunter, chess master, cook.

Climbing was a crucial part of Crowley's identity and if he had been less egocentric and a little less selfish, he might have been remembered as one of the great Himalayan pioneers.

Even though the 1905 Kangchenjunga expedition had ended in disaster, it had arguably been far more successful than the 1902 attempt on K2, where Eckenstein's team barely left the glacier. Under Crowley's leadership they had put up four high camps and reached some 21,500 ft, a significant achievement for 1905, on what would later be dubbed the hardest mountain in the Himalayas.

As for the Lepchas, like all the porters and Sherpas of the period, they were mountaineering's hidden footmen, who played a vital role but lacked the means to tell their own story. Nowhere in any account of the 1905 expedition are the names of the dead Lepchas recorded. The death of five men on the expedition made it the deadliest of any Himalayan expedition so far and sent out a clear signal of the extreme dangers of climbing at high altitude. It wasn't, however, the only lethal incident associated with the 1905 expedition.

In a strange postscript, later that year a Calcutta newspaper included a report on the "Alleged assault on a European". According to the article, half a dozen "badmashes", local villains, had attempted to rob an unidentified traveller. He in turn had shot and seriously wounded two of them before they fled.

That mysterious European was Aleister Crowley. Like that later anti-establishment hero Hunter S. Thompson, Crowley was very keen on guns. He had a case full of rifles and shotguns back at Boleskine and when travelling usually carried a Webley .38 for self-protection. The attack in Calcutta, Crowley later wrote, was only the latest in a series of "outrages against Europeans, but I was the only outragee who came out on top".

Crowley never went on any further expeditions but even in the late 1920s when at the height of his decadence and drug-taking he was running a commune on the island of Sicily, he still regularly took his guests climbing in the local hills. When seven porters were killed on the 1922 Everest expedition, he wrote a highly critical letter to the British press, complaining that it was a re-run of Kangchenjunga and that as in 1905, the real mistake was to have roped everyone up.

Three years later Crowley came up with his own plan to climb Everest accompanied by the notorious American journalist, alcoholic and certified madman, William Seabrook. Crowley envisaged hiring a pilot to drop them off on Everest's south east glacier with all the necessary tents and supplies. Having built up their health to the utmost, they would then attempt to "rush the mountain".

Nothing came of it and Crowley never returned to the Himalayas, but in 1929, a full twenty-four years after the 1905 expedition, he was contacted by a German climber who was equally bent on climbing "the five treasuries of the snow". His name was Paul Bauer, and his attempt on Kangchenjunga in 1929 would be described by the Alpine Journal "a feat without parallel, perhaps, in all the annals of mountaineering."

CHAPTER TWO
The Struggle for Kangchenjunga

In the summer of 1922, Dr Gustav Muller, a prominent official of the Alpenverein, the Austro-German Alpine Club, rose to the podium to pose a series of questions to the club's annual assembly:

> What is the source of the mountains' attraction, their value for and influence upon us? How come even those mountains that could fill us with terror attract us with all their might? How come especially our best young people return to these barren, wild, defiant, dark fellows and feel attracted by their repulsive nature? How come even we old folks feel happy and content among jagged rocks and glacial mazes?

The answer, he declared, was that mountains provided a space for modern man to free himself from the temptations of worldly success and instead focus on higher goals. Mountaineers, he declared, "desire inwardness, profoundness, ethics, heart, mind, ideals. We seek open space for our soul in the mountains." As Muller went on to explain, there was much more at stake however than just personal spiritual development. Like many other prominent members of the Alpenverein, Muller believed that mountaineering could and should play a central role in Germany's national renewal. Prefiguring the title of Adolf Hitler's notorious book, *Mein Kampf* or *My Struggle*, he argued that mountaineering was ennobling *precisely* because it was so difficult:

> Struggle is everywhere in the mountains... Only when the German people and especially German youth recognize struggle as the eternal law of the world and will search for no other reward than the awareness that they have acted the way they were supposed to in the fulfilment of their duty in struggle, distress, and danger, only then will we Germans again be able to call ourselves a great people and become invincible.

Muller's rhetoric might sound overblown to modern ears but for the men and women inside the auditorium who spontaneously rose up to sing the national anthem, his speech struck a deep chord. In 1922 Germany was a broken country, humiliated and economically crippled by the treaty of Versailles. The Great Powers had imposed limits on its army and navy and disbanded its air-force. Its national currency was heading towards hyper-inflated worthlessness and its industrial heartland was about to be occupied by troops from France and Belgium. Germany had no overseas territories and precious little national pride. It was a country desperately in need of revival, and if Germany's mountaineers could play a role, then as far as the collected members of the Alpenverein were concerned, all the better.

Like a lot of men who make heroic speeches, Gustav Muller was not planning to lead the charge himself, but he knew that there was a huge appetite for and interest in mountaineering in Germany, and that both in the auditorium and the hills beyond, there were young German climbers who were more than willing to throw themselves into battle with the world's great mountains for the sake of national pride and personal redemption. No-one personified that idea more than Paul Bauer, a climber whose epic battles to climb Kangchenjunga would bring him world-wide fame.

Paul Bauer

Paul Friedrich Bauer was as different in character from Aleister Crowley or Jules Jacot-Guillarmod as could be imagined. He was born in 1896 in Kusel in the Rhineland, close to the border with France. When the First World War broke out in 1914, he volunteered for the German army and rose through the ranks from private to company commander. Bauer's war ended in 1917 when he was captured and sent to Britain as a prisoner of war. Two years later, he was shipped back to Germany and demobbed back into civilian life, a moment of searing humiliation, as he later wrote in the introduction to his book *Himalayan Quest*:

> In November 1919, in a station building on the Rhine guarded by coloured French soldiers, I was summarily commanded to remove the uniform which I had worn for five years, and in incredibly shabby 'civvies' issued by the Government, a simple cap on my head and carrying my entire possessions in a sack on my back , I made my way home - an experience, the bitterness of which is only slowly evaporating.

On his return to Munich, Bauer briefly joined one of the militias who battled it out on the city's lawless streets before he eventually enrolled at the university to train as a lawyer.

For Bauer and his fellow students, the economically depressed cities of Bavaria and beyond were painful, alienating places, which only reminded them of Germany's national shame. Whenever possible, they would escape to the cliffs and valleys around the city to camp out and try to forget about Germany's defeat and the privations that followed. As Bauer later wrote, "The city, the whole of Germany which for five long years we had stood ready to defend, but which now had grown so terribly strange to us, lay behind us, miles away... We had fled to nature from a strange world that was crashing around us."

Tall and thin, his spectacles never disguising his intense stare, Bauer might not have expressed himself quite so floridly as Gustav Muller of the Alpenverein, but he was equally convinced that mountaineering was good for the soul. At the very least, he believed, it could teach the classic German ideals of selflessness and camaraderie, the same ideals that had informed his time in the army. In a much-quoted comment,

Bauer made explicit the connection he felt between soldiering and mountaineering:

> When we had to hand over our rifles, our orphaned hands reached out for our ice-axes.

In 1922 Bauer and a friend from Munich headed off for a bicycle-powered budget expedition to the Swiss and Italian Alps. For six weeks they lived in a handmade tent, surviving mainly on provisions brought from Germany. It was a glorious introduction to Alpine mountaineering, which included ascents of the Matterhorn and Monte Rosa and ten 13,000 ft peaks.

A few years later, Bauer graduated and began work as a notary but his passion for mountaineering remained. In July 1928, after spending two years saving, writing applications and poring over all the books they could find, he and three friends set off for the Caucasus mountains of the USSR, following in the footsteps of that other Kangchenjunga pioneer, Douglas Freshfield. Their first target was Dych Tau, the second highest mountain in Europe. They didn't succeed and were rebuffed by several other high mountains but their extended trip to the Soviet Union was a thrilling introduction to expeditionary mountaineering, which left Bauer eager to go even further. Almost inevitably his sights turned towards the Himalayas, home to most of the world's fourteen 8,000m peaks.

In the early 1920s three well-funded British expeditions had gone out to reconnoitre and then attempt to climb Everest but as Bauer later pointed out in his expedition book, long before Mallory and Irvine, three German brothers, the Schlagintweits, had travelled extensively in the Himalayas and had once held the world altitude record for their attempt on Abi Gamin on the border of northern India and Tibet in 1855. The Schlagintweits, had not actually reached the summit but their high point of 22,259 ft had not been surpassed for several years. Bauer was determined to smash that record and outclimb the British.

Though money was scarce in the late 1920s, Germany had the world's biggest Alpine club with thousands of members. When Bauer approached officials to ask if they might help fund a German expedition to the Himalayas, he got a positive, though not over-generous, response: if he and his comrades could pay forty per cent of the cost, the Alpenverein offered to cover the remaining sixty. This still left Bauer with a lot of money to raise but he considered it just one more challenge.

After sounding out his friends at the Munich Student Climbing Club, Bauer put together a strong party of nine climbers. One member, Ernst Beigel, had been with Bauer in the Caucasus and another, Eugene Allwein, had been part of a German expedition to the Pamir mountains of Russia, but most of them had never climbed outside of Europe. All however were tough, experienced Alpine climbers who, as Bauer wrote, had lived through "the bitter aftermath" of WW1 and were used to roughing it.

Each man agreed to cover his share of the expedition costs but there was never the kind of formal contract that Aleister Crowley had drawn up in 1905; Bauer was the unquestioned leader. The others, he wrote, were like the crusader knights of old, "a band of proud, determined, self-confident men… united in fanatical devotion" and willing to submit to "a kind of military discipline and unquestioning obedience".

Unlike the lavish British attempts on Everest, from the outset Bauer was determined that his would be an austerity expedition, with everything pared down to the bone. If at all possible, he proclaimed, their attempt would cost somewhere between one tenth and one quarter of the cost of a typical Himalayan adventure. If any reporter should ever describe them as "the best equipped expedition that ever left New York", Bauer declared, parodying the newspaper coverage of American Arctic expeditions, he would feel like an utter failure.

In the months before their departure, the members of Bauer's team read up on previous Himalayan expeditions in order to ascertain the most efficient and lowest cost options for everything from equipment to food. Sisters and mothers were roped into darning and sewing and each climber was required bring a bag of spare clothing for the porters. The most important thing as Bauer knew, was to keep the weight of their baggage as low as possible. When one German brewery offered to supply them with crates of free beer, Bauer declined their offer knowing that it would require them to hire more porters. Even the smallest items such as sewing needles and boot nails were scrutinized and subjected to the same minimalist zeal. When the British Consul in Munich inspected their baggage, he couldn't believe they were a climbing expedition and classified them as mere tourists because they appeared to be carrying so little equipment.

On June 23rd 1929 they said their goodbyes to their friends and families in Munich and set off for Italy to catch the midnight boat from Genova to India. Unlike Crowley and Jacot-Guillarmod who began their Kangchenjunga adventure as veterans of six months in the Karakoram, Bauer and his friends had never even visited the East and found themselves continually amazed by its sounds, smells and peoples.

When their ship docked at Port Said, Bauer allowed everyone to dip into their slender expedition treasury to visit the city's bars and bazaars only to find themselves ripped off by "baksheesh sharks" who sold fruit and whisky at vastly inflated prices. Back on ship, they sailed through sandstorms and only narrowly avoided a Biblical-scale swarm of locusts. One First Class passenger died and was buried at sea, though whether he was felled by the heat, excessive consumption of alcohol or some mysterious "tropical frenzy", no-one seemed to know.

Three weeks after they had set off, as their ship approached Colombo in Sri Lanka, Bauer received a telegram from the government of India, informing him that they had been given official permission to enter Sikkim and make an attempt on Kangchenjunga or one of the lesser peaks nearby. Though it might sound remarkable, especially when you consider Bauer's obsession with efficiency and economy, he had left Germany without knowing precisely where he was heading, and had done a paper reconnaissance of both Kamet and Nanga Parbat in case his options were limited. When the telegram added that if he chose Sikkim, their baggage would not be subject to any import duty, Bauer's mind was made up: Kangchenjunga it would be.

Even as they arrived in India, Bauer could not quite forget the First World War. Approaching the port of Madras, he recalled how fifteen years earlier in 1914, the German light cruiser *Emden* had bombarded the harbour and set its huge oil tanks ablaze. Its Captain later wrote that he had commenced shelling in order to disturb English commerce, damage English prestige and "arouse interest among the Indian population".

There were many in Germany who felt much more sympathy for the people of India than for their colonial masters, but throughout his life Bauer had huge respect for British mountaineers and regarded the English as "our closest blood relatives in the world". Bauer made a vow to avoid talking about politics or religion and got on so well with all the officials he met that he ended up flying a Union Jack above his mess tent at Base Camp.

As was becoming common practice for Himalayan expeditions, the German expedition's starting off point was Darjeeling but unlike Aleister Crowley, who languished there for almost a month, Bauer and the German team managed to get in and out of town in just three hectic days.

After unpacking and repacking their equipment, they hired ninety nine porters. Fifteen were veterans of previous British attempts on Everest. As with his climbing team, all of whom he knew personally, Bauer insisted on selecting all his porters, rather than handing over responsibility to the Himalayan Club, a new organisation which had been set up by British climbers to help recruit and keep track of Sherpas and porters. He knew that their co-operation would be vital to the success of the expedition and from the beginning tried to pay as much attention as possible to their welfare. After the expedition doctors, Allwein and Kraus, had given them a thorough physical examination, Bauer made his selection from a large crowd of men, many of whom had travelled dozens of miles hoping to get a job. Bauer couldn't speak any of the local languages so he had to rely on his gut instincts, honed by army service, to choose the best men.

Bauer didn't have permission to enter Nepal, so he was committed to climbing Kangchenjunga for the first time from the Sikkimese side. Having read about the trials and tribulations of Crowley and Jacot-Guillarmod's 1905 expedition, he was not too concerned about avoiding the perilous South West Face, but not only did he have to plan a different route up the mountain, but he also had to take a different route to its base. Instead of following the Singalila ridge and crossing over into Nepal, he and his team would first head for the leech infested, malarial forests of the Teesta Valley. This would immediately involve a drop in altitude of 6500 ft followed by several days of ascent and descent through valleys and ridges that barred the way to their promised mountain.

On July 31st, an advance guard of fifteen porters assembled in front of Bauer and Lt-Col Tobin, a British officer who had agreed to act as the German team's transport officer for the approach march. Each man was presented with a 60 lb pack and 15 rupees, which most promptly handed over to their wives who, Bauer observed, rewarded them with a ceremonial white scarf and a parting glass of rice wine.

Three days later, it was Paul Bauer's turn to be presented with a white scarf as he and the remaining German members of team said goodbye to the grandly titled police superintendent of Darjeeling, Mr Laden La, and marched off towards the steaming dank forests of the Teesta Valley. Though as the crow flies, Kangchenjunga was less than fifty miles away, over the next 14 days, by Bauer's calculation, they would march almost 120 miles and endure almost 45,000 feet of ascent and descent just to get to Base Camp.

When Bauer first studied a map of the region, he thought that a daily average of 12 miles, was too little but as he soon realized, for anyone carrying a heavy pack, it was the maximum that could be achieved. Initially he and the other Germans were surprised and rather embarrassed by the relative luxury of Sikkim's newly refurbished Dak Bungalows, the official rest stops for colonial officials. Initially they'd baulked at the smiling servants offering hot baths and freshly laundered shirts but it wasn't long before they too were soon behaving like "perfect English gentlemen".

Unlike 1905, when Crowley and Jacot-Guillarmod had suffered constant and frequently heavy downpours for almost the whole of their approach march, Bauer encountered very little rain. As a first timer in the Himalayas, he was amazed by the landscape. It was, as he later wrote, like a trip through "fairyland" where every rock and every inch of ground seemed to be covered in exotic ferns and lianas which stretched from the ground right up to the highest treetops. Occasionally he caught glimpses of huge peaks in the distance, but for the most part the surrounding mountains were hidden by dense foliage and curtains of cloud.

After eight days of relentless marching they arrived at Lachen, the last significant settlement in Sikkim, and watched the local people gaze with quiet fascination at their baggage. Their porters had been promised a two-day break, while the 'Sahibs' took stock of logistics. So far nothing had been lost and all the promised foodstuffs and supplies from Sikkimese merchants had turned up on time.

A day after they arrived, while most of the expedition rested, Bauer and three other members of his team left the village for the final stage of their journey into the mountains accompanied by Nursang, the only porter familiar with the area. Ahead lay the Zemu valley and then the Zemu glacier where they planned to establish Base Camp. Thirty years earlier Douglas Freshfield's party had hacked their way through the dense forests that filled the valley but since then only one European, the Scottish explorer and climber Dr. Alexander Kellas, was known to have visited the area.

Bauer's outfit included a curved sword bought a year earlier in the Caucasus as well as several bayonets; it wasn't easy however to cut through the dense undergrowth and walls of rhododendron bushes. Occasionally they chanced upon small huts and clearings, which they later discovered were used by herdsmen and traders travelling back and forth between Sikkim and Tibet, but apart from the ever-present chorus of crickets, the forest was eerily empty. When late on the second day they finally encountered a small group of four men and one woman, huddling in a tiny hut, the locals were even more surprised to see these strange foreign visitors than the Germans were to find them. Bauer gave them each a cigarette, a biscuit and a lump of sugar but the Nepali woman just couldn't stop giggling.

Their new acquaintances directed them towards a path which ran through the forest but it soon petered out and they once again found themselves having to force a way through until they eventually found a riverbank which lead them to some open ground at the head of the valley. Dense mist and low cloud blocked their view of the huge Zemu glacier itself but they were sure that this was the end of the rainforests.

Having found the route in, Bauer was now ready for the main party to move up and establish Base Camp. So far everything had gone smoothly but when he returned to Lachen, Bauer found himself in the middle of an ugly and distinctly noisy porter crisis. The more experienced Everest veterans were arguing for more pay than the humble 'coolies' and their demands had stirred up the less experienced men too.

Bauer's expedition cash box was an old rifle case, but though it appeared to be quite large, money was tight and he knew that if he gave in too easily, more demands would follow. The Germans had come prepared to do a lot of their own carrying, but Base Camp was several days away from Lachen so there was no chance they carry their supplies in under their own steam.

For two days the dispute rumbled on but Bauer maintained his cool and took careful note of most difficult porters. Eventually he agreed to a raise for anyone who had to carry a load on the glacier itself and a small bonus for the men who were now heading back to Darjeeling but as the next opportunity presented itself, he got rid of the principal malcontents.

They set up Base Camp next to a large tarn, Green Lake, which Freshfield had spotted back in 1899. Its altitude was a breathless 14,300 ft, just 1500 ft feet short of the summit of Mont Blanc, the highest peak in Western Europe, and a higher point than Bauer had reached in 1928 in the Caucasus. After spending so much time at much lower altitudes on the approach march, it took several days for everyone to adjust to the thin air but there was plenty to do. While relays of supplies continued to arrive, Bauer and the other Germans built walls from turf and tree branches, to protect their tents from the wind. Soon they had a larder and a livestock pen to house a small herd of fifteen Tibetan sheep purchased from a merchant in Lachen. In order to bless the site, the porters raised a fallen tree trunk on nearby rocks and festooned it with scarves and prayer flags.

Initially the surrounding mountains remained cloaked in mist and cloud but after a few days, Bauer woke to find the camp alive with shouts. For the first time the skies were clearing, revealing Siniolchu, a very striking 22,598 ft peak to the south east and then Kangchenjunga itself in all its glory. As Bauer later recalled, it was a stupendous sight:

> We gazed up at something unreal, and slowly and hesitatingly our hands lifted the telescope, that we might with cold calculation pass in review those ridges and faces which we had studied pictorially a thousand times at home, and which might hold our fate in any tiny notch.

On August 18th, Bauer and a party of four climbers and three porters set off to make their first proper reconnaissance of the mountain. After a three-day march they were high up on the Zemu Glacier, face to face with the enormous challenge they had set themselves.

In front of him stretched two of Kangchenjunga's huge ridges descending dramatically from its summit. To the right was the North Ridge, an extended spine of rock which ran from a lesser mountain to the north called the Twins to Kangchenjunga's main peak before carrying on southwards through two of its secondary summits and then rising up again at Talung Peak. To the left there was the slightly shorter East Ridge, which back in 1899 Douglas Freshfield had declared impossible.

Unlike Aleister Crowley, Bauer had carefully read *Round Kangchenjunga* and had spent a lot of time studying Freshfield's maps and photographs. He agreed with his British predecessor that the most likely route to the summit lay up the North Ridge but without permission from Nepal to cross into their territory, he couldn't access it via Freshfield's suggested route

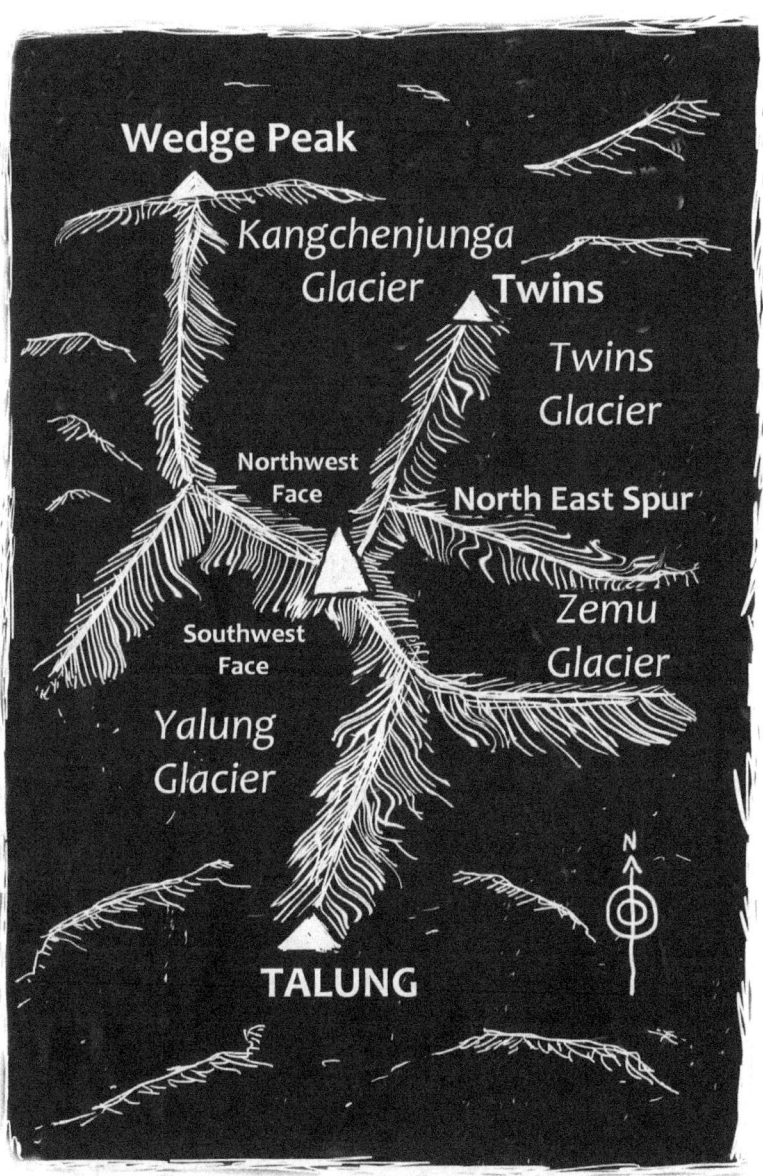

The North East Spur and the glaciers of Kangchenjunga

from the North West. Instead they would have to stay on the eastern, Sikkimese side.

The East Face was too steep for a direct ascent but jutting out into the Zemu glacier there was a high rock buttress which joined the North ridge about 3000 ft below the summit. Freshfield had described it as both "a marvel of mountain architecture" and something that was "utterly repulsive" to the climber. Unsurprisingly, he didn't think it would "go".

Bauer wasn't so negative. After making a careful study of the photographic evidence back in Germany, he concluded that the buttress could be climbed. If all went according to plan, the "North East Spur", as he christened it, would be his stepping-stone onto the North Ridge. It would enable his climbers to avoid the dangers of the East Face and ultimately make a rapid ascent to the summit.

Up close, however, Bauer realised why Freshfield had been dubious. By his estimate, the North East Spur was about 2800 ft high and several hundred feet long. Its flanks were extremely steep and subject to regular rockfalls, and from what they could see from below, the crest was covered in strange, jagged towers of ice. As Bauer later recalled in an article for the *Himalayan Journal*, his first impression was one of sheer awe:

> The sight was terrible. We turned back silently.

It wasn't the perfect start and to make matters worse on the way back to Base Camp Bauer decided to leave the others and take a short cut. Like many "good ideas at the time", it did not turn out to be a wise move. Within half an hour he found himself wandering through a maze of crevasses interspersed with huge piles of glacial debris. With the sun beating down relentlessly and the sky unusually clear, he found it impossible to judge distances. Rocks that seemed to be very close took forever to reach, and he could see no sign of any tents.

When after several hours Bauer failed to turn up, his teammates had become increasingly anxious. Had he fallen into a crevasse? Was he completely lost? They were just about to send out search parties when they spotted him through a telescope, arriving at the top of a distant glacial moraine. Everyone breathed a collective sigh of relief but there was little cheer back at Base Camp. A second party which had gone out to reconnoitre Simvu, a very dramatic smaller peak nearby, had singularly failed to get anywhere and had come back complaining that their maps were seriously inaccurate.

Their first forays into the glaciers of Sikkim had not brought the Germans much joy but Bauer had neither the porters nor the time to up sticks and move Base Camp to another location and still didn't have permission to enter Nepal and revisit Crowley and Jacot-Guillarmod's 1905 route. He briefly considered a change of plan, turning their attention to nearby Siniolchu, but after getting within sight of Kangchenjunga, as he later wrote, "it would have been cowardice to first try our strength on its satellites."

In spite of these early setbacks, everyone on the team was feeling fit and the clothing and equipment they had brought from Europe was holding up well. Bauer paid off most of the remaining porters but retained seventeen of the strongest men, including five Everest veterans, and equipped them with ice axes, boots and crampons and everything necessary to go high. Then a week after their first reconnaissance, on August 26th Bauer set off again for the North East Spur with a larger party, determined to probe its defences properly and, it all possible, reach its crest.

After setting up Advance Base at 17,300 ft, their first task was to forge a route through a dangerous icefall which barred their way to the Spur. Then they started the climb proper. It took two attempts to get anywhere near the top but after three days, Bauer and one of the strongest German climbers, Karl Von Kraus, a medical student from Munich, reached a ledge just 300 ft below the crest. On the next day a second party attempted to follow in their footsteps but they too were forced to stop a few hundred feet from the top. A day later, a third party of four Germans and three porters mounted an all-out attack, but when eventually they got to a point where all seven men were more or less standing on top of each other's shoulders in a vertical line, Bauer called a halt and retreated down the mountain, leaving his deputy, Eugene Allwein, to take a final but equally unsuccessful crack at the problem. Clearly the North East Spur would be no pushover.

Back at Advance Base the collective mood was low. For the first time doubts were creeping in about Bauer's judgement. He consulted his maps and sent down instructions that a small party should take a closer look at the East Ridge and see if there was a way onto it from the Zemu glacier, but even if that were possible, it would be a much harder route to the summit. As Bauer knew, his only real option was to try again. Unlike Freshfield or Crowley, he didn't see his expedition as simply a private affair. Having persuaded the German Alpine Club to part with funds, Bauer felt bound to come back with some tangible results. As well as his own pride, national prestige was at stake.

So a day later, the Germans tried again. This time they succeeded in placing an intermediate camp almost a thousand feet up the flank of the Spur, climbing in the face of brutal weather. A night of thunder and lightning was followed by a day of snow and blizzards but rather than retreating, they carried on into the storm.

Bauer's team on the North East Spur

Higher up, the flanks of the Spur were covered in oddly shaped snow and ice formations, which projected out from the rock. In normal circumstances Bauer would have avoided them, but these weren't normal circumstances. Unless they were willing to take a big risk, they would not reach the crest of the North East Spur, never mind the summit of Kangchenjunga. So they began cutting a path through, not just around, the ice formations. Remarkably, they discovered that the strange projections and cornices were able to hold their weight. Though they weren't able to reach the top on the first day, Bauer was confident that their new approach would enable them to get much higher. Their daring paid off: on their third attempt, on September 6th they finally stood on top of the North East Spur.

Any sense of triumphalism was short lived. No sooner had they got there than the weather deteriorated. This time the blizzards were so severe they were forced to retreat all the way back down to Advance Base to watch as the snow obliterated the hundreds of steps they had painstakingly cut.

To add to the misery, Bauer was suddenly felled by excruciating toothache. The team's quartermaster, Joachim Leopold, had deliberately reduced their medical kit to the bare minimum and had not included any dental forceps, so Bauer's inflamed tooth had to be extracted using a pair of boot pliers. In the end, it took two hours and the combined might of the team's two doctors and its vet to extract the troublesome molar.

Back in Darjeeling, news of the expedition's progress came in fits and starts and was invariably several weeks out of date. When their British Liaison Officer, Harry Tobin, returned to Darjeeling in late August, he was pleased to tell journalists how the Union Jack was proudly flying next to the German flag above Bauer's mess tent. On September 11th the *Statesman* reported that Tobin would shortly be replaced by Edward Shebbeare, a British forestry manager, who had also been Transport Officer on the 1924 British Everest expedition. The same article noted that the Germans had agreed to hold back the names of any climbers who reached Kangchenjunga's summit, in order to emphasise the collective nature of their endeavour. This, the report said, was "in accordance with the highest traditions in mountaineering" adding that the

German party was in rude health and good spirits, "singing mountaineering and national songs in the evenings, fit as can be and only anxious to get going in real earnest". On the mountain the truth was very different.

The bad weather had continued with more snowstorms and blizzards. After all the setbacks and bad luck, other men might have abandoned the attempt but Bauer and his Munich alpinists refused to give up. They climbed back up the North East Spur, re-cutting all the steps in the ice that had been filled in by the snowstorms. On September 16th, a month after their first reconnaissance, Bauer and two other climbers, Beigel and Kraus, stood on top of the long fought for crest for the second time. It was a great moment but if they thought it was going to be straightforward from then on, they were very wrong. The long crest was continually interrupted by tall pinnacles and icy towers up to 180 ft high. The same strange formations that they had encountered lower down were here but on an even bigger scale. The only way to make progress was behave like coal miners, tunnelling their way through the ice when they couldn't hack the pinnacles down.

At one point, four of the Germans took turns to dig out an eight metre *vertical* tunnel into one ice formation that would have otherwise been impossible to circumvent. As Eugene Allwein recorded bitterly in his diary, it was a relentless slog, nothing like the climbing they were used to in the Alps:

> The work was terribly hard and exhausting and after a while one had to adopt the back and knee technique to squeeze into in the ever widening chimney in order to reach the roof, and as you hacked, the loosened snow and ice fell down into your face and over your shoulders while the melted snow water soaked into your clothes no matter how well you had done yourself up.

Not only did they dig tunnels through the hard packed snow but they found themselves excavating small ice caves to sleep in. With temperatures dropping well below zero at night, they found that their snow-holes were warmer than tents. Gradually their icy dwellings became bigger and more elaborate, with multiple chambers separated by decorative arches, and enough space to hold up to eight men.

As September ground on, the German team advanced steadily, setting up three more camps, higher and higher up the ridge crest. Unlike Aleister Crowley, Bauer had several top-class climbers in his team who were able to alternate the lead climbing. Their new British liaison officer, Edward Shebbeare, arrived at the end the of the month with the unexpected news that the Nepali government had changed their minds and had given them permission to enter their territory but by then Bauer was wholly committed to the Sikkimese route and feeling more and more positive every day. As far as he could see, they had conquered all the major difficulties and as soon as they ascended from the Spur onto the North Ridge itself, they would be in a position to make an all-out attack on the summit.

On October 2nd, four of the strongest climbers established a new camp at 23,057 ft on a wide piece of open ground and excavated a large ice cave next to it. Bright and early next morning, two of them, Eugene Allwein and Karl Kraus got away at 7.00 a.m. and moved swiftly upwards until they came to a point on the Spur where the crest dipped down before rising back up to the North Ridge. It was 11.00 a.m. and according to their best estimates they had reached around 24,256 ft, significantly higher than the North Col on Everest. They felt strong enough to carry on but didn't think they would be able to reach the site for the next camp and return in daylight. So after a final glance at the route ahead, they turned back, confident that they would be able to finish the job on the next day.

Back at Camp 10, Allwein and Kraus told everyone the good news. As Bauer took stock, he felt quietly confident. He now had five German climbers and four porters at Camp 10. There were two other members of his team immediately below and one man back down at Base Camp directing the continual relay of supplies up the mountain. In terms of food and fuel, he reckoned that he had enough for ten men for five or six days, as well as tents and sleeping bags to equip two further camps. There was a further 5000 ft to the summit, but over the last ten days the weather had significantly improved. It still snowed lightly almost every day, but there had been no heavy storms or blizzards and according to meteorological records for the region, it was likely that the monsoon was well and truly over. If their luck held, they had at least two weeks to make their final ascent before autumn turned to winter.

That night Bauer decided to celebrate. Ernst Beigel, the expedition's cook, dipped into his rucksack and brought out a small present for every member of the team, porters included. There were cigarettes for some men, pipe tobacco for others, and delicacies for those who didn't smoke. Amazingly, Beigel had even carried up several kilos of fresh apples, enough for everyone to have three each. In spite of their early setbacks, Bauer's shoestring expedition had already done remarkably well. Allwein and Kraus had already set a new German altitude record and if their hunch about the weather turned out to be correct, there was ample time to reach the summit.

The celebrations were premature. As they slept, a huge storm system was brewing on the horizon which would eventually cover not just Kangchenjunga, but the whole of Sikkim. The next day when Bauer looked out of his tent, he was shocked to see that the sky had turned livid green. Lower down, torrential rainstorms were destroying roads and tracks, making movement between villages virtually impossible. High on Kangchenjunga, the heavy clouds that filled the sky were soon disgorging their contents in a snowstorm that lasted two days. Bauer had no alternative but to sit the storm out, but as a precaution, he sent down two of his team, Kraus and Thoenes, and their porters in order not to use up too much food at Camp 10.

Two days later on October 6th, the snow stopped abruptly and Bauer's hopes rose but realistically he knew that the only way to reach the summit was to abandon his usual "safety first" approach and make an all-out dash for the top. He split the team again, sending Beigel and Aufschnaiter down while he and Allwein attempted to get as far as they could with two porters, Keddar and Pasang. Even if they couldn't reach the main summit Bauer wanted at the very least to get from the North East Spur onto the North Ridge itself.

When they set out next morning, they had enough food and fuel to last for four days but immediately ran into problems. Though the surface had developed a hard crust, it easily gave way, leaving them to sink into thigh deep snow. Allwein and Kraus's path from three days earlier had been obliterated, and it took two hours to ascend just three hundred feet. Eventually they decided to cache their rucksacks and carry on unencumbered for another two hours aiming to stamp a path and return on the following morning but they only managed to reach 23,780 ft, five hundred feet short of Allwein and Kraus's high point. For Bauer the view was nonetheless magnificent. To the north and east they could see the far-off mountains of Tibet and Bhutan, and nearer at hand the tips of Simvu and Siniolchu poking out from the clouds below. Bauer was thrilled to see that even their porters, who were usually indifferent to the pleasures of mountaineering, were enraptured by the vista.

It would have been foolhardy to carry on before the snow had time to consolidate, so they returned to their ice cave at Camp 10, hoping there would be no more snowfall that night. The Demon of Kangchenjunga ignored their wishes: it started falling at 7.00 p.m. and didn't stop for the whole night. When they woke up on the following morning it was obvious they could go no further. As Bauer later wrote:

> Within 24 hours we had had at least two metres of fresh snow. This was the graveyard or all our plans. While only a day ago we still had thoughts of advancing, today it requires all our nerve to even consider the possibility of getting down.

Bauer's team was spread out all along the crest of the North East Spur, and if anything, further down the mountain, the situation was even worse. Ernst Beigel and Peter Aufschnaiter, the team's only Nepali speaker, had managed to reach Camp 9 on the night of October 7th after a brutal struggle. They slept fitfully in frozen clothing but rather than staying put, on the following morning they attempted to continue down the mountain in awful weather and very poor visibility. In places, the snow was armpit deep and they were constantly dodging avalanches, one of which took Aufschnaiter's rucksack with it. Several hours later, they managed to reach Camp 8 but on the way down to next camp, Beigel was sent tumbling down the mountain when a cornice collapsed beneath his feet. Aufschnaiter managed to hold him by jumping over the ridge crest to the other side, but Beigel lost his rucksack too, and with it their tent. After spending a freezing night in the open with not even a sleeping bag between them, they continued their descent but Beigel was soon showing signs of severe frostbite in his heel and several of his toes.

On October 8th, seven weeks after establishing Base Camp, Bauer finally acknowledged that the expedition was over but he insisted on being the last man to leave the ice-cave that had been their home for almost a week. After Allwein and their two porters had headed down, he took out two flags from his rucksack- the German tricolour and the Union Jack. If everything had gone according to plan, he would have unfurled them on the summit, but this year at least, there was clearly no chance of achieving his goal. Just making it down to Base Camp would be an achievement in itself. After saying a final prayer, Bauer said goodbye to Camp 10 and left to join the others.

As they descended, Allwein took the lead, sometimes having to plough a man size furrow through the snow. The two Sherpas, Keddar and Pasang, followed with Bauer playing anchor-man at the rear. There was too much loose snow for crampons to be useful but Allwein donned a pair of large overshoes, hoping they would give him a better grip. He and Bauer were carrying 40lbs each while their two porters shouldered around 80lbs apiece; whenever they veered off the path that Allwein stamped for them, they sank down and had to be hauled out.

To clear some of the loose snow, Allwein deliberately started small avalanches but it was a high risk technique and the porters were not quite as confident as he was following in the wake of an avalanche. It was no surprise to Bauer when he felt a sharp tug on the rope. Keddar and Pasang had both slipped. He managed to hold onto them but they were winded by their fall and even more rattled. When Bauer himself came a few hours later, Pasang managed to hold him but by the time they reached the next snow cave, the Sherpas were completely unnerved.

The entrance to Camp 9 was blocked by over six feet of snow. It took over an hour and a half to dig their way in, but once inside they were able to enjoy a relatively warm evening. Next morning however their increasingly anxious porters found the going even harder and were simply unable to get down one particularly steep section. Bauer had no alternative but to send them back to the snow cave while he and Allwein stayed on to cut steps in the icy snow and improve the route.

Next morning they tried again but only after Bauer had been through the contents of their rucksacks to remove anything not deemed essential. He packed the rejects into two bags and threw them down towards the glacier, 5000ft below. One bag snagged on a ledge, the other went all the way, disgorging its contents onto the ice. Bauer was more concerned about the fate of the other members of his team. He had kept a careful watch on the way down but had seen or heard nothing of the other parties, save a note at Camp 8 from the Berliner Alexander Thoenes, written a few days earlier. It was not encouraging. Thoenes wrote that one of his porters had developed frost-bite in his fingers and that snow conditions were so bad that no-one could possibly climb back up the ridge crest to help them.

Finally, after a huge effort, a day later they arrived at the 'Eagles' Nest' and found the others, more or less intact. Kraus and Thoenes and their porters seemed in reasonable health, but in spite of valiant efforts from their comrades, Beigel and Aufschnaiter were in terrible shape. Beigel's toes were deeply frost bitten and Aufschnaiter had severe snow-blindness. Rather than risk being trapped on the mountain in case of another snow-storm, the next morning they carried on down. That evening they found themselves celebrating their escape at Advance Base with a feast of tinned corned beef, frozen potatoes and several cartons of clarified butter.

For the next four days, the sun shone brightly but there was so much snow that it was an agony to get across the Zemu glacier to Base Camp. Beigel could barely walk so they rigged up an improvised stretcher out of two tent-poles. Though Bauer tried once again to cull all but their most important equipment, the porters gathered up anything he threw away, so that one man ended up carrying more than 100lbs. For Bauer the disappointment of not reaching his goal was tempered by the pride that he felt in his by now close-knit team and the way they had performed in such adverse conditions.

Next year, he decided, they would return to finish the job off but even as they left Kangchenjunga, fantasising about future expeditions, the weather went from bad to worse. As they trudged through the rainforests of Sikkim it snowed remorselessly leaving the rhododendron bushes and bamboo thickets swaddled in a blanket of snow. It looked picturesque but conditions were treacherous. Instead of avalanches, they were continually menaced by landslides, which roared down the valleys in torrents of mud and rock.

On October 20th, about a week after they had left Base Camp, and just before they reached Lachen, the first Sikkimese village, they were stopped in their tracks by the biggest landslide yet. As Bauer later wrote, it was as terrifying as anything they had faced on Kangchenjunga:

> The detritus of the mountain, loosened by the rain, was hurtling headlong into the valley. The whole earth seemed to be trembling. There was nothing whatever we could do: we just had to stay there and trust to luck.

After that, they had no further close shaves but 'civilisation' took a while to get used to. When they reached the nearest Dak Bungalow, Bauer was greeted by the friendly face of a British circuit judge, doing his rounds. His first question, whether they wanted to start with tea or whiskey, left Bauer utterly non-plussed. For the last three months, he and his men had lived a very basic existence, but here they were, unshaven and unkempt, entering a world of white tablecloths and starched linen, trying to make small talk with a local official.

On the return journey through India, they slowly got accustomed to the manners and luxury of the British Raj. Beigel headed for hospital in Calcutta to have his frost-bite treated, but the others took the return journey at a more leisurely pace, spending time in Gangtok and Darjeeling where they were feted and feasted.

Bauer was pleased to discover that their efforts had been closely followed in the British and colonial press, though in truth many of the reports were more speculative than accurate. There had been rumours that the 'Abominable Snowman' had menaced the expedition, coupled with real concern for their safety when the whole of Sikkim was plunged into terrible weather in early October.

As the details of their story emerged, Bauer and his men were hailed as heroes both in Germany and beyond. Britain's redoubtable *Alpine Journal* published not one but two accounts of their expedition in both 1930 issues. The second, finished with an extraordinarily appreciative comment from the editor, Colonel Edward Strutt:

> We must again express our sincerest thanks to Dr Bauer for the privilege of being able to publish the narrative of a feat beyond parallel in the all the annals of mountaineering.

Bauer was both flattered and surprised by all the attention and was soon planning a return trip. Next time there would be no equivocation or exploring of other routes, they would head straight for the North East Spur and go all the way to the summit.

What he didn't realise was that a young American might have already beaten him to the prize and that even if he hadn't, a German rival was in the midst of preparing a much bigger expedition. Kangchenjunga might only be the third highest, but for the moment at least, it was the best-known mountain in the world.

CHAPTER THREE
A Mountain God

When E.E. Farmer strolled into his office, William Ladd wasn't quite sure quite what to make of him or what advice he could offer. Ladd was an experienced mountaineer who had climbed extensively in the Rockies and the Alps. He was the president of the American Alpine Club and a respected Professor at Columbia medical school. Farmer was tall, clear-eyed and square-jawed but when it came to climbing, he was a complete unknown. Yet as Farmer soon announced, he was about to leave for the Himalayas.

Though it might be easy to think of the early history of high altitude mountaineering as essentially a team affair, with earnest leaders and selfless team members sacrificing their personal ambitions for the good of the whole, it wasn't always quite like that. There were always individuals who preferred to travel alone with a handful of porters, setting their own itineraries and personal challenges. The Scottish chemist and oxygen pioneer, Alexander Kellas, made eight Himalayan expeditions between 1907 and 1921. On his first trip he brought two Swiss guides, and once he joined forces with the noted British climber, Henry Morshead, but for the most part he was a solo traveller.

Kellas concentrated on smaller peaks in Sikkim and Kashmir but there were also men willing to pit their wits, and their bodies, against true Himalayan giants. In 1890 the Italian, Robert Lerco, engaged a small party of Balti porters and headed into the Karakoram mountains aiming to become the first European to set foot on K2. No-one knows quite how high he got because his diaries were destroyed in a fire, but forty-four years later in 1934, Maurice Wilson, a traumatised veteran of WW1, set his ambition 1000 ft higher, with a solo attempt on Everest. He managed to get up to 22,700 ft, before perishing in his tent at the foot of Everest's North Col.

When it comes to Kangchenjunga, the honours for the first maverick solo attempt go to that young American, Edgar Farmer. As he admitted to Bill Ladd in the winter of 1929, his mountaineering experience was limited and he had never really encountered snow and ice outside of the streets of Manhattan but over the last few years he had studied Himalayan climbing in detail and Kangchenjunga in particular. This he believed was preparation enough to make the first ascent. Ladd wished him the best of luck and wrote a brief note to record his strange encounter.

It's impossible to know what inspired EE Farmer to want to attempt Kangchenjunga or what he expected to hear from William Ladd. He left no records or diary. When he turned up at Ladd's office, Paul Bauer was still at the preparatory stage, so there was no press interest in the mountain. Whatever his motive, a few months later, good to his word, Farmer travelled out to India. He followed the time-honoured trail to Darjeeling where he met a young tea planter, recently arrived from Britain, George Wood Johnson. Wood Johnson also had high-altitude ambitions and had already made one foray into the Himalayas but though he was able to recommend a guide, a Sherpa called Lobsang, he was too busy to take any time off himself.

When Farmer eventually tracked down Lobsang, he didn't come clean about his real mission. Instead he told him that he wanted to trek to Dzongri, the small Sikkimese settlement close to the border with Nepal and spend a couple of weeks photographing the nearby peaks. Lobsang agreed to accompany him and hired two Sherpas and several other porters to carry Farmer's equipment. In early May they left Darjeeling with food and fuel for around five weeks.

Nothing more was heard of the eager young American until Lobsang and the other porters returned in June. They had Farmer's cine camera but as for their client, he had disappeared, they said, while making an unauthorised solo attempt on Kangchenjunga. Lobsang was very worried that his reputation would suffer and that he might even be accused of foul play so he immediately contacted the Darjeeling police and sent Farmer's camera to Wood Johnson, hoping that once the film was developed it would corroborate his account. He could not be sure but he didn't think that Farmer had survived.

Lobsang's police statement was a sad tale of delusion and misadventure. He told how Farmer had left Darjeeling pledging not to cross over into Nepal but never having any intention of honouring his promise. Like everyone else, Lobsang and the other Sherpas had believed that Farmer's aim was simply to take film and photographs. After all, though he had climbing equipment and spare clothing for himself, Farmer had brought no crampons or ice axes for anyone else.

After several forays into high passes overlooking Kangchenjunga they had crossed over the Kang La. At the time Lobsang had not realised that it marked the border between Sikkim and Nepal but it was soon clear that Farmer knew exactly where he wanted to go. After marching them up the Yalung glacier he had ordered his Sherpas to set up a second camp closer to the foot of the mountain. The next morning, Farmer insisted on carrying on, but it wasn't long before Lobsang started to feel the effects of the altitude. Eventually, after a nasty fall when climbing across some rocks, he had told Farmer that he could not go on but rather turning back, the young American simply handed over his cine camera and asked him keep filming as he climbed up towards the lower slopes of Kangchenjunga.

The Sherpas had watched incredulously as Farmer clambered over the intervening rocks and icy ridges until the clouds descended and hid him from sight. They waited for another few hours, expecting him to return, but when the cold became too intense, they headed back to their tent and begun cooking, expecting the young American to stumble in at any moment.

Farmer didn't reappear that night but first thing next morning when they returned to the foot of the mountain, Lobsang had climbed up a small hill and had seen him, far away but seemingly still going strong. Farmer had crested a distant ridge and then disappeared once again into the mist. As the afternoon wore on, low cloud had settled on the mountain until they could see nothing, so they had headed back to camp.

For the next two days, they had kept their vigil but they saw or heard nothing more of Farmer and had become convinced that he was not coming back. When their food ran out they had no alternative but to leave the glacier and return to Darjeeling. Lobsang was subsequently hired by Paul Bauer for his expedition later that summer, but it doesn't seem as if the German team were ever told about the missing American.

It took several months for Farmer's friends and family in the USA to realise that something had gone very wrong but even if they'd had the means, it would have been very difficult for them to have instigated any kind of search for their missing relative without travelling out to India themselves. There were no official mountain rescue networks and America had no diplomatic mission in Nepal. All they could do was wait for the next Kangchenjunga expedition to look for clues to his fate. Considering that Paul Bauer's 1929 expedition was only the second in the mountain's history, and that the previous attempt had been twenty-four years earlier, it looked as if they might be in for a long wait.

Then on Monday February 17th 1930, the *Times* of London made a dramatic announcement, devoting no less than three pages to news that the "strongest mountaineering expedition that has ever visited the Himalayas" would shortly be leaving Europe "to attack the world's second highest mountain, Kanchenjunga". The *Times* might have got the mountain's ranking, and its spelling slightly wrong but over the next four months, there would be intensive coverage of the latest Kangchenjunga expedition, based on reports from their special correspondent embedded in the team. When EE Farmer's family heard the news, they sent a telegram to the expedition leader, imploring him to find out whatever he could of their missing relative. Fittingly, considering all the hullaballoo in the press, the man in charge of this epic new venture was nick-named G.O.D. by his friends: Günter Oscar Dyhrenfurth.

Though German by birth, Günter Dyhrenfurth was an entirely different character to Paul Bauer. A handsome, cosmopolitan man with smiling eyes and an Errol Flynn moustache, both Günter and his wife Hettie were of Jewish ancestry. They shared none of Bauer's intense nationalism and when they saw how right-wing, anti-Semitic politicians were coming to the rise in the 1920s, they had left Germany and emigrated to Switzerland.

Günter and Hettie Dyhrenfurth

Hettie was a noted sportswoman in her own right, best known as a champion tennis player. Petite with a fashionable bob hair-cut and impeccable dress sense, she was not a natural born mountaineer but it was impossible to live in the Dyhrenfurth household and not become part of her husband's Himalayan dreams. According to the *Times*, by the time he set off for Kangchenjunga, Günter had already climbed no less than 700 peaks in the European Alps and the Tatra mountains, his tally including 56 first ascents and new routes. The Dyhrenfurth's honeymoon in 1911 had consisted of a joint ascent of the Matterhorn, with Günter taking the tough Italian route from Valtournenche, while Hettie climbed the 'yak route' from Zermatt up the Hörnli ridge. Thereafter they spent the following decades thinking about a trip to the Himalayas but as they soon discovered, it was not so easy to turn their dream into reality.

Günter Dyhrenfurth was not another E.E. Farmer. He was never going to make a solo attempt on Kangchenjunga, he wanted to lead a big, expensive Everest style expedition that would guarantee success. He spent years trying to get funding from the Austro-German Alpine Club, but its committee had repeatedly said no. Unsurprisingly, he was very disappointed when Paul Bauer stole a march on him in 1929. The only consolation was that Bauer's unsuccessful but courageous attempt had prompted an upsurge in press and public interest. This enabled Dyhrenfurth to put together a small consortium of media interests to fund his expedition in 1930, including the *Times*, the Scherl publishing house of Berlin and the Trans Ocean Film company.

Unlike Bauer's tight-knit group of friends from the same Munich climbing club, Dyhrenfurth's team was resolutely international, a miniature 'League of Nations' according to the *Times*. From Switzerland came his deputy, Marcel Kurz, a world authority on winter mountaineering and Charles Duvanel, the expedition cameraman; from Germany came Hermann Hoerlin and Uli Wieland, both gifted young climbers, and Helmut Richter, an authority on high altitude physiology. From Austria came Erwin Schneider, a geologist who was known as one of the leading young continental climbers, and from Italy the enigmatic Enrico Gaspari, who accompanied the expedition as far as India and then left, as the *Times* reported, for unspecified "personal reasons". As with Bauer's expedition, Britain was heavily involved in logistics, supplying no less than three transport officers: Lt Col Harry Tobin, the secretary of the Himalayan Club who had also accompanied Bauer, J.S. Hannah, an official from the Bengal railway, and George Wood Johnson, the same tea-planter who had helped E.E. Farmer to get under way.

Frank Smythe

The final member of the team was Frank Smythe, a young British climber and skier who had gained a reputation for daring ascents in the Alps. Frank was the prototype modern mountaineer, a dashing all-action hero with a raconteur's way with words on the page and in the lecture hall. Smythe joined Dyhrenfurth's expedition as both a member of the climbing team and as the *Times*' anonymous "Special Correspondent".

As was the practice of the day, he wasn't allowed to sign his own dispatches and had to write about himself in the third person but Smythe's subsequent memoir, *My Kangchenjunga Adventure*, easily outsold books by Dyhrenfurth and his wife, and became for many the definitive account of the expedition.

Having agreed to invest a substantial sum of money, the *Times* syndicated its coverage around the world and made sure the expedition got as many column inches as possible. On February 19th, it reported that Frank Smythe had just been given a farewell dinner by the Ski Club of Great Britain where luminaries such as the former Alpine club president, Sir Martin Conway, had joined well-wishers to send him off to "the hardest mountain in the world." On the following day Frank left London for Venice to join Dyhrenfurth and his wife in the advance party. As his train got ready to leave Victoria station, the legendary leader of the first two British Everest expeditions, General Charles Bruce, gave him one final piece of advice: "Don't forget to worm your porters." It was a line that could have come straight of William Bowman's celebrated parody, *The Ascent of Rum Doodle*, but as the *Times* editorial insisted, there was nothing playful about this expedition:

> The task before them will call for every atom of strength and endurance and mountain craft and every pound of energy they that they possess...it is an undertaking of peculiar difficulty.

The voyage out was Frank's first real opportunity to get to know his new leader. Although he was not quite as authoritarian as Paul Bauer, he soon discovered that Günter Dyhrenfurth did have a penchant for giving orders, insisting that everyone should take part in early morning exercise sessions and at one stage getting them all to climb the ship's mast for the benefit of the expedition cameraman. Frank Smythe was not amused and over the next few months increasingly found himself taking umbrage at his leader's autocratic style.

On March 9th, the advance party arrived in Bombay along with six and a half tons of supplies and equipment. At a press conference, Dyhrenfurth told reporters that he had been dreaming about Kangchenjunga for twenty years and planning the current expedition for more than three. Unsurprisingly there was a lot of interest in his wife Hettie. The idea that she might soon be battling her way up Kangchenjunga's ferocious north ridge and spending her nights sleeping in a snow hole, was certainly enough to pique press interest. Before the team left town, their baggage was loaded into a specially hired train compartment though sadly, pressure of space forced them to abandon 500 bottles of beer donated by an anonymous philanthropist. As Paul Bauer noted a year earlier, Himalayan expeditions required true sacrifices.

In Delhi, they had lunch with the British Viceroy of India, Lord Halifax. Mahatma Gandhi's campaign for Independence was in full flow and the Viceroy was much vexed. As with Bauer in the previous year, the German climber Hermann Hoerlin found himself torn between gratitude towards his British hosts and sympathy for the native Indians and their struggle for independence. Presciently, Hoerlin wrote in his diary that he was very fearful that if independence ever came, there would be a lot of conflict between the Hindu and Muslim communities.

After a brief sight-seeing trip to the Taj Mahal and the temples of Benares, Frank Smythe left the Dyhrenfurths to hurry ahead to Darjeeling to meet Wood Johnson and begin organising their porters and supplies. Following a hair-raising ride on the back of Wood Johnson's motorbike which involved multiple breakdowns and being stalked by a tiger, Smythe arrived in town only to find that their specially commissioned rail truck had been delayed.

There was still plenty to do. As well as experienced Sherpas for the high-altitude work, they needed a small army of general porters to carry their provisions into Base Camp. Smythe had a letter of recommendation from General Bruce which made an immediate impression on the local Sherpas and Bhotias. They still remembered the old soldier who had led the early British Everest expeditions, and were very glad to meet Frank, who they erroneously thought was Bruce's grandson. As for the Darjeeling weather, it was not quite as bad as it had been for Crowley and Jacot-Guillarmod in 1905, but Frank Smythe still had to wait for several days to catch his first sight of Kangchenjunga at the tail end of a fierce thunderstorm. When it finally did appear, Frank was not disappointed, appearing as he wrote "like a vision, massive and deadly still, illuminated by moonlight".

The main body of the team arrived in Darjeeling at the end of March , followed a few days later by the expedition's baggage. Whereas Bauer had travelled light and pared everything down to the minimum, Dyhrenfurth's approach was decidedly more lavish. As well as a large wireless to receive weather reports and keep everyone entertained at night, they had a brand-new gramophone and a well-stocked collection of both jazz and classical records. Each member of the team was issued with a full set of cold weather clothing and a handmade tent, complete with its own national flag. In addition to regular food, there were tins of caviar and foie-gras, plus cases of whiskey and rum and vast quantity of chocolate, donated by no less than three different manufacturers.

Though the expedition was well outfitted, there was one crucial thing it didn't have: permission to enter Nepal. Having read of Bauer's travails on the North East Spur, Dyhrenfurth had decided instead to take up Douglas Freshfield's suggestion and make his attempt from the other side of the mountain. The Nepali authorities, however, resolutely refused to grant him permission.

The 1930 Team:
Above: Hoerlin, Schneider, Wieland, Smythe, Dyhrenfurth, Kurz, Wood-Johnson
Seated: Richter, Hettie, Duvanel

In Delhi Dyhrenfurth had sought assistance from British diplomats, but they had not succeeded in changing anyone's mind. Dyhrenfurth and his transport officers, had no option but to reformulate their plans and head for the Sikkimese side of Kangchenjunga, hoping to succeed where Bauer had failed.

Hettie Dyhrenfurth was the expedition's quartermaster. With 180 crates to break down into porter loads, she had her work cut out for her but she was organised and efficient and charmed everyone with her enthusiasm. When the expedition doctor found that their porters were reluctant to be vaccinated against smallpox, she volunteered to have the first jab in order to demonstrate that it was painless.

With their loads packed and ready to go, Dyhrenfurth hired 150 porters and 60 pack ponies and was just about ready to leave for the North East Spur when out of the blue a letter arrived from the Maharajah of Nepal, informing him cordially that in view of the cosmopolitan character of the expedition "which has for its object the cementation of international friendship and good-will among the countries concerned", he had changed his mind entirely. The Dyhrenfurth party would not only be permitted to enter Nepali territory to attempt the mountain as originally planned via the North West face but would also be given every assistance possible. "His Highness," the letter finished, "hopes the expedition will be a great success in every way."

This was very good news, but very bad timing. Just a few days before they were due to leave, all the expedition's transport plans had to be torn up and hundreds more local porters recruited. In 1929 Paul Bauer had needed ninety men to carry stores to Base Camp on the Sikkimese side, but Dyhrenfurth and his chief transport office Harry Tobin reckoned that to get to their proposed Nepali Base Camp on the other side of the mountain, they would need close to four hundred men, plus a substantial mule train. Just to carry the expedition's film stock, required around forty men.

Apart from the extra cost, there simply weren't enough good porters available, so Dyhrenfurth was forced to take on dozens of so-called "bazaar wallahs" who were glad of the advance pay but had no real idea of what they were being asked to do. Maintaining this many men in the field, and feeding them, was obviously going to be a problem, so Dyhrenfurth sent a telegram to the Maharajah of Nepal asking him if more recruits might be available when they crossed the border, and if they might be able to replenish their food stocks at Ghunsa or Tseram, the last big Nepali villages before Kangchenjunga. The Maharajah agreed to both requests and promised to send a court official to assist them but knowing how sparsely populated this region of Nepal was, Dyhrenfurth remained nervous.

To make matters more complicated, his chief transport officer Harry Tobin told him that because of the huge size of the party, it had to be split into three, in order not to place too much stress on the villages and camping grounds they would be using during the approach march. Though no-one realised it at the time, this was a disastrous suggestion which would cause them countless problems in the weeks to come. For the moment though, it was crucial to get going as quickly as possible.

On April 6th, the first group of 220 porters left Darjeeling to be followed at two day intervals by the remaining 250 men. If all went according to plan, Dyhrenfurth estimated that it would take them about eighteen days to reach Base Camp. The third siege of Kangchenjunga had begun in earnest and for a brief moment the whole of the town seemed to be on the move- everyone, that was, who was in a fit condition to continue.

Frank Smythe met the first stragglers barely a mile out of town. He and the other Europeans had been scheduled to leave on Day 2, in between the first and second big convoys, but it wasn't long before they started encountering porters from the first group who had spent their advance pay getting as drunk as possible. Wood Johnson stayed back to hustle them on but from the beginning porter discipline was poor. Dyhrenfurth had employed no less than four sirdars, or head porters, but only Lobsang, the Sherpa who had been with Paul Bauer and EE Farmer, had any real leadership quality.

Like Crowley and Jacot-Guillarmod before them, Dyhrenfurth's team found themselves under attack from armies of leeches in the sweaty lowlands of Sikkim, but this time around the weather was relatively benign and there were none of the torrential rains that had made life so miserable in 1905. But whereas Crowley's expedition had dropped down into Nepal relatively quickly, Dyhrenfurth's team took a different route, tramping for almost nine days through the forests of Sikkim gradually gaining in altitude, until in the midst of a blizzard they reached the village of Dzongri close to the border, just below Kang La pass. It was here that the expedition's problems really started.

The Kang La is 16,373 ft high, almost 600 ft higher than the summit of Mont Blanc. To make it even more challenging, in the spring of 1930, the winter snows had not yet cleared and lay deep on the ground from 14,000 ft upwards. Getting over the Kang La was hard enough for a European, wearing proper boots and cold weather clothing, but for the porters, most of whom were scantily clad and even more miserably shod, the prospect of carrying a sack that weighed anything between 60-80 lbs over one of the highest passes in the Himalayas, was daunting to say the least. Dyhrenfurth had taken around seventy pairs of Bavarian boots but there were clearly far more porters who needed them. As Frank Smythe noted, it was hardly surprising that around fifty men from the first group chose to desert rather than face the Kang La.

After a fitful night's sleep, at daybreak on April 16th, Dyhrenfurth led the remaining porters from the first party up the icy slopes leading to the pass. Following a by now familiar pattern, the morning was warm and bright, but this only increased the difficulty. The sun bounced off the snow, burning their skin and dazzling their eyes. Frank Smythe soon began to experience what the British Everest climbers of the 1920s had dubbed "glacier lassitude": the sudden loss of energy when hiking through airless icy valleys. When Smythe finally reached the crest of the Kang La, he was suffering from such a bad headache that he had to leave Wood Johnson to manage the porters, while he quickly dropped down into the valley below.

The descent was like a journey from winter into spring, as the snow and ice of the Kang La was quickly replaced by verdant meadows, criss-crossed by streams. They set up camp in a field above the village of Tseram, at the same spot where Douglas Freshfield had stopped on his epic circumnavigation in 1899. There was a newly built yak herders' hut but alarmingly there was no sign of the Nepali court official, or Subadar, who was supposed to meet them with fresh porters and much needed food.

Wood Johnson and Smythe set off for the village with an interpreter, hoping to find the Nepali Subadar and investigate

A Mountain God

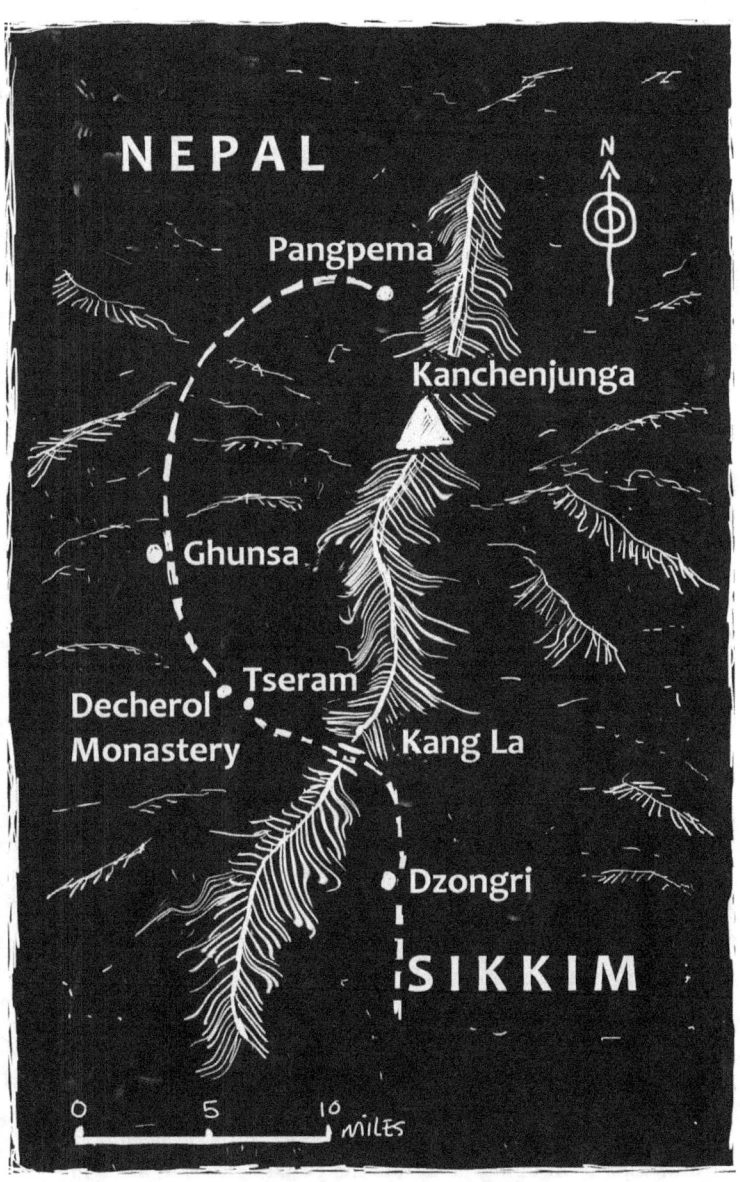

The Route to Base Camp 1930

the rumours sent to them by his family that EE Farmer might have passed through or even still be living at the nearby Decherol monastery. Eventually they found a friendly and well-informed yak herder but he had no good news on either count. The Subadar, he said, had indeed arrived at Tseram but after waiting for several days had headed back down the valley. As for the mysterious EE Farmer, he confirmed that the Decherol monastery had indeed once stood close by at the end of the massive Yalung glacier but it was long abandoned and had been a ruin for at least thirty years. The Yak herder did remember that many months earlier the young American and his Sherpas had camped some distance from the village, presumably to avoid being spotted, but other than that, he had heard or seen nothing of E.E. Farmer.

Back in camp, there was better news on the Subadar front. Their interpreter, a Gurkha officer called Tickeram Thapa, had gone ahead found their man. The official had declined to return straight away, but had promised to come up on the following day. It wasn't clear whether he would be accompanied by additional porters and the much-needed supplies but they had made some progress at least.

The next day the Subadar arrived in camp, alone. In *My Kangchenjunga Adventure*, Frank Smythe gave a beautifully down beat description of the hapless official, who undoubtedly would have been much happier back in the balmy hills of Kathmandu:

> He proved to be a thin-faced, sad, somewhat anaemic looking man, with a long thin, straggling and ill-nourished moustache. He was clothed in baggy white breeches and a black jacket. The only indication of any rank was the Nepalese coat of arms in gold above his turban.

Though the Subadar did not have any supplies with him, he was very helpful when it came to their troublesome porters. On hearing of all the desertions and ill-discipline, he assembled the men and told them the Maharajah of Nepal had decreed that Dyhrenfurth and the Europeans had to be given all assistance possible, and that if this did not happen, heads would roll – literally.

Logistics remained Dyhrenfurth's most pressing problem. The expeditions of the 1930s were not equipped with walky-talkies; the only way for the different convoys to communicate with each other was by runner, and when news eventually came in, it was not good. The second party, with the largest group of porters, was still camped several miles back on the Sikkimese side of the Kang La pass. Not unreasonably, they were refusing to cross over into Nepal unless they too were issued with boots. The only solution was to collect up all the footwear worn by the first group of porters and carry them back over the pass to be reused by the second.

While all this was underway, Dyhrenfurth, decided to press on with the Subadar towards the next village, Ghunsa, where he hoped to purchase additional food. To get there, they had to cross four more high passes including the Mirgin La. At 15,000 ft, it wasn't quite as high as the Kang La, but it too was covered in deep snow. When they reached the top, they were greeted with a hailstorm and a barrage of thunder. Dyhrenfurth and the Europeans had come equipped with skis which would have made the descent much quicker but they rarely used them for fear of demoralising the porters. During the crossing, the unfortunate Subadar lost one of his shoes in a snow hole and spent so much time searching for it, that he developed first-stage frostbite.

Two days later they reached Ghunsa and set up camp just outside the village. In one of the expedition's most bizarre moments, a porter suddenly drew his kukri and for no obvious reason stabbed another man. He was eventually disarmed and taken to the mess tent, only to escape and pick up a large stone with which he threatened to smash Frank Smythe's skull. Only after another fierce struggle was the madman finally subdued.

They were the first Westerners to visit Ghunsa since Douglas Freshfield in 1899, but Dyhrenfurth's fascination with the village was tempered by his continued worries about the parlous state of their supplies. There was no sign of any food dumps or any replacement porters, without which they could not proceed to Base Camp. As Frank Smythe wrote in a dispatch for the *Times*:

> It has been an expedition in itself getting here, and we have been taught many lessons. Himalayan climbing is incidental compared with the problems of transport...

The Nepali Subadar, by now nursing a very sore foot, revealed that though he had amassed plenty of food and provisions for the expedition, his stash was much lower down the valley and nowhere near their proposed route. There was no alternative but to threaten him with a bad report to the Maharajah. Much chastened, the Subadar in turn harangued the headman, who to everyone's relief, finally admitted that there was plenty food available – if they were prepared to pay for it.

A deal agreed, that night several members of the team assembled at the headman's house hoping to try out the local hooch, marwa, a mixture of water and fermented hemp seeds drunk through a straw from a tightly lidded wooden pot. Frank Smythe, who hadn't tasted alcohol for several weeks, found it surprisingly easy to drink and decidedly potent when consumed in sufficient quantity.

On the following day, while recovering from their hangovers and waiting for the headman to rustle up the promised supplies of food, they visited the local monastery. Unlike the ruins at Decherol, Ghunsa's monastery was thriving perhaps, Frank Smythe wondered, because its resident monks had abandoned their vows of celibacy and were living freely with the local villagers. In Dyhrenfurth's honour, they donned masks and brought out horns and drums to perform a traditional 'devil dance'. In return the expedition gramophone was extracted from its packing case to introduce the monks to the wonders of twentieth century 'tinned-music'. The assembled lamas were particularly impressed by their 78-rpm recording of the 1929 hit record "Sunnyside Up", and wouldn't let the members of the expedition leave before they had drunk yet more marwa.

By the end of the day the headman had put together a large mound of food and the Subadar had promised to go back down the valley to bring up the stores that had already been requisitioned. Confident that they now had enough to continue towards the mountain, they marched out of the village on the following morning, leaving their Gurkha officer in charge of the supply dump with instructions to send material on as soon as more porters became available. Three days later, on April 28th, almost three weeks after leaving Darjeeling, they reached a small plateau of rough grass at Pangpema, about five miles from the foot of Kangchenjunga. This, Dyhrenfurth announced, was a perfect site for Base Camp.

It was a cold desolate spot, a patch of rough grass at 16,569 ft surrounded by soaring peaks. By day it could be warm and airless, by night the temperature dropped as low as -38 degrees C. Dominating the skyline was Kangchenjunga, its huge 10,000 ft high North West face, looming down on the glaciers below. Initially, from a distance the summit didn't look impossible, but the more they studied it, the more they realised what a challenge they had set for themselves.

The bottom of the face was at around 18,000 ft. Then at around 22,000 ft there was the first of three huge terraces running across the face, the last of which was approximately 26,500 ft high. Back in 1899, Douglas Freshfield had enjoyed the same view and come away convinced that though it would be almost impossible to climb directly up the North-West face because the avalanche danger, there might be a way to get onto the North Ridge from this side of the mountain via a saddle on the far left hand side, which connected Kangchenjunga to a lesser peak called The Twins. If this proved to be the case, Freshfield thought the North Ridge would provide a comparatively straightforward route to the summit.

Dyhrenfurth concurred, though he had decided on a slightly more complicated approach, which involved scaling the bottom of the North West face as far as the first terrace and then traversing left on to North Ridge. Then after sticking to the ridge for several thousand feet, they would cross back onto the North West face and work their way rightwards across the third terrace. If all went well, they would then set their final camp below the summit pyramid and when the weather look propitious, head for the top. It was a complex and demanding plan and no-one was under any illusion that it would be easy to pull off, but having read about Bauer's travails on the North East Spur and Crowley's disastrous attempt on the South West Face, there was clearly no "yak-route" to the top Kangchenjunga.

Before anything could happen, first they had to properly establish Base Camp. At 16,500 ft, Pangpema was high enough to cause several members of the team to develop altitude sickness so, rather than force the pace, Dyhrenfurth elected to spend a few days building shelters for the porters and organising their stores and equipment. When their superstitious Sherpas saw the Europeans pick up rocks to build a wall for the mess tent, they erected a tall pole nearby and covered it in prayer flags to protect themselves from the multitude of devils who must have been disturbed.

In order to speed up their acclimatization, Helmuth Richter, the team's doctor and physiologist, offered to drain two hundred cubic centimetres of blood from each climber and then issue them with iron-rich liver pills. He claimed his experimental treatment would help them cope with the reduced air pressure at high altitudes and that if they continued to chew handfuls of liver pills, their red blood cell count would increase. Only Dyhrenfurth and the team's cameraman Charles Duvanel took Richter up on his offer, but neither showed any immediate improvement in their performance.

Though the presence of the Nepali Subadar had done much to reduce their porter problems, Dyhrenfurth was still concerned about how they would cope with the rest of the expedition. The night before they left Base Camp to start the climb proper, he asked Wood Johnson to convene a meeting. Dyhrenfurth had no soothing words and chose instead to throw down the gauntlet. "You have had a hard time," he asked Wood Johnson to tell the assembled men. "You will get a much harder time and you will be faced with privations and danger. Let any man who wants to, go back to Darjeeling". Fortunately, most of malcontents had left already, and the men who remained were willing to continue.

Dyhrenfurth's main problem was food. Through the offices of the Nepali Subadar and the headman of Ghunsa, they had now obtained large quantities of roast barley, the staple diet of the Sherpas, but most of the provisions for the Europeans still had not arrived. There were some packages with the second party but the bulk of their tinned food had been assigned to the third convoy, the mule train commanded by Harry Tobin, which at that moment was languishing several days away on the other side of the Kang La in Sikkim.

It was never going to be possible to take the mules over the high pass, so Tobin had arranged with Dyhrenfurth that a number of porters from the first two convoys, would come back across the Kang La, unload the mules and carry their stores back to the expedition. Unfortunately, neither Tobin nor Dyhrenfurth had told the two other transport officers Wood Johnson and Hannah, so none of Tobin's supplies had arrived. To tide them over, a local farmer offered to sell them one of his yaks. Wood Johnson dispatched the unlucky creature with Dyhrenfurth's rifle, but their European stomachs found the yak meat very difficult to digest and when it was served up at every mealtime, they soon came to hate it.

The International Himalayan Expedition, or IHE, as Dyhrenfurth liked to call it, had not got off to a good start. The logistical challenges of getting a large party of climbers to Kangchenjunga Base Camp had proved much greater than anticipated, and the difficulties had been compounded by a mistaken decision to split the party into three. Like all

Himalayan ventures, Dyhrenfurth's expedition was a race against time. If they were to have any chance of getting to the summit before the monsoon hit, they would have to move very quickly.

So at 9.00 a.m. on May 1st 1930, three days after setting up Base Camp, a slightly ailing Günter Dyhrenfurth led his climbers and Sherpas up the glacier toward the vast North West face to begin the attempt. As they moved higher up the Kangchenjunga glacier, the scenery grew more and more dramatic, with towering peaks surrounding them on three sides, none of which had yet been attempted, never mind climbed.

As for Kangchenjunga itself, the closer they got, the more it seemed to loom over them but even after several hours of gradual ascent, they still couldn't get a full view of the base of the mountain. Rather than push too hard on the first day, Dyhrenfurth decided to stop and establish their next camp but it wasn't easy to find a safe spot. They needed to find somewhere far enough away from the avalanches that regularly thundered down the nearby slopes but they soon realised the whole glacier was riven with crevasses. Dyhrenfurth found one particularly well-hidden crevasse the hard way, when a snow bridge gave way as he was crossing it. He fell in up to his waist and might have gone a lot further if the lip of the crevasse had not held.

Frank Smythe was happy to have moved up to Camp 1. He felt fitter and was relieved to have escaped the afternoon winds that battered their tents at Base Camp. The task ahead, however, looked increasingly daunting and to add to the tension, Smythe and Wood Johnson were becoming increasingly irritated by their leader and his pompous ways. Every morning he would wake everyone up by blowing a small alpine horn, much to Smythe's discomfort and disgust. When Wood Johnson had the temerity to steal it from his tent, Dyhrenfurth simply produced another one and continued with his early morning reveille.

As they ventured further up the glacier, if anything things looked worse and worse. Far from discovering easy slopes at the foot of the mountain they found themselves looking up at a tall horseshoe-shaped wall of icy cliffs, which seemed to extend all the way around the base of the mountain as far as the adjoining peaks. By Smythe's judgement, the icy barrier was 600–800 ft high, a formidable challenge made even more dangerous by vast protruding flakes of ice and enormous icy seracs which sat above the cliffs, poised to collapse at any moment.

Reconnaissance over, they set up a second camp a few hundred feet higher up the glacier but still, they hoped, far enough away from the face to be avalanche-proof. Their new home was an even colder spot, a small huddle of tents in the middle of a vast snowy wilderness.

That evening Wood Johnson came up with more porters but there was no good news from the second or third convoys. One unlucky Sherpa, Ondi, got separated from the main party and fell into a crevasse. He shouted for help but at first the others could not hear him. When they eventually came to his rescue, he emerged frost bitten and deep in shock. The expedition's woes continued when later that evening Marcel Kurz, one of their strongest climbers, announced that his earache was so bad, he would have to retreat down to Base Camp as soon as possible.

The next day, the route finding went on, with Frank Smythe and Wood Johnson probing further up the glacier towards the base of the mountain. To their relief they realised that there were some breaks in the seemingly endless ice-cliffs, but getting up onto the first terrace was not going to be easy. As ever, the challenge was to find a fail-safe route which could be used regularly by porters to carry supplies up to the higher camps. It would have been too expensive to equip all of them with crampons and proper climbing boots, so the first task for the lead climbers was to chop steps up the steep sections. As Frank Smythe found out however, the ice was both very hard and strangely rubbery. Just to cut a few steps took an enormous effort.

To make the job even harder, the cold weather clothing supplied by Dyhrenfurth was both heavy and cumbersome. Their boots weighed in at 8½ lbs per pair, and with the addition of crampons the total weight of their footwear came to over 12 lbs. Frank Smythe later criticized Dyhrenfurth for not taking on board the lessons of previous Everest expeditions. Instead of several light-weight layers which could be varied according to the conditions, they had been issued with heavy, inflexible jackets which quickly became very sweaty when a climber was working hard. In total Frank calculated that his climbing kit came to 32½ lbs, almost a quarter of his bodyweight, so for much of the time, he used his own much lighter boots and wore several layers of Shetland jumpers under a wind-proof outer jacket.

Though Frank Smythe adjusted well to high altitude, the shock of falling into a crevasse had weakened Günter Dyhrenfurth. By the morning of May 4th, he had such a severe throat infection that his voice was reduced to a whisper, so he followed Marcel Kurz down the mountain to Base Camp, leaving instructions with Smythe and the others continue work on the ice-wall. Though for the time being, he could no longer take part in the climbing, Dyhrenfurth remained convinced that if they could find a way up to the lower terrace, they would then be able to get onto the North Ridge and from there get high on the mountain.

Frank Smythe did not query Dyhrenfurth's instructions directly, but like Aleister Crowley before him, he had come to realise that the 'objective' dangers faced in the Himalayas were far greater than anything encountered in the Alps. Both the mountains and risks involved in climbing them were on a much greater scale. However, whereas Crowley dismissed the dangers breezily, Smythe was increasingly wary. "I have experienced fear many times on many mountains," he later wrote, "but never the same dull, hopeless sort of fear inspired by this terrible wall of ice….Kangchenjunga is something more than unfriendly, it is imbued with a blind unreasoning hatred towards the mountaineer."

The Sherpas were also clearly intimidated. Though several were veterans of previous Everest expeditions, no-one had seen anything like this.

There was still no good news from the rear of the expedition, and if anything, the situation was worse. The group of porters sent back over the Kang La pass to collect all the loads from Harry Tobin's mule train had instead gone back to Darjeeling after looting one of the team's supply dumps. This had prompted Tobin to attempt to lead a smaller party over the Kang La himself but he had fallen and badly hurt his arm. To add to his woes, his head porter, Naspati, had also fled to Darjeeling after his assistant died of exposure during an earlier attempt at crossing of the Kang La.

Fearing they might never get their much-needed supplies, Dyhrenfurth sent orders to Wood Johnson to come back down and join Hannah, the other transport officer. Together they would make one last push to find Tobin and retrieve all the equipment and provisions he was carrying. In the meantime, the climbing team would have to continue dining on yak meat.

After Wood Johnson said his goodbyes, Smythe returned to the ice-wall with another of the German climbers, Uli Wieland, to continue their painstaking step cutting. Several of their Sherpas had been with Bauer in the previous year; they all agreed that the work being done now at the foot of the mountain was even more arduous than anything they had experienced on the North East Spur.

Smythe estimated it would take five days to get to the top of the main ice cliff and on to the first terrace but the weather continued to torment them. On May 5th, a much-recovered Erwin Schneider arrived in camp full of energy and went straight into battle. His enthusiasm helped them make good progress but on the following day a heavy snowstorm obliterated all the steps he had helped cut. No-one was ready to give up quite yet and no sooner had the snow-storm reached a crescendo than the sun came out, banishing the grey clouds that had been hanging over the mountain.

Dyhrenfurth was still too ill to come back up from Base Camp but on the following evening another of the German climbers, Hermann Hoerlin, arrived at Camp 2 allowing Smythe and Wieland to take the next day off to rest and recuperate. Hoerlin and Schneider made steady progress and came back confident that next day they would reach the first terrace. In order to boost morale they gave the Sherpas extra rations, with a promise that they would be sleeping in a new camp on the following night.

After a day off, Frank Smythe was rested but still uncertain about what would happen next. Though it was good to hear of Hoerlin and Schneider's progress, he still worried that the ice cliffs were too exposed. Even if they did manage to reach the first terrace, they would have to send heavily laden porters up the same, dangerous route for several weeks to come to stock the upper camps. That night he finished a long, rather gloomy dispatch for the *Times*, highlighting the dangers they faced and a growing feeling of dread:

> Were one of those catastrophic ice avalanches- the collapse of a hanging glacier- such as are common in the Himalayas, to take place we would be brushed like a speck of dust from the earth...As I write, avalanche after avalanche is roaring off Kangchenjunga, each one seeming to proclaim defiance and warning.

After a torrid night plagued by nightmares, Smythe handed over his article to a waiting runner but he was too exhausted to get back into the fray. Instead, he stayed in his tent when the others broke camp as scheduled on the following morning.

The Austrian Erwin Schneider was first out accompanied by Chettan, one of their most experienced Sherpas. Nicknamed 'Satan', he hailed from the Solu Khumbu region of Nepal, the Sherpa heartland, and was a veteran of previous British Everest expeditions and Paul Bauer's Kangchenjunga expedition of 1929. Square jawed and solidly built, unlike most of their Sherpas he had cut off his pig tails and wore his hair short, European style. Chettan was a very strong Sherpa but he too was nervous about climbing the ice-wall. He warned

Schneider that he thought it too dangerous but if the Sahibs were willing to attempt it, he felt it was his duty to carry on.

Next out of camp was Charles Duvanel, the expedition cameraman, and his tripod bearers. It had been an unusually warm night and the morning was very misty but Duvanel sensed that May 8th was going to be an important day for the expedition. Top of his list was to get good shots of Hoerlin and Wieland and the main group of Sherpas coming towards camera.

Several hundred feet lower down at Base Camp, Günter Dyhrenfurth was still suffering from a sore throat and remained unsure when he would be able to re-join the main body of the team. His wife Hettie was busy as ever, organising the porter loads to go up the glacier. In two days' time, it would be their nineteenth wedding anniversary and to cheer Günter up, she was planning to present him with a Sacher Tort, provided that the expedition's chief cook, Tendechar, was capable of doing the baking.

So far Hettie had endured a difficult expedition. As the team quartermaster, she had been in the thick of all the logistical struggles that had made the approach march so difficult. Everyone agreed that she had done a good job, but clearly it had not gone smoothly. Add to that a few days of altitude sickness followed by an unexpected fall into an icy cold stream and Hettie could hardly claim that her first expedition had gone perfectly, but at least now she was now much recovered. Whatever her husband's frustrations, she was enjoying the bustle of life at base camp. All she needed now was good news from the advance guard and their anniversary celebrations would be complete.

At Camp 3, Frank Smythe was in his tent, working on his next dispatch. The others had left, leaving him and the cook to watch them disappear into the distance. If all went well, the advance party would set up camp that night on the first terrace and next morning he and the cook would follow.

Then, suddenly, Frank heard something.

Up at the ice-wall, Erwin Schneider had just crossed the narrow snow bridge that stretched over the huge crevasse which guarded the foot of the mountain. As he waited for his Sherpa Chettan to follow, he looked up at the final stretch of the ice-wall, plotting their next moves. Suddenly he saw an immense section of that wall begin to move. As he stared up in utter astonishment, it toppled forward and began breaking into huge chunks.

Within seconds, the collapsing wall created a massive avalanche of snow and ice which looked certain to devastate everything in its path. Schneider held out no hope that he would survive — he would either be crushed by the huge ice blocks, forced back into the crevasse or suffocated by the cloud of snow that would follow in the avalanche's wake. With a bang he was knocked off his feet and thrown backwards towards to what he assumed was certain death.

For Frank Smythe, several hundred yards further down the glacier, it felt as if time was now running in slow motion. It was, he later wrote, like watching a piece of film jammed in a projector. He could just about see his team-mates, tiny figures menaced by a vast avalanche moving inexorably towards them, long tongues of ice projecting out in front of the main cloud. He watched in horror as they were engulfed in a wave of snow. Then suddenly Frank Smythe snapped out of his reverie and yelled at the cook, "Run!". At 20,000 feet it was easier said than done. They managed to get just 20 yards out of camp, before collapsing in the snow. Then miraculously, as suddenly as it had started, the avalanche stopped in its tracks, not far from his tent.

Higher up the glacier, the cloud of snow and ice had settled, leaving an uncanny silence in its wake. To his amazement, Erwin Schneider realised that he had survived. He looked up and saw a few flimsy looking sections of rope hanging from the ice-wall, the tattered remains of several days' work. Then he hauled himself up and began crabbing his way around the lip of the huge crevasse at the foot of the ice wall. The snow bridge which he had crossed a few minutes ago had been smashed to pieces, but he found another crossing point at the far edge and gingerly worked his way over before heading down the mountain.

Frank Smythe and the cook were at the same moment making the opposite journey, climbing up towards the avalanche. They had no idea what had happened to their team but doubted that anyone had survived. To Frank's immense joy he was soon proved wrong. Most of the climbers and the Sherpas were still standing and there was no sign that anyone was seriously injured. Charles Duvanel, the expedition, cameraman later told Frank how he had instinctively run to the left when he saw the avalanche approaching and miraculously had managed to avoid it.

As he surveyed the scene, Frank saw one Sherpa, Nemu, wandering around looking for the load that he had hastily abandoned a few minutes earlier. Initially Frank was confused and angry. He barked at Nemu that he should search for survivors not equipment, but as he acknowledged, the Sherpa was as much in shock as anyone. "Who were killed and who were alive did not matter," Frank later wrote. "He had abandoned the load entrusted to him by the sahibs. Very likely he was temporarily unstrung by this terrible experience, for life had been measured from death by a matter of inches, but somehow his action was typical of the man."

In the distance Frank spotted Wieland making his way up a slope towards a dark object, which seemed to be wedged between two blocks of ice. It was Chettan's hand. The others swiftly dug him out and immediately began giving artificial respiration, but even though they continued for an hour, Chettan's head injuries were so severe it was a hopeless task. All that remained was to find Erwin Schneider's body.

Then, to everyone's astonishment Schneider appeared out of nowhere, with the scarcely believable tale of how by sheer luck he had avoided death. As Frank Smythe collected the survivors' stories he mentally reconstructed the path of the avalanche as it swept diagonally from right to left, obliterating the steps that he and others had so painstakingly cut. According to his estimate, the debris covered almost a square mile. With the Sherpas reporting more cracks appearing in the ice-wall, they quickly buried Chettan in a nearby snow hole and after a brief ceremony retreated down the mountain to Camp 1, leaving an ice axe to mark their fallen comrade's grave.

On the following morning, a Sherpa ran down to base camp with a note outlining what had happened. As Hettie Dyhrenfurth recorded in her expedition account, it was devastating news for everyone:

> I will never forget this day! I was paralyzed and all my courage and enthusiasm for achieving the goal was broken.

Günter Dyhrenfurth went up to discuss what to do next. At a tense meeting he briefly mooted the idea of renewing the attack, but unsurprisingly there was no enthusiasm from the men who had survived the avalanche. Dyhrenfurth's second suggestion was to try climbing a ridge further to the west. It would be free of avalanches, he argued, and even if didn't lead directly to the main peak, it might enable them to reach one of Kangchenjunga's secondary summits. Initially Frank Smythe had mixed feelings. As he wrote in a dispatch for the *Times*, Chettan's death had un-nerved everyone, but they weren't prepared to admit total defeat:

> Our blood is up; we intend to get as far as possible up the mountain. But what a mountain it is! Surely no great Himalayan peak has every weak spot so jealously guarded.

Their second attempt however was short-lived. Frank Smythe, Hoerlin and Wieland managed to climb a steep couloir to the crest of the North West ridge, but as Frank later wrote, it was "the most terrible ridge that I have ever set eyes on. It consists of huge rock towers and the amazing knife-edges of ice, common to Himalayan arêtes. In all its 4000 ft I do not think there is a single place where a camp might be pitched." Smythe was sure it was hopeless but it took Dyhrenfurth another day to accept that their attempt on Kangchenjunga was over. As he climbed down with Smythe another huge avalanche roared down the mountain as if to remind them just how dangerous it was.

Dyhrenfurth pondered what to do next. They still had two to three weeks of climbing before the monsoon was due and after much struggle, had finally managed to get hold of the provisions from the second and third convoys. It was time,

Dyhrenfurth decided, to abandon Kangchenjunga altogether and instead focus on lesser peaks nearby. This final phase of the expedition was much more successful, yielding the first ascent of Kamthang and Jonsong Peak, by no less than six members of the team. At 24,344 ft it was the highest mountain then ascended, a real achievement for a team who only a few weeks earlier had almost been wiped out.

After that, Frank Smythe headed back home with an advance party, leaving Günter Dyhrenfurth to complete some geological work and various members of the team to climb several other smaller peaks. By the middle of June, the monsoon was upon them and it was time for everyone to leave. Three months after he'd set out with all those hundreds of porters, Dyhrenfurth returned to Gangtok, the capital of Sikkim, and was royally entertained by the Maharajah. A few days later he reached Darjeeling and said goodbye to the porters and Sherpas who had been working for them for so many months.

Though they were not returning as all conquering heroes, the extensive coverage the expedition had received ensured there were plenty of hands to shake and official functions to attend. When they reached Calcutta, Dyhrenfurth gave a speech to the Himalayan club celebrating the harmony between the four different nations present on the expedition, commenting that it set an example of "the spirit of friendship and co-operation among the nations" at a time of increasing tension in Europe.

In general, the British press was very positive about the expedition, portraying it as a valiant attempt which had only failed because of the difficulties of their goal. Everyone from the grandees of British mountaineering such as Francis

Younghusband to contemporary climbers like Teddy Norton agreed that it showed that Kangchenjunga was a much more difficult mountain than Everest. The most critical coverage of the expedition came from within, and in particular from Frank Smythe. Throughout the expedition he had enjoyed an uneasy relationship with Dyhrenfurth and as he came to write articles and books in the aftermath, his misgivings came to the fore. Smythe was openly critical of Dyhrenfurth's choice of equipment and expedition clothing, but much more seriously he laid the blame for the porter Chettan's death on Dyhrenfurth's poor leadership, and in particular his decision to make his team attempt the ice wall. As Smythe wrote in the *Alpine Journal*:

> It seems a bitter thing to say, but he perished needlessly and uselessly, and a man such as he, perhaps the finest of all Himalayan porters, can ill be spared.

In his defence, Dyhrenfurth replied in the *Himalayan Journal*, that initially Smythe had approved of the route up the ice-wall, and argued that history had shown that Himalayan expeditions were inherently dangerous:

> It is ridiculous to speak of responsibility, as though someone had been guilty of a crime! War with these Himalayan giants entails hard and relentless fighting; the most careful leading can never guarantee that such fighting will cost no lives. Have not the Everest expeditions, which were prepared with the minutest care, also cost a number of lives? Nobody dreams of holding the leaders of Everest expeditions responsible for the price. "C'est la guerre!"

Smythe's most interesting comments came much later, in his 1945 book *The Spirit of the Hills*. Back in 1930, much had been made of the international quality of the expedition, but Smythe noted that far from producing a more harmonious team, it made individual members more competitive and less likely to use good judgment. As he wrote plaintively, remembering the days spent on the ice-wall:

> It was a suicidal route. Hope diminished, the work went on. The leader returned to the base camp suffering from the effects of altitude. Before doing so, he sent the climbing party forward. No single member of that climbing party liked to be the first to waver: we were too inexperienced in Himalayan mountaineering. Also it was an international expedition, and the leader had provided each nationality with a flag to spur him on. Thus the attempt to climb Kangchenjunga became a "siege" and a "war" in which safety and enjoyment were at a discount.

In spite of his misgivings, for Frank Smythe Kangchenjunga was just the beginning of a long and illustrious career as a high-altitude mountaineer. In the following year he came back to the Himalayas to set a new world record, reaching the summit of Kamet, a 25,446 ft peak in the Garwhal region of India. After that he took part in three British Everest expeditions, his greatest success coming in 1933 when he got within 1000 ft of the summit. For Smythe, the Kangchenjunga expedition was also the launching point of a very successful career as a mountaineering author. His book, *The Kangchenjunga Adventure*, was widely reviewed and sold over 3,000 copies in its first few months.

Günter and Hettie Dyhrenfurth returned to the Himalayas in 1934 on a second international expedition. This time they avoided Kangchenjunga, heading north east into Baltoro region of modern-day Pakistan. They successfully scaled five peaks over 24,000 ft with Hettie setting a new women's altitude record on Sia Kangri. None of Dyhrenfurth's books ever sold as well as Smythe's, but he did succeed in making two films: *The Throne of the Gods*, a documentary based on Charles Duvanel's footage of the 1930 Kangchenjunga expedition and *The Demon of the Himalayas*, a drama that was partially shot on the Dyhrenfurths' 1934 expedition.

To further add to their esteem, the Dyhrenfurths were awarded gold medals at the 1936 Berlin Olympics to honour their 1934 expedition. Günter flew to Berlin to accept the prize but he refused give a Nazi salute to Goebbels and Hitler. Hettie did not accompany him. By 1936 she had separated from her husband, emigrating to the United States with their children while Günter elected to stay in Switzerland and eventually remarry.

As for Kangchenjunga, the 1930 expedition significantly increased its fame. The esteemed letter writers to the *Times* never quite agreed the correct spelling of its name, with the *Times* itself always dropping the 'g'. After much deliberation it was accepted that Kangchenjunga was the third, not the second highest mountain in the world, with K2 acknowledged to be around 25 ft higher but as most commentators agreed, size wasn't everything. Though its summit might have been around 1000 ft lower than that of Everest, it was universally agreed that Kangchenjunga was the world's hardest mountain.

Though he would return to the Himalayas many times, Frank Smythe came away from Kangchenjunga with very negative feelings. "There is nothing friendly about a Himalayan peak," he wrote with real intensity. "You feel that it is coldly hostile and that it resents intrusion. It allows no latitude, it seizes upon the slightest mistake. When you have reached its summit, you have finished with it. There is no desire to renew acquaintances, or make a friend of Himalayan peaks, they resent familiarity and always they will kill you- if they can." But if he intended his words to put other mountaineers off, he was very wrong. Within six months a new team would arrive at Kangchenjunga, led by someone who disliked Günter Dyhrenfurth far more than he ever did: Germany's true 'Demon of the Himalayas', Paul Bauer.

CHAPTER FOUR
Monsoon Story

For thousands of years, every summer the Indian sub-continent has been gripped by the monsoon. As warm air rises over the deserts and plains of central India, cooler air over the Indian Ocean flows northwards, picking up moisture as it crosses the Arabian Sea and the Bay of Bengal. When that mass of damp air eventually reaches the Himalayas, it is forced upwards, producing rain and snow in torrential quantities.

The numbers are phenomenal: 90% of India's rainfall comes in the summer months between June and September; up to 3.3 metres of rainfall was logged in a continuous three week period in Kerala in 1924 and more recently over thirty six thousand lightning strikes were recorded in Andhra Pradesh in southern India in just thirteen hours during a pre-monsoon storm in late April 2018

The monsoon is not entirely predictable. Huge fortunes are illegally gambled on the precise date of its arrival and departure; in some years the rains fail, bringing drought, in others there is so much precipitation that it causes severe flooding.

Generally though, between early June and late September, it's the rainy season.

For farmers the monsoon rains are crucial to help their crops grow; for town planners they are an occupational hazard which continually threaten to overwhelm their drains and flood their cities. For mountaineers, the monsoon sets the rhythm of the climbing year. When it rains on the plains, it snows on the heights, making the Himalayas particularly dangerous in the summer.

As Himalayan mountaineering developed in the twentieth century, the year was split up into a longish spring pre-monsoon season, starting in late March and finishing at the end of May, and a slightly shorter autumn season beginning in September and ending in late October when the approach of winter made it simply too cold to climb. There was no high-altitude mountaineering during the monsoon, or at least there wasn't until an article appeared in the *Times* on Christmas Eve 1930. Under the headline "Kanchenjunga: A New Bavarian expedition" (the Times continued to drop the 'g'), it announced that the German climber Paul Bauer would soon be returning to the Himalayas, to clear up some unfinished business:

> Bauer intends to leave Europe early in June, and the attempt on Kanchenjunga will be made in August and September, towards the end of the monsoon period. This bold experiment of climbing during the monsoon season will be watched with the greatest interest by mountaineers, as there are those who believe that the best chance of success on Mount Everest would be to attempt that peak during the monsoon season or immediately after it ends. Tea-planters living around Darjeeling tell of a clear period during the monsoon, when the upper part

of Kanchenjunga is sometimes visible for as long as two weeks. On the other hand, experienced Himalayan mountaineers hold that there is no chance of success at this season, owing to the quantity of fresh snow on the mountain and the generally unsettled weather.

Two years previously, the early arrival of heavy winter snows and very low temperatures had put paid to Bauer's first attempt. By arriving in the middle of the summer, he hoped to gain enough extra time to go all the way to the summit.

Bauer had watched Dyhrenfurth's international expedition fail on the North West face and had no intention of repeating his mistakes. He would return to the other side of the mountain and renew his attack on the North East Spur with an exclusively German speaking team. If things went according to plan, they would establish Base Camp in the middle of July, make a rapid ascent and reach their 1929 high point by the end of the month. This would give them the whole of August and September to cross over on to the North Ridge, establish two further camps and then strike out for the summit. At the very least, Bauer expected to gain two to three extra weeks. As the *Times* reported, opinions were divided within the mountaineering world with some believing him foolhardy and others applauding his courage, but as ever there was only one way to find out.

In the two years since the first German expedition, Bauer had continued to practise as a notary but the political and economic situation in Germany had become ever more turbulent. The Wall Street crash of 1929 had further weakened the economy and an era of high unemployment had contributed to the rise of extremist parties on the right and left. Bauer was even more convinced that mountaineering could play a role in Germany's national renewal and that it was his duty and the duty of every German climber to give their everything to the cause. As he later wrote in *Himalayan Campaign*, he didn't climb for pleasure – he saw it as a "personal obligation".

The 1931 Team:
Behind: Aufschnaiter, Allwein, Thoenes, Leupold, Fendt, Von Kraus
Seated: Bauer, Beigel

Bauer left Germany on May 25th 1931 with another very strong party. It included five members of the 1929 expedition, as well as four new men, all members of the Munich University Alpine Club. The youngest was new boy Hermann Schaller, a twenty-five-year-old student; the oldest was Bauer himself, now aged thirty-four. Two members of the party, Eugene Allwein and Hans Hartmann, couldn't travel out with the main group but promised to move as quickly as possible once they got away from Germany. Bauer didn't consider inviting anyone from Günter Dyhrenfurth's team and in press articles leading up to his expedition, he barely mentioned his rival. The two men were united in a growing mutual antipathy, which, as time progressed, would become increasingly vehement.

Though he resolutely ignored Dyhrenfurth, Bauer had benefitted from all the publicity and attention paid to his rival's recent attempt. Once again the Alpenverein offered to support his expedition but this time round he was able to raise extra money by selling the press rights to *The Times* and an expedition book to the German publishing firm Knorr and Hirth.

The extra money didn't however mean a more lavish approach. Though not quite as austere as his penny pinching 1929 trip, Bauer's return to the Himalayas was far from luxurious. There were no cases of chocolate or tins of foie gras to tickle his climber's palates when the going got tough. There were no gramophones to keep them entertained in the evening. Instead they took extra rations of dry biscuits and some newly purchased surveying tools. Much of their gear was leftovers from 1929 which had been stashed in Darjeeling and further up country at the village of Lachen. The only significant development in terms of equipment was the decision to take a new style of felt-lined boots which were both warm and, at 4.1 lbs, considerably lighter than the footwear commissioned for the Dyhrenfurth expedition.

Bauer had written ahead to the Himalayan Club to ask for help and had been very warmly received. He continued to have great respect for British mountaineers and after his team's performance in 1929, that admiration was reciprocated. Unlike Dyhrenfurth, Bauer sorted out his travel plans and permissions well in advance and drew up a detailed plan for the approach march. When he arrived in Darjeeling at the end of June, his first supply convoy was standing at the ready, and within a few hours had moved off with several hundred pounds of food. Getting the rest of his Sherpas and Bhotias going, however, was more complicated than Bauer had hoped.

Many of them were veterans of the previous year's expedition but the Sherpas in particular were not happy. They complained that Dyhrenfurth had not paid them properly and, to make matters worse, that he had paid Bhotia porters more than Sherpas. The Bhotias and Sherpas were ethnic Tibetans who had migrated to Nepal and India. Both groups were very strong at high altitude, but by the early 1930s the Sherpas had acquired a reputation for being more disciplined and more skilful. In order to right the wrongs of 1930, they insisted that Bauer should employ only Sherpas. Eventually, after a lot of arguing and the intervention of the local police chief, the dispute was settled but it was not the start that Bauer had been hoping for.

Disharmony amongst the porters was matched by poor weather. By the time they were fully underway the monsoon was in full flow, making the roads between India and Sikkim frequently impassable. Bauer couldn't complain, after all he had made the decision to travel and climb during the monsoon, but as they ventured deeper into the forests of Sikkim, the weather grew worse with frequent storms which sometimes raged for six to eight hours. Their only comfort was that the heaviest rains came mainly at night but the approach march was a miserable experience for everyone, apart from the leeches.

In spite all the discomforts, the team made swift progress. This time, Bauer had employed just over two hundred porters, split into four groups, but there were no Kang La's to cross or high passes to conquer. By July 6th, the final two Germans in the team, Allwein and Hartmann, had arrived from Germany and joined Bauer at Lachen. In a gruelling feat of endurance, they had managed to travel by rail, lorry and foot some 1500 miles from Bombay to Sikkim in under a week.

The main body of the team reached base camp on the Zemu glacier a week ahead of schedule. Bauer remembered it as a very striking spot but was even more impressed after the monsoon rains. Though they had reached over 14,000 ft, they were surrounded by a miniature forest of juniper and rhododendron bushes, interspersed with carpets of Alpine flowers and huge fronds of giant rhubarb, up to six feet high. None of them had ever seen anything like it.

After much hullaballoo, most of their porters were paid off and sent home, but 30 were retained for high altitude work and another 20 were kept on to act as runners and do any necessary carrying between base camp and Lachen. Five days later on July 13th Bauer re-established Advance Base close to the foot of the North East Sur.

It had taken just under seven weeks to get from Munich to within sight of their old adversary and Bauer was revelling in a warm nostalgic glow. As they established camp they found ropes, candles and lanterns which had been lost in the snow two years earlier but revealed by the recent warm weather. The topography had changed slightly with several of the huge stones against which they had pitched their tents, having migrated 150 ft further down the glacier. It was still a splendid location though, as Bauer wrote in the *Times*:

> The wild and sublime grandeur of the panorama which surrounds our camp is something so overwhelming that it cannot be taken in on any one occasion in its entirety, but can only be appreciated in its separate phases at various times of night and day.

The North East Spur reared up in front of them, intimidating and steep as ever. Second time around though, it didn't make Bauer catch his breath. He scanned its flanks, picking out the sites of their previous camps and higher up tracing the route they had pioneered along the ridge crest. The Spur was now a known quantity, a familiar foe whose strengths and weaknesses he thought he understood.

As predicted, for the main part, the skies were cloudless and blue but it was much warmer than Bauer had expected and it wasn't long before the high temperatures began to throw up unexpected problems. The snow and ice that covered the slopes above them started to soften and eventually melt, releasing hundreds of rocks and stones that had previously been frozen in place. When the Germans tried to climb up to the 'Eagles' Nest', their old Camp 7 halfway up the Spur, they found themselves regularly bombarded by fusillades of stones.

Bauer carefully scanned the route, looking for places they could take shelter but the rock-falls were so persistent and so dangerous that he had no alternative but to call a temporary halt to climbing. Instead he posted sentinels at the bottom of the Spur and instructed them to record the frequency of avalanches and rockfalls to discover whether there was any pattern or regularity. After two days of observations, they worked out that the only safe period to climb was between 5.00 and 8.00 a.m. in the morning, when there was enough light to move safely over the still frozen snow. With such a limited climbing window, work slowed down considerably but they persevered.

As they got closer to the ridge crest, they found the same fantastically shaped ice features that had so impressed them in 1929: huge icy ribs that projected outwards like enormous fish-bones, tall towers and small cones of ice and, most unworldly of all, strange formations which resembled giant mushrooms. After three days they had prepared a route from the Eagles' Nest to the top of the crest but the unusually warm weather continued to create problems. The steps they painstakingly cut in hard packed snow quickly became soft and slushy and very treacherous. Icy cornices which one day seemed strong enough to take the weight of two men, the next day broke away easily under their feet. During the whole of August the temperature only dropped below zero three times and to everyone's amazement it was so warm that it even rained at the top of the Spur.

To make things even worse, the unseasonably damp weather was a breeding ground for infection and illness. One of Bauer's best and most experienced climbers, Eugene Allwein developed sciatica and was forced to rest. Several porters came down with tonsillitis and one man, Babu Lall, a veteran of the 1929 expedition, fell seriously ill and died on the way down to Base Camp, from a mysterious condition later diagnosed as Blackwater fever.

Though the members of the Kangchenjunga expedition didn't know it, the unusually hot and damp weather was causing health problems all over Bengal and Sikkim with outbreaks of typhus and dysentery recorded in many villages.

It took until August 9th, almost a month of climbing and carrying, before Bauer felt ready to establish Camp 8 on the crest of the Spur, on a flattish terrace at around 20,700 ft. It was an important moment for everyone, the beginning of the next stage of the expedition so Bauer decided to move up en-masse, with five German climbers and several porters all heading upwards from the Eagles' Nest and a smaller intermediate camp a few hundred feet above.

The first to reach the terrace were the two Berliners, Hans Hartmann and Karl Wien. They arrived at 2.00 p.m. and stamped down the snow before pitching their tent. About an hour behind came Hermann Schaller and two Sherpas followed by Bauer and Pircher and their detachment of porters. Fresh faced and intense, Schaller was the youngest and least experienced member of the team but he was he strong, fit and very enthusiastic. His two Sherpas, Pasang and Tsin Norbu were both heavily laden, carrying tents and cooking equipment.

About 300 ft below Camp 8, Bauer stopped to watch as Schaller tackled the most difficult section of the climb, a narrow couloir on the flank of the Spur which lead up to the terrace where the first tent had been pitched. As Schaller disappeared behind a rocky rib, Bauer watched Pasang follow in his path, leaving the last man, Tsin Norbu, at the bottom of the couloir belaying the others. It was a tricky bit of ice climbing but the three men were carefully roped up and Tsin Norbu was solidly anchored next to a large rock.

Then suddenly, out of sight, Pasang slipped.

As Bauer watched in shock and horror, Pasang tumbled into view followed a few seconds later by Schaller who arced through the air, passing over Pasang until they both came crashing down at the foot of the couloir. For a brief moment Bauer hoped that the rope might just hold but as they bounced helplessly into the air and then continued falling, it simply could not support their weight. Within seconds the rope had snapped, leaving Schaller and Pasang to fly out of control down the flank of the North East Spur, with an avalanche of dirty snow following in their wake.

One of the Sherpas in Bauer's party, Bagde, was a close friend of Pasang. He screamed and for a moment it looked as if he too was planning to throw himself into the abyss. Bauer was so worried that he was forced to tie Bagde to a rock before climbing up to Camp 8. There he found the other two Germans, Hartmann and Wien, resting inside their sleeping bags, oblivious to what had happened below.

Bauer didn't tell them straight away but insisted that they should follow him back down. Only when they saw the still distraught Bagde and the other Sherpa, Norbu, did Hartmann realise that something terrible had happened. It was too late in the day to reach their tents, so they hacked out a perch in the snow and sat down to spend a miserable night huddled together to keep warm. Schaller and Pasang had been carrying the bulk of the expedition food; all that was left was a handful of sweets and some dried apricots.

After a painfully long night, they were on the move again, climbing down to the Eagles' Nest, where their descent coincided with the arrival of a supply convoy from below. Bauer told them the bad news and then ordered everyone to strike the camp and return to Advance Base. Before they did any more climbing, they would all spread out over the glacier below to search for the dead men's bodies.

Allwein and Aufschatter found them next day in the glacier basin. Bauer watched from above as they carried the corpses through the snow. Pasang was severely disfigured but apart from injuries to his head and right arm, Schaller looked strangely placid. When Bauer reached them on the following morning, he helped tidy up the dead men's clothing and crossed their arms. Then they wrapped Schaller in his sleeping bag and carried the two corpses to a rocky island in the middle of the glacier.

The Sherpas dug holes in the hard soil and then buried their comrades after a brief ceremony. It was the second year in a row that men had died on Kangchenjunga, and though the accident wasn't as deadly as the avalanche which had hit Jacot-Guillarmod's party in 1905, it was a huge blow to team morale.

Earlier in the expedition Schaller had written a fateful sentence in his diary:

> Kangchenjunga is the highest goal for a mountaineer, worth risking one's life for.

As a team, they had discussed what they would do in the event of an accident and everyone, Schaller included, had agreed that it should not prevent them from continuing but as Bauer now discovered, dealing with their collective grief and somehow motivating everyone to start again, was immensely difficult.

First he sent a runner back to Kalimpong with a telegram for Schaller's parents, along with a short dispatch for the *Times* which appeared a week later on August 21st. In an obituary published that week, Schaller's youthful excitement struck a poignant note:

> The death of Herr Hermann Schaller, of the Kangchenjunga Expedition, which cut short a young and promising career, will be deeply felt by a wide circle of personal friends and mountaineering comrades .... Letters which he wrote home since leaving Munich, were all full of his high hopes and his delight in the many experiences of the adventure. The fine qualities of courage, endurance, and unselfish devotion to the common interests which he displayed during the last few weeks make his untimely death a heavy loss to the other members of the expedition.

The climbers and Sherpas came together to build a tall cairn next to the gravesite to commemorate their fallen comrades but the expedition was divided as to what to do next.

Tsin Norbu, the only survivor of Schaller's party acted as the porters' spokesmen. He argued that it was useless to continue and that they should abandon Kangchenjunga and climb an easier peak nearby. Why carry on, he asked, when the mountain was in such a dangerous state and when there was so much illness in the team? Allwein had improved but was still suffering from sciatica and almost everyone had coughs and colds. Two of the other Germans, Yoachim Leupold and Wilhelm Fendt were both severely ill, Leupold with malaria and Fendt with a raging fever, later diagnosed as paratyphoid.

There was no good cheer in their letters from home either. In the summer of 1931 Germany was in the middle of a severe financial crisis. The currency situation was so bad that the Bank of England had to intervene to prop up a number of German banks. Most of the expedition's cash had been raised in Germany and there were payments still to be made. With one climber having a seriously ill father back home, and another hearing news that his wife had just had a daughter, Bauer felt under huge pressure to call off the expedition – but he felt compelled to continue. As he wrote in a dispatch the Times:

> Sorrow for his death must not make us faithless to the task set us and we knew that he would wish us to go on. A few days before the accident he had said that all his thoughts were concentrated on the summit of this formidable mountain.

Fortunately, in spite of their grief, the other German climbers all agreed with Bauer that the expedition must go on. Work started again in earnest on August 16th, two days after the burial, with two of the newer members of the team, Karl Wien and Hans Pircher climbing back up to the Eagles' Nest. The Sherpas were still unhappy and Tsin Norbu decided to leave the expedition altogether but Tendechar, the expedition cook, managed to persuade three of the strongest men— Kami, Ketar and Pemba— all veterans of 1929, to stick with Bauer and his team as they pushed back up the mountain. A few of the other Sherpas agreed to carry loads between Camp 6 at the foot of the Spur and the Eagles' Nest, but refused to go any further.

Their first big challenge was to cut a new route to Camp 8. It was obvious to Bauer that no Sherpa would ever risk the couloir where Schaller and Pasang had died, so there was no alternative but to find a more direct route along the top of the ridge, an option they had rejected initially because it looked so difficult. At some points it was knife edge thin, elsewhere it was blocked by the mushroom shaped formations they had encountered on the flanks. Clearing a safe path required endless painstaking work but finally on August 24th, after eight days of hard labour, they were able to reoccupy the first terrace and re-pitch the tents at Camp 8.

Ahead lay another 4,000 vertical feet of difficult climbing just to get to their high point of 1929. The main challenge was once again to find a way over, or if necessary through, the ice towers that crowded along the ridge crest in front of them. They did not seem to be quite as high as they had been in 1929, but it was still an immense struggle to find a safe route through or around them. A few times Bauer's men spent days chipping away at the base of a tower until it came crashing down but often the towers were so big they had no alternative but to tunnel right through them.

By the end of August, the lead climbers were ready to move up to Camp 9, on the next terrace, about 1000 ft higher up. The supply train up the mountain was moving steadily but Bauer was increasingly worried about man-power. Wein, Pircher and Hartmann were making solid progress on the ridge, but their three high-altitude Sherpas, whose job was to keep them fuelled and provisioned, were already showing signs of exhaustion. They begged Bauer to persuade some of the other Sherpas to come up and help carry supplies to the lead climbers.

So on September 1st, Bauer began the long climb down to Base Camp on the Zemu glacier with his 'personal' Sherpa, Kami. They were very glad to get a good meal from the expedition cook, Tendechar, but the situation on the Zemu glacier was far from perfect. Two of the Germans, Fendt and Leupold, were still too weak to do any further climbing and as Bauer acknowledged, in normal circumstance should have been on the way back to Germany. The good news was that

Eugene Allwein had recovered from his sciatica and was keen to return to the fray and, even better than that , two more Sherpas, Dordshi and Pasang (the second Pasang on the team) were willing to accompany Bauer back up the North East Spur to join the others on the high-level carries.

No sooner however had the two Sherpas agreed to go back, than the heavens opened. For almost a week it snowed so heavily that Bauer couldn't leave Base Camp. The weather finally broke on September 8th and the following day they began the long slog back up mountain. Bauer's initial hope, that they would be well established on the North East Spur by the end of July, had clearly been far too optimistic. When he reviewed progress, they were still two weeks ahead of their position back in 1929 but the continual delays were wearing down even his iron resolve. As he wrote longingly in a dispatch for *The Times* dated September 10th, they desperately needed bit of good luck:

> We now hope that this snow is the last outbreak of monsoon weather in this forsaken tract, and that a fortnight of fine weather will enable us to make the final assault on the summit before more snow and the cold force us to descend.

Fortune, however, was not on his side.

When, after a long slog, Bauer and the two Sherpas got within sight of Camp 8, Pasang and Dordshi utterly lost their nerve, knowing they were so close to the place where the accident had occurred just a few weeks earlier. Pasang in particular was terrified that he would perish like his namesake and pleaded with Bauer to let him turn back. It was so late in the day that either they would have to bivouac on the spot or push on through. Bauer chose the latter, but though they reached Camp 8 safely, next morning the two Sherpas were still in no shape to continue. Pasang had developed snow blindness after taking his goggles off and Dordshi was still totally demoralised. Bauer didn't have a spare man to escort them down, so he left them in the ice cave at Camp 8 with blankets and enough food and fuel to survive for several days, promising to come back as soon as possible.

As he continued up with just Kami in support, there was one bit of good news from above. In his absence, the others had pushed on to just under 23,000 ft to set up Camp 10. They were hoping to set up Camp 11 at close to 25,000ft, surpassing their maximum altitude from 1929. The porter crisis however had intensified with Ketar and Pemba, the two Sherpas who had done most of the carrying, collapsing in tears when they heard Pasang and Dordshi would not be coming to their assistance. Bauer realised that without them it would be futile to carry on, so he decided to rest Pemba and Ketar at Camp 9 for a few days, in the hope that a little time off would boost their morale.

The other compensation was that they were now at in an amazing setting, which appealed to the Romantic in Bauer:

> One lived here upon an almost ethereal platform raised high above the world, and separated from it by vast abysses, while gentle slopes led up to higher regions. One was nearer the sky than the earth...Although we felt utterly worn out, the fact that we were actually standing up there, gave us new strength.

They had enough supplies for a fortnight and sufficient equipment to establish three more camps. As he predicted, Ketar and Pemba cheered up immeasurably after a few days off and, mercifully, the weather remained settled. On Sept

16th, they were on the move again, both porters and climbers carrying 30 lb loads. It was the last throw of the dice. If the weather held, it was just about feasible to get to the summit, but the pressure was starting to take its toll.

Bauer's own moment of crisis came a few hundred feet below Camp 10. The terrain was not difficult but Bauer noticed that he was moving very slowly and feeling utterly exhausted. After three hours of hard graft he managed to climb just under 900 ft on a route that was by then well established. His climbing partner, Peter Aufschnaiter, was so concerned by his leader's slow progress that he had no alternative but to tell him to turn back. It was a moment that Bauer had never thought would come. For the last two years Kangchenjunga had been his obsession, but if he carried on at this slow pace he would both endanger himself and the whole expedition. Reluctantly he began to descend but before long he found himself feeling weaker and weaker until he got to a point where he realised he just wasn't strong enough to reach Camp 9 alone and that Camp 10 was in fact closer.

He turned around but as he struggled upwards, step after agonising step, he caught sight of a range of mountains to the north, close to where the Scottish explorer Alexander Kellas was buried. Ten years earlier in 1921 Kellas had died from a heart attack, en route from Sikkim to Tibet to take part in the first British Everest expedition. It was a sad lonely death which had shocked the mountaineering world. If he didn't make it to the next camp, Bauer feared he would share the same fate and become his expedition's next casualty.

Drawing on all his reserves, Bauer made it to the snow cave at Camp 10 only to discover it was empty. The others must have carried on up the ridge. He soon realised why: the ice cave at Camp 10 was furnished with neither sleeping bags nor blankets, and unlike most of their snowholes which were invariably far warmer than any tent, was split by a huge crack through which the freezing wind blew.

Bauer found a medicine chest and a stash of milk tablets and spent the night crawling around trying to keep warm, guzzling down pans full of warm milk and handfuls of Kardiozol pills, a potent respiratory aid. He survived, but as he later wrote, it was the worst night of his life. The next morning, as soon as he could summon up strength, he retreated back down the mountain to the sleeping bag he had left at Camp 9.

While their leader was having a torrid time, the others were still going strong. They had excavated another large ice cave, Camp 11, a little higher than planned at 25,100 ft. This meant they had now gone past their high point of 1929 and were about to start on virgin territory. After Camp 10, the ice towers and strange mushrooms had largely disappeared, enabling them to make much more progress.

On September 17th the two Berliners, Hans Hartmann and Karl Wien, left Camp 11 and climbed up to the highest point on the North East Spur which they christened 'Outpost Peak'. At 25,262 ft, they were now just 3,000 ft below the summit of Kangchenjunga and about 1000 ft above their high point of 1929. The skies were astonishingly clear, allowing them to see a long way into both Nepal and Tibet. It would have been a triumphant moment, if it hadn't been for what they saw next.

In all the photographs they had pored over back in Germany, it had looked as if the North East Spur joined the north ridge of Kangchenjunga in one continuous sweep but as they now discovered the path upwards was more complicated. After Outpost Peak, the North East Spur actually dropped down and twisted north-westwards before broadening out into a small plateau. The plateau looked like the ideal site for their twelfth camp but the long slope at the far end which led up to the North ridge was covered in a deep, fragile looking layer of snow. It already showed signs of having begun to avalanche and looked distinctly precarious.

Hartmann and Wien returned to Camp 11 to discuss what to do next, but the day's clear skies were followed by a bitterly cold night. They were all nursing coughs and colds, and Hans Hartmann's toes were looking distinctly frost-bitten. After enduring an excruciating night, the next morning he was unable to leave his sleeping bag. Allwein and Wien headed up to take a closer look at the slope which lead to the North ridge.

Up close, the prospects seemed even worse. Not only was it steep but part of the slope bulged outwards, making it even more dangerous. Allwein, an avalanche expert, studied it intently but could find no safe route up or feasible way to avoid it. If they'd had an avalanche gun, they could have deliberately brought the snow down, if they'd had time they might have waited for the slope to spontaneously collapse but they had neither and to make matters worse it had started to snow again. There was no chance of carrying on, Allwein announced reluctantly, the way ahead was just too dangerous.

Back at Camp 11, Hartmann argued that if Bauer had been with them, he would not have turned back so close to their goal but as Wien wrote in his diary, "What good are these discussions... we must reconcile ourselves to the facts." Back in 1929, they had found themselves stranded in their tents high up on the North East Spur, split into several parties and unsure whether they would be able to get back down in the midst of heavy snow-storms. They had managed to escape but only just. Once again heavy snows were threatening to hamper their retreat, so reluctantly they turned back.

A day later they found Paul Bauer at Camp 9. He was much recovered, glorying in the magnificent setting and hoping for positive news from above. When Allwein told him what they had found, he was devastated. Had they really made so many sacrifices only to be defeated for a second time? It was a demoralising end to the expedition but Bauer accepted that ultimately they had made the right decision. As he later wrote in an article for the Himalayan Journal:

> We might have ventured a final assault in which all was staked on a single card, but even so we must have waited; and a long wait at those heights, if it is possible at all, demands fresh forces. In consequence of these considerations, we felt that there was no option but to renounce final success. An immediate attack on the slope would have been senseless and inexcusable.

Their retreat was not so panic stricken as two years earlier, but it was a dismal, depressing experience. At Advance Base, they found a letter from Schaller's mother telling them how worried she was for their safety after the death of her son. To further remind them of the risks, in the same postbag there was a plaque which had been commissioned by the Himalayan Club to commemorate the deaths of Schaller and Pasang.

The others went up to install the plaque next to their burial place, but for the second time on the expedition Bauer was too weak to accompany them. Instead he lay down below the rocky island in the middle of the Zemu glacier and found himself hallucinating that he was back in the German army at the end of WW1, staring up at his former battalion commander, unable to speak because of a gaping wound in his chest. This was not how he had envisaged his Kangchenjunga adventure ending.

On September 28th he sent a runner to Kalimpong to announce the end of the expedition and on the following day they broke camp and began the long journey back home. A week later, The *Times* made a formal announcement of the disappointing news:

> Information has been received that the German Himalayan Expedition led by Herr Paul Bauer has been obliged to abandon its assault on the summit of Kanchenjunga after attaining a height of 26,000ft. At that height. the climbers discovered an unexpected 500ft. wall was unassailable owing to the danger of avalanches. This news was dispatched by runner from Camp V1 on September 28. Thus the extremely formidable character of Kanchenjunga as a giant that rebuffs assault is again confirmed.

The German team reached Darjeeling in mid-October and then headed back to Europe via Calcutta, trying to put a brave face on it. "The greatest thing," Bauer wrote in his memoir, "is to have fought for such a goal, without shrinking, without fearing, to the last."

Once again the expedition received a lot of praise for its efforts, both in Germany and Britain. If anything, the editor of the *Alpine Journal*, was even more effusive in his assessment of the second attempt than he had been about the first:

> To comment at length on the great 1931 struggle would be mere presumption. It will be sufficient to state that for skill, endurance, cold-blooded courage and especially for judgment, the expedition will stand as the classical model for all time.

In 1932, *Himalayan Campaign*, Bauer's account of his two Kangchenjunga expeditions was published to great acclaim and awarded a Gold medal at the Los Angeles Olympics.

Bauer began his account of the second attempt with a call to arms, imploring German climbers to treat Kangchenjunga like Everest, and turn it into a national goal:

> Having once forced a breach, German climbers should concentrate all their efforts upon Kangchenjunga, which in more respects than one, is the world's most important mountain.

Bauer's passion was untiring but his obsession with Kangchenjunga was not shared by all German climbers. When he got back home there was no support for another expedition to the mountain that seemed impossible to climb. In 1932, Willy Merkl led the first German expedition to Nanga Parbat in the Western Himalayas, the world's ninth highest mountain and another chapter in German mountaineering began. The expedition was not successful, but it was soon followed by four further attempts. For a generation of German climbers, Nanga Parbat became their Schicksalsberg, their "mountain of destiny".

As Bauer saw it, the only reason why Nanga Parbat was now preferred over Kangchenjunga was the simple fact that at 26,660 ft it was 1500 ft lower and perceived to be an easier climb. To an extent though, it was his own fault. Bauer's nationalist rhetoric had turned mountaineering into a matter of national pride, and after two unsuccessful expeditions to Kangchenjunga there was no appetite for yet more failure. As Germany's mountaineers soon found out to their cost, however, there was no such thing as an 'easy' 8000m peak. By the end of the decade, more than twenty-five climbers and

Sherpas had died on Nanga Parbat, and no-one had reached the summit.

A much uglier side to Bauer appeared later in the 1930s when the Nazis came to power. They soon began a programme of compulsory "Gleichschaltung" or Nazification of all aspects of German life, including sports such as mountaineering. Bauer joined the party and was appointed leader of the German Mountaineering and Hiking Association. He rose to become deputy leader of the Alpenverein and the German Himalayan Foundation, an organisation set up to finance further Himalayan expeditions.

Günter Dyhrenfurth, Bauer's old rival, was still very active but he got no funding from any official body and naked hostility from Paul Bauer. When Dyhrenfurth's film, *The Demon of the Himalaya* was released, Bauer was in the forefront of opposition, denouncing it in a letter to the Reich film office as "Jewish businessmen exploiting the current interest in far-away mountains".

In spite of this, Bauer retained the respect of British climbers. When Frank Smythe wrote an article for *The Himalayan Journal* in 1935 on the "The Problem of Kangchenjunga", he finished by declaring that Bauer's route up the North East Spur was probably the best way to the top, adding:

> When Kangchenjunga is climbed, it is to be hoped that it will be climbed by Herr Bauer and his party, for their great efforts of 1929 and 1931 have rendered them worthy of treading the summit of that most noble and magnificent mountain.

But it was not to be.

Bauer returned to the Sikkim in 1936 to lead a small training expedition aimed at introducing a new generation of German climbers to the Himalayas but there was neither the support nor the resources to make another attempt on Kangchenjunga. Instead they made the first ascent of Siniolchu, a striking but much lower peak.

Two years later, Bauer bowed to the inevitable, and left Germany to lead the fourth, unsuccessful, German expedition to Nanga Parbat. It would be his last ever visit. In the following year Hitler sent German forces over the border into Poland and Paul Bauer re-enlisted to work as an instructor and member of the Gebirgsjager, Germany's Alpine troops. The Himalayas would have to wait. For now and the foreseeable future, the world was at war.

Part II
The First Ascent

CHAPTER FIVE
The Sport of Imbeciles

At first light on June 3rd 1950, Maurice Herzog and Louis Lachenal wriggled out of their sleeping bags, donned their frozen boots and crampons, and slowly began climbing upwards towards the summit of Annapurna, a striking mountain in central Nepal. It was too cold to heat water for breakfast, but fortified by Maxiton, a powerful amphetamine, Herzog and Lachenal ploughed on, alternating the lead as they got ever closer to their goal.

An experienced Chamonix guide, Louis Lachenal could feel his feet becoming frost-bitten. He wanted to turn back and asked Herzog what he would do if he had to abandon the attempt. Herzog instantly replied that he would carry on alone. Annapurna was not just a mountain, it had become Herzog's spiritual 'ideal' and he wasn't going to give up so close to the end. Lachenal felt it his duty not to leave his partner so on they went until they reached the summit at 2.00 p.m. after six hours of climbing.

At 26,545 ft, Annapurna is around 1500 ft lower than Kangchenjunga, but it was the first ever 8,000m mountain to be climbed. Other climbers had been higher, Teddy Norton reaching 28,126 ft on Everest back in 1924, but no-one had stood on the very summit of one of the world's great mountains. Herzog and Lachenal had made history, breaking through a key psychological barrier, the four-minute mile of high altitude climbing. When they returned to France they were acclaimed as national heroes and were soon famous around the world.

The Second World War had brought a temporary halt to high altitude climbing but it also saw the development of new, much-improved cold weather clothing, nylon ropes and more reliable oxygen equipment. A new generation of Himalayan climbers emerged who were greater risk takers than their predecessors. They were determined to settle old scores with mountains their countrymen had failed to climb in the 1920s and 30s. In 1953 the ninth British expedition succeeded in putting Hillary and Tenzing on the summit of Everest and five weeks later the great Austrian climber, Hermann Buhl, reached the top of Nanga Parbat on the sixth Austro-German expedition. A year later in 1954, Lino Lacedelli and Achille Compagnoni hacked their way to the top of K2, forty-five years after the Duke of Abruzzi led the first Italian expedition in 1909.

Who though would be the first person to climb Kangchenjunga?

The two most recent expeditions had been led by the Germans, Paul Bauer and Günter Dyhrenfurth, but both men were now in their fifties and neither had the means to organise a new attempt. The general assessment of Kangchenjunga, that it was hardest of the world's top three mountains, did seem to have been born out in practice. Both Everest and K2 had almost been climbed in the 1930s but no-one had got closer to the summit of Kangchenjunga than Bauer's team in 1931, and they really hadn't got anywhere near. But as Fridtjof Nansen famously said, "The difficult is what takes a little time; the impossible is what takes a little longer". The 'can do' spirit of the late 1940s meant that Kangchenjunga would not be left alone for too long.

The first mountaineer to declare an interest was Norman Dyhrenfurth, Günter Dyhrenfurth's son. He had emigrated to the US with his mother in 1937 and served in the army during the war. In 1948 Norman wrote an article for the American Alpine Journal entitled "What are the Chances of Climbing Kangchenjunga?" It began with a bold statement:

> No mountain on the earth can surpass Kangchenjunga for size, magnificence and awe-inspiring grandeur.

In the following pages, he went on to review the expeditions of the 1920s and 30s and list the possible routes to the summit. He was doubtful of his father's approach from the North West and thought that Paul Bauer's route up the North East Spur was extraordinarily difficult. More promising, he wrote, would be to try the West ridge, approaching either from the Ramthang glacier or from the South West, via the Yalung glacier. No-one had tried the Yalung approach since 1905 and the ill-fated expedition led by Jacot-Guillarmod and Aleister Crowley but if all went well, Norman would shortly be heading for Nepal to put his theories to the test.

Nothing came of it but Norman wasn't the only climber who wanted to visit the Yalung, the huge glacier that runs down from the South West Face. In 1951 Gilmour Lewis, a young Welsh mining engineer then based in India, spent several weeks in the area with a Swiss friend, George Frey, and a party of Sherpas led by Tenzing Norgay, who in a few years would soon win world-wide fame on Everest. They climbed one of Kangchenjunga's satellite peaks and even ventured onto the lower reaches of the South West Face itself.

Frey died later that summer in a climbing accident that almost killed Tenzing, but two years later in the spring of 1953 Lewis returned to the Yalung with John Kempe, a British headmaster based in Hyderabad. Kempe climbed the north peak of nearby Kabru, from which he was able to closely study the South West Face, while Lewis trekked up the Yalung glacier to take a look from below. Both came back convinced that if a party could reach the "Great Shelf", the huge terrace that ran across the mountain from around 23,000 ft, it might well be able to reach the summit.

Getting to the Great Shelf, however, would not be easy. The most direct approach was via a huge icefall, a frozen river made up from hundreds of enormous blocks of ice which creaked and groaned as they spilled down the mountain. Traditionally mountaineers had avoided icefalls because they were so dangerous, but after the success of the Everest expeditions of 1952 and 1953, which began with a crossing of the infamous Khumbu icefall, Kempe and Lewis thought that it might be possible to climb Kangchenjunga's equally ferocious ice-fall.

Initially they hoped that a British newspaper might fund a reconnaissance expedition but they drew a blank. Though disappointed, Kempe and Lewis decided to press on regardless, albeit on a smaller and cheaper scale. What they didn't realise was that back in England, in the spring of 1954, another British mountaineer was thinking long and hard about Kangchenjunga. His name Lieut. Col. John Hunt and, in his case, money was no object.

Hunt was the army officer who had led the 1953 Everest expedition. He had spent the six months following his triumph touring Britain and then the rest of the world, celebrating his team's success on Earth's highest mountain. As a result of all those public appearances and the books, films and articles generated in the aftermath of Everest, a vast amount of money had been raised.

There were various suggestions as to how to spend it, ranging from giving the money to the expedition's sponsors to distributing it amongst the climbers but in the end the Everest Committee decided to set up a new body, The Mount Everest Foundation, whose aim would be to encourage "the exploration of the mountain regions of the Earth." The first beneficiary of this aim, or so Hunt wished, would be a major British expedition to Kangchenjunga.

It was something that he had been dreaming about since 1932 when, as a young soldier in the Indian army, he had first seen Kangchenjunga from Darjeeling. With tightly cropped pale red hair and a clipped moustache, outwardly Hunt appeared like an archetypal 'pukka chap' but he was an unconventional soldier who preferred butterfly collecting and mountaineering to socialising in the regimental mess. In 1937 he'd used his leave to spend several weeks exploring the peaks and passes around Kangchenjunga with a friend, before severe weather and illness had forced him to retreat.

When in the spring of 1954 Hunt heard about John Kempe's planned trip, he began to formulate a plan. If Kempe came back with positive news about the South West Face then he would organise a more comprehensive reconnaissance for

1955, to be followed up in the following year by a full blown expedition. Hunt had learnt a lot on Everest in 1953 and was very keen to put those lessons into practice on Kangchenjunga. Firstly though, he wanted to see how John Kempe got on.

1954 was going to be a busy year in the Himalayas. There was an American expedition to Makalu, a New Zealand expedition to the Barun Valley, a Japanese expedition to Mansalu and a British expedition sponsored by the *Daily Mail,* whose aim was to establish once and for all whether the Yeti existed. None of these efforts however were as impecunious as John Kempe's shoestring expedition to Kangchenjunga.

He assembled a small party of British climbers and begged, borrowed and rented the bare bones equipment needed to venture onto the world's third highest mountain. Three members of his team - John Tucker, Ron Jackson and Gilmour Lewis - took a budget boat trip from Britain; the remainder – Kempe, Trevor Braham, and the expedition doctor Don Matthews – were already based in India.

In the early spring of 1954, they convened at British mountaineering's new home from home: Rungneet tea plantation near Darjeeling. It was the residence of Mrs Jill Henderson, the Honorary Local Secretary of the Himalayan Club. All the recent British Everest teams had stayed at Rungneet and for a penniless expedition like John Kempe's, its comforts were particularly welcome.

Accompanied by seven Sherpas and six busloads of general porters, Kempe and his team set off for Kangchenjunga in mid-April. As he admitted, lack of money meant that they could not afford to hire the best Sherpas and had to make do with whoever was available. As with so many of the 1930s expeditions, they had trouble with their porters early on, with twenty men leaving just a few days into the expedition. Kempe pressed on but, as he confided to his diary, he soon grew tired of all the logistical problems and the sheer grind of the approach march:

> Climbing in the Himalayas is really for imbeciles. In the Alps after four days one can return to civilization, read a book and return to the climb with a lot to think about. In the Himalayas there is no rest, it is always too uncomfortable to read anything very serious though I have a feeling that a maths book would have given me more to think about than anything. And one is usually too tired by the evening or too busy to settle down and read.

Just beyond the village of Tseram they spotted the now even more ruined Decherol monastery, but though they encountered a couple of yak herders who remembered meeting Frank Smythe in 1930, there was no new information about the lost American climber, E.E.Farmer. Kempe had planned to refresh the expedition's larder at Tseram but there was no food available so he had to send his head Sherpa Ajeeba off to nearby farms to buy provisions at exorbitant prices. They could not afford to buy a yak for fresh meat but were able to procure a small sheep whom they christened Octavius. Before long their hunger overcame their petting instincts and Octavius was dispatched and eaten.

Once they reached Base Camp, Kempe identified a series of potential routes up Kangchenjunga from their base in the Yalung glacier. The most direct still seemed to be via the icefall but on closer examination, he realised that it was split in two: the Lower Icefall stretching from 18,000 ft to a small plateau at 20,000 ft and the larger but slightly less steep,

Upper Icefall, which continued for the next 3000ft to the foot of the Great Shelf.

In order to get a better look, Kempe and the British climber Trevor Braham climbed up as far as Pache's grave, the main camp site for the Crowley expedition of 1905. It was an eerie spot, covered in black lichen and the scattered remains of old packing cases and kerosene tins. A rough wooden cross made from a broken ski, marked the grave of Alexis Pache, the Swiss army officer who had died along with three porters. As John Tucker wrote in his expedition memoir:

> The whole area gave the impression that the party had only just left and the two men (Kempe and Braham) found it hard to appreciate that they were standing at the scene of a tragedy which had been enacted fifty years ago and fifteen years before they themselves were even born.

Kempe was no fan of Aleister Crowley and his direct route up the South West Face but he wanted to discover whether the icefall was climbable. If so, it could provide a route onto West Ridge. As he and his party sat in his tent preparing to make their first foray, the whole of Kangchenjunga seemed to be on the move with large avalanches thundering down from above. When they ventured upwards, Kempe found the icefall a noisy, threatening environment. Even if they could find or force a passage, he was unsure it could be used repeatedly by heavily-laden porters.

As an alternative, his teammate Gilmore Lewis suggested they should make their way up a large rock buttress adjacent to the icefall which, though very steep, looked a little safer. It proved to be surprisingly straightforward and they even found a good camping spot on top, but they couldn't find an easy way to get back onto the South West Face. Kempe was relatively confident in the skill of his Sherpas when climbing on snow and ice, but few of them had any technical experience on steep rock. He was debating what to do next when fate intervened.

First the expedition doctor, Don Matthews, was caught by a small rock fall which left one of his hands badly smashed up. Then a day later, a huge avalanche thundered down the South West Face and almost flattened Advance Base camp and the Sherpas who had been left in charge of it. There was no alternative but to descend and move the damaged tents several hundred yards lower down.

Rather than return to the rock buttress straight away, Kempe agreed to allow two members of his team, Trevor Braham and Ron Jackson, to try a completely different approach on the other side of the glacier. Braham thought there might be a way onto Kangchenjunga's North ridge, the unrealized goal of Paul Bauer and Günter Dyhrenfurth. It too was not to be. Like Matthews, Braham was hit by falling rocks which sent him bandaged and bleeding back to Base Camp.

As May headed towards June, Kempe realised that they had done what they could on Kangchenjunga, so he switched focus to Talung, a 24,107 ft peak nearby. Climbing Talung would be an achievement in itself and also promised another very good vantage point from which to examine the South West Face. In the end atrocious snow conditions denied them the summit but they were afforded a magnificent view of Kangchenjunga, which they photographed and scanned with their binoculars.

Ultimately, Kempe's party did not come away with a definitive new route but they thought that a better-equipped party might be able to get higher on the South West Face and that at the very least it deserved a bigger and more thorough reconnaissance.

Back in Darjeeling, they were met by a cable from John Hunt. He had by then secured funding for both his 'reconnaissance in force' in 1955 and a large scale expedition in 1956 but before he committed a lot of time and money he wanted to know whether the South West Face was indeed feasible. Kempe's subsequent report was encouraging but inconclusive. Hunt was in a quandary. He had already sounded out future members of a Kangchenjunga team but could he really be confident of success?

To add to his problems, Hunt knew by then that he would not be allowed to lead the reconnaissance. He had been on leave from the army for most of the last two years and though the top brass had delighted in the prestige of having a serving officer at the helm on Everest, they weren't so happy with the idea of their renowned Lieutenant Colonel disappearing yet again in 1955. Hunt was planning to resign from the army within a few years and certainly was committed to the main 1956 expedition, but someone else would have to take charge of the reconnaissance. So he wrote a letter to the world's most famous mountaineer, his friend Ed Hillary, who was then in Nepal's Barun Valley with a team of New Zealand climbers.

"What we have in mind," Hunt wrote cheerfully, "is a high powered reconnaissance in the spring of next year, equipped and otherwise capable of getting very high, and therefore testing fully the chances of reaching the top; this would be followed by a full attempt if the reconnaissance shows it to be worthwhile."

Ed Hillary seemed the ideal candidate. He was interested in Kangchenjunga, a top class mountaineer and someone whose fame would add lustre to the proceedings.

There was just one problem.

By the time John Hunt's letter reached Nepal, Ed Hillary was being invalided of the Himalayas. High up the Barun Valley, one of his Kiwi teammates, Jim McFarlane, had fallen into a crevasse and Ed had damaged several ribs trying to rescue him. News of his injuries percolated back to Darjeeling and eventually on to London, growing more and exaggerated in the retelling. Far from awaiting his reply, John Hunt was asked to write Ed's obituary for the *Times,* in case he never came back at all.

The prophets of doom were wrong of course but in the early summer of 1954 Ed Hillary had no intention of staying on in Nepal or making a return trip in the following year. He was newly married, ill and homesick and having spent most of the previous two years living out of a proverbial rucksack, had severely neglected the bee-keeping business that he ran with his brother Rex. The 1955 Kangchenjunga reconnaissance would have to find another leader.

Fortunately John Hunt already had a plan B. If Ed couldn't do it, then hopefully British climber Charles Evans could.

Evans had been Hunt's deputy on Everest and was such a good friend of Ed Hillary that he had been invited to take part in the New Zealand Barun Valley expedition. When that expedition folded, Evans had decided to stay on and at that very moment was tramping across Nepal with one of the New Zealanders, Norman Hardie, and six Sherpas. Apart from coffee, they carried hardly any western food, subsisting instead on tsampa, the coarse barley that the Sherpas loved, and home brewed beer.

At a village just outside Kathmandu Charles met Dawa Tenzing, his friend and favourite Sherpa. Dawa had worked as a high-altitude porter on both the Everest 1953 expedition and their more recent escapade to the Barun valley. He had a pile of letters and a telegram from John Hunt addressed to both Ed and Charles, confirming that the Nepali government had given permission for two Kangchenjunga expeditions in 1955 and 1956 and asking if either man would consider leading the reconnaissance.

Ed had scrawled over it: "Not me. Over to you, Charles."

It was an unexpected but utterly serendipitous invitation. Charles had a successful medical career back in England, but had been dreaming about Kangchenjunga for years. Unlike Ed Hillary, he was fighting fit and unlike John Hunt, he could take time off in 1955. He rang Hunt in London, asking to see Kempe's report but conditionally saying yes to his offer. His two caveats were that he should be allowed to choose his own team and, crucially, that the expedition should be equipped with enough oxygen to go truly high.

Within a month both Charles' requests had been approved, and preparations were being made for the first major British expedition to the Himalayas since Everest.

CHAPTER SIX
Valley Boy

May 26th 1953 was a day Charles Evans would remember forever, the day he almost became the first man to climb Everest. Almost.

He and Tom Bourdillon had been chosen as the spearhead of the British expedition, the first pair to take a crack at the summit while Ed Hillary and Tenzing Norgay waited in the wings. If Charles and Tom succeeded, they would crown the efforts of eight previous British teams.

They were awake at 5.00 a.m. and ready to go at 6.00 a.m. They didn't waste time with breakfast, instead swigging back some lukewarm lemon squash made the evening before. It had been a freezing cold night but both men were confident and ready to go.

Above them soared Everest's South East ridge. Two thousand feet of it had already been explored by the Swiss climber Raymond Lambert and Tenzing Norgay a year earlier. They had stopped at around 28,2000 ft ; Charles and Tom's task was to climb the remaining 800 vertical feet to the summit of the world's highest mountain.

Everything was prepared. Charles and Tom were the two best British climbers on the expedition. They were equipped with the most innovative oxygen sets then available, designed by Tom and his father Robert Bourdillon. The weather was calm and the skies were blue. All they needed was a bit of luck.

At 6.00 a.m., Charles emerged from their tent, strapped on his oxygen set, breathed deeply and got ready to move off.

Nothing.

Within seconds he had torn off his face mask and was inhaling hard and then he was back in the tent. One of the delicate valves that controlled the flow of oxygen was frozen solid. Tom thawed it out with a candle and Charles tried again.

The same thing happened.

Tom spent the next hour and a quarter frantically trying to work out what had gone wrong. Eventually he solved the problem, but when they finally left camp, they were significantly behind schedule. For the next 2,000 ft everything went remarkably well but when they changed their oxygen and soda lime canisters, the problems started again. Instead of breathing pure oxygen, Charles found himself climbing one of the steepest sections of the South East Ridge breathing an unpalatable mixture of oxygen and carbon dioxide. It was amazing that he was able to keep going, but when they reached 28,700 ft, Everest's lower South Summit, Charles knew straight away that he wouldn't be able to make the final three hundred feet to the true summit.

So he and Tom Bourdillon had become embroiled in the world's highest altitude argument. Tom wanted to continue, but Charles as adamant that he couldn't go on with a faulty oxygen set and that even if Tom's was working perfectly, it was too risky to carry on solo. Ultimately, Tom had seen sense and changed his mind, but the descent to their team-mates on the South Col had been a little more than harrowing and a little less than miraculous. As Tom later wrote, they had yo-yoed their way back down, repeatedly falling while trying to hold each other on the rope, then falling again, until they reached the bottom, bruised and frozen but otherwise astonishingly unscathed.

Everyone was overjoyed to see them back in one piece but the night that followed was purgatorial, Charles and Tom crammed into a tiny tent with John Hunt, with no sleeping oxygen and the temperature dropping below freezing point. On the following morning, they went down leaving Hillary and Tenzing to climb up to a higher camp, from which two days later they made the first ascent.

Back in Britain, Charles and Tom were hailed as heroes but though they were proud to have been part of the Everest team, coming a close second was not the same as making the first ascent. In the years that followed, many mountaineers asked the awful 'what-if...?' questions. What if both their oxygen sets had worked? What if they had started like Hillary and Tenzing from a higher camp? What if Tom had continued alone?

Both men bitterly regretted their failure but life had to go on. Tom had a young wife Jennifer who he was desperate to get home to, Charles had plenty more adventures planned and knew that Everest would not be his last trip to the Himalayas. He spent the first half of 1954 on a lecture tour to the US, and the second half in the Barun Valley with Ed Hillary's New Zealand team.

When John Hunt's cable turned up unexpectedly with the offer to lead the 1955 Kangchenjunga reconnaissance, Charles had not needed much persuasion to say yes. Having served as deputy on several other expeditions, this time he would be able to do things his way. It would be a chance to prove himself as both a leader and climber. The expedition was billed as a reconnaissance but what if they could go all the way to the top? Any lingering feelings of disappointment over Everest would disappear if he led the first ascent of Kangchenjunga. But could he?

Charles was used to success, but he wasn't a 'thruster' in the mould of John Hunt or Ed Hillary. Of medium build with a mop of sandy hair, he had a dry wit and an easy smile, an archetypal man's man who everyone seemed to like. He was born in Wales in October 1918 and like too many of his generation never knew his father, a solicitor who was killed in August 1918 while serving in France in the final months of WW1. Charles was brought up by his mother Edith. She did not remarry, instead devoting her life to her son. Charles spent his early years in the Welsh valleys, never speaking English and riding to school on a pony.

It was an idyllic existence but Charles' uncles, all doctors, were convinced he needed a 'proper' education so it was agreed that he should go to Shrewsbury school. Edith uprooted herself too, moving to the nearby town to be close to her son and save the costs of enrolling him as a full boarder. After Shrewsbury, Charles went on to study medicine at Oxford, before joining the Royal Army Medical Corps, with whom he served with distinction in the brutal Burma campaign.

His first sight of the Himalayas had come in late December 1945 when on leave from the army he had trekked along Sikkim's Singalila ridge towards Kangchenjunga. Other officers spent their time off in the clubs and flesh-pots of Calcutta but a mountaineer since youth, Evans had followed all the pre-war Himalayan expeditions and was particularly keen to meet the legendary Sherpas, who he had read so much about.

He didn't get much help from officialdom. Charles was told by an Indian clerk in Darjeeling that no maps of the Singalila ridge were available and warned that it would not be possible to camp out because of the many wild animals poised to "eat up any travellers". If he did insist on going on a trek, the clerk informed him, he would be required to take both a cook and a Sherpa because in order to maintain prestige, British travellers were required to employ several servants.

In spite of all the bureaucratic hurdles, Charles eventually got underway with a single twenty-year-old Sherpa called Lobsang who was hired as porter and general factotum. Though the weather was mixed, Kangchenjunga did not disappoint. Charles' first sight of the mountain came when the clouds lifted to reveal a huge white mass set against a pale blue sky. It was a vision of the sublime. "My feelings were deeper than I could have imagined," he wrote many years later.

For the next week Charles tramped along the Singalila ridge as it wound its way north, Sikkim on one side, the forbidden kingdom of Nepal on the other. At one stop, he was visited by the local police chief, who warned him against straying into Nepal. "I wouldn't dream of it," Charles replied succinctly. Lobsang turned out to be a picaresque figure who used his kukri to chop wood, clean his toe-nails and spread butter. He carried 60 lbs of kit and bedding, three times more than Charles, but was invariably much faster.

It was Charles' first time at high altitude. He frequently found himself breathless but, as he wrote many years later, it was a life-changing experience:

> Measured in one way I had achieved nothing, but I had seen mountains of a size and splendour that no amount of reading, no photographs could have made real to me. I had found a closeness that makes relationships with Sherpas easy; I had found that I could live in this country on what I could find in villages by the way; and I had found something I could not describe but which I knew would make further expeditions easier.

Charles was so enchanted that he considered leaving medicine and applying for a job at the Survey of India but was advised there was no point in joining an institution whose future looked so shaky. Instead he returned to Britain to become a surgical registrar at a hospital in Liverpool. Within a few years he had decided to focus on neurosurgery, heading up a specialist unit for Merseyside. Charles was very good, and in 1953 was appointed Hunterian professor of the Royal College of Surgeons, a very prestigious role.

His success in the medical world was all the more surprising because by then he was spending so much of his time in the Himalayas. Charles had made his first proper foray into Nepal in 1950, when he joined a party led by the famous pre-war British climber Bill Tilman, to make an attempt on Annapurna II, a subsidiary of the main summit. The following year he returned for an expedition to Deo Tibba, before joining the hapless Everest training expedition to Cho Oyo in 1952 and then the Everest expedition of 1953.

Now, in the summer of 1954 Charles began to put together a team to take on Kangchenjunga. The obvious place to look was the old Everest team but as Charles soon discovered, the options were limited. His old partner, Tom Bourdillon, and Wilfred Noyce, another leading British climber of Everest 1953 fame, had already announced that after committing themselves to 'the main expedition' in 1956 they would not be available for the reconnaissance. It was obvious that Ed Hillary would not be coming either and nor would most of the other members of the Everest team.

Charles' solution was ingenious. Instead of signing up all the big names of the British mountaineering world, he would base his team on men who had something to prove. Four of his recruits – Norman Hardie, John Jackson, Tony Streather and Neil Mather – were rejects from the 1953 Everest expedition. As for the other three, George Band had been the youngest member of John Hunt's Everest team but had spent much of the expedition laid low by a severe gastric infection; Tom Mackinnon was a veteran Scottish climber, who, aged 44, would not have been considered for Everest. Charles' last and most controversial choice however was Joe Brown, a 24-year-old self-employed builder from Manchester, who would never even have been nominated in 1953.

From its earliest days, mountaineering had been regarded as a middle and upper-class sport for the simple reason that its first 'playground', in the words of Sir Lesley Stephen, was the Alps. If you wanted to climb in the mountains of France and Switzerland, you had to have both time and money. There were a few 'tradesmen' like the engraver Edward Whymper and the builder A.F. Mummery, who had become famous British mountaineers, but by and large most were middle class professionals – lawyers, soldiers, doctors – and occasionally members of the aristocracy.

The Alpine Club, the most important mountaineering institution, had its base in Pall Mall, one of posh London's social hubs. Applicants for membership were blackballed if they had not done the required number of climbs or were considered unsuitable. Most of the mountaineers who went on the major Himalayan expeditions of the twenties and thirties were Alpine Club men, paid up or in the making. Six members of the 1953 Everest team were graduates of Oxford or Cambridge and nearly all of them had gone to public school. Joe Brown came from an entirely different background.

Like Charles Evans, he had been brought up by a single mother after his father died when he was just eight months old but that's where the similarities ended. The youngest of seven children, Joe's first playground was the back streets of inner-city Manchester. Oxbridge was never an option. Joe left school at fourteen to work as an apprentice plumber and in 1954 was still living at home. His introduction to climbing was the stuff of local legend. In 1946, he and his mates had climbed the rocks next to Kinder Downfall in the Peak District, protected by a rope which had come from a building site. Getting to the top and then hauling the others up was hugely exhilarating and soon Joe was spending all his weekends and holidays on the crags and peaks of Snowdonia and Northern England. "When I first climbed," he remembers, "it was like a thunderbolt, I didn't want to do anything else."

He joined two local groups – the *Valkyrie Club* and its successor the *Rock and Ice* – and eventually partnered up with Don Whillans, an even younger local plumber who was equally passionate about climbing. Together they made a series of outstanding ascents in North Wales and the Peak district, before taking their first trip to the Alps in 1954. They amazed local French mountaineers by storming up the West Face of the Petit Dru, then widely considered to be one of the most difficult climbs in the Alps.

On the same trip Joe and Don met some students from the Oxford University Mountaineering Club who told them all about the upcoming Kangchenjunga expedition – not that they offered any hope that they might take part: "Tom Bourdillon was there who had been on Everest and we got onto the subject of Kangchenjunga and he said that it was all done and dusted, meaning that it was all ready to go, all the members were chosen, and none of us had any thought that it was a possibility for us to be chosen."

Joe might have been told that the team was all but selected, but in October that year, the postman knocked on his door with a life-changing telegram: "Invited Kangchenjunga stop Letter to Follow stop Charles Evans." Joe couldn't believe it but Charles had heard a lot about Joe's exploits in the Alps and had decided to take a chance on him. Within a few weeks Joe was on his way to meet Charles at his hospital in Liverpool. He tried hard to put his latest recruit at ease, explaining his plans and then giving him a quick tour of the operating theatre. Charles pointed to his surgical tools and joked that they were pretty much the same as what Joe would use on a building site. Quick as a flash, Joe picked up one of his drills and quipped back, "You're kidding, mine would do a far better job than this."

Joe's biggest problem was money. Charles explained that all their travelling expenses and food would be covered by a grant from the Mount Everest Foundation, but added that £20 (about £500 in today's money) would be enough for pocket money. That was a lot for Joe and having just been away for the summer in the Alps, he didn't have any spare cash. His only option was to sell the climbing gear that he had just bought in France to his friends.

The other team members, who all had full time jobs apart from George Band, weren't quite so worried about money. Tom Mackinnon was a pharmacist, John Jackson a teacher, Tony Streather, a career soldier. The second youngest member was Neil Mather, another climber from the North. He lived with his parents in Bury and worked for the British Cotton Industry Research Association in Manchester. His boss, who went by the unlikely name of Mr F.C. Toy, was thrilled that one of his employees was going on a major expedition. As he told the *Bury Times*, "When he gets to the top of the world, the textile technologist will at last have arrived where he ought to be." Mr Toy was so enthusiastic that he agreed to keep Neil on half pay for the duration of the expedition, no matter how long it took.

From the beginning, Charles' unofficial deputy leader was Norman Hardie, a civil engineer who had moved from New Zealand to Britain in 1950. Wiry and bespectacled, Norman was a keen hunter and outdoorsman. He was a friend of Ed Hillary, having met him in 1948 in New Zealand during a famous mountain rescue on La Perouse, a dramatic peak in the centre of South Island. Norman was the only member of the Kangchenjunga team who was worried about its status as a reconnaissance. It was unlikely, he tormented himself, that anyone who went in 1955 would be invited by John Hunt to return in the following year, but what if they found the perfect route? How unfair would that be? For the moment though, Norman kept his concerns to himself- there was plenty more pressing work to get on with.

The preparation period for Kangchenjunga was less fraught than it had been for Everest but there was still a lot to be done. Most of their clothing and equipment were based on designs from 1953 but several items, notably their boots and oxygen sets, needed significant improvement. Alf Bridge, one of the backroom boys from Everest, was appointed Expedition Secretary. He was a Mancunian, who had been a very good climber in his youth though never a member of the Alpine Club. Aged 52, he felt too old to put himself forward for the expedition, but he was a great supporter of Joe Brown, encouraging his protégé both financially and morally. Alf was also a good friend of Eric Mensforth, the boss of Normalair, the company that provided the oxygen sets for Everest and who were now offering to help with Kangchenjunga.

In December, three months before their scheduled departure, Norman Hardie was seconded to work full time with Alf at Normalair. In 1953 the Everest team had endured a lot of problems with their oxygen sets. Bottles leaked, valves and tubes froze up and there was no easy way to regulate the flow of oxygen. Norman's brief was to ensure they had a more reliable set with a greater range and more flexibility. As with Everest, mountaineering's favourite 'boffin', the pioneering sports physiologist Griff Pugh, was brought in to advise on oxygen and diet.

Charles was determined to change their approach to food. In 1953 high altitude rations had been organised into one-man packs, but as he knew from experience, high altitude made a climber's appetite fickle and unpredictable. So instead of packing everything into single units, Charles opted for bigger ration packs that could accommodate different tastes. As he wrote in the *Times*, "'the man who likes ham and hates cheese can eat all the ham, while his friend eats all the cheese, and neither man is forced to eat small amounts of each, a practice on a mountain which usually results in his eating the small bit he likes and throwing the other away." Having proved himself an adept, if not always keen quartermaster on Everest, George Band was given the job of organising the expedition food. He sent polite begging letters to the usual British companies and was rewarded with complimentary food and equipment.

The 1955 Team
Top Row: Tony Streather, Norman Hardie, George Band, Tom Mackinnon, John Clegg (expedition doctor)

Bottom: Neil Mather, John Jackson, Charles Evans, Joe Brown

In January the whole team met for a training weekend in Snowdonia to familiarise themselves with each other and their climbing equipment. All went smoothly. As George Band increased the pace of his letter writing, more and more supplies came in and were boxed up, ready for India. There was no time however to organise a leaving party. Joe Brown wrote to his clients to tell them that he'd be available for building work on his return, Norman Hardie arranged for his wife Enid and a friend to meet him in Nepal after the expedition was over, Charles performed his last operations and on February 12th they all convened at Liverpool docks to embark on the *SS Circassia*, the pride of *Anchor Line's* Eastern Service.

It was a cold, miserable winter morning with ice on the roads and a distinct chill in the air but nevertheless John Hunt was there to see them off, along with Edwin Herbert, the president of the Alpine Club. A photographer from the *Times* arrived to take a group photograph of the latest intrepid British Himalayan expedition and then, without more ado, they were on their way.

The *Circassia* was a small but luxurious passenger liner which boasted a swimming pool, a cocktail bar, a lavishly appointed lounge and 600 yds of promenade deck. There was accommodation for 321 first class passengers and 80 steerage berths, though on this voyage there were only 200 travellers. As George Band noted in his diary, the passenger list included no less than 27 Christian missionaries. Even though George himself was the son of missionaries, he was not enchanted by their company, commenting in his diary, "A quiet voyage on the whole. "

For Joe Brown, their passage to India was the beginning of a great joyous adventure that he still couldn't quite believe was happening. "The memorable thing was the meals, the amount of food and variety. For breakfast there was every type of bread, cereal, eggs and bacon, and some things that were unavailable back home at the time – it was just incredible. I was aware that I had a lot to learn socially, like on the ship when you'd get a table placing that had umpteen pieces of cutlery, and I'd say to John Jackson, 'Which should I use for this?' and he'd say 'It doesn't matter'. The voyage was just an incredible holiday."

In between huge meals, the team did get down to some serious play. Not content with swimming and swinging on the rails above the pool, Joe Brown invented the strange sport of 'bottom skipping', in which contestants sat on deck and attempted to propel themselves into the air by flexing their glutes while swinging a rope beneath their buttocks as many times as possible. In movie footage shot by Charles Evans for the expedition film, Joe is shown 'bottom-skipping' manfully, with a rope in one hand and a cigarette in the other.

Every day, they would cram into Tony Streather's cabin to take Hindi lessons. Tony had spent the early years of his military career in India and was a good linguist and a patient teacher. The rest of their time was spent reading, writing and taking it easy. George Band had several thousand words to write for a book about his recent trip to Rakaposhi in Pakistan, while Charles Evans worked on a chapter about camping for a 'how-to-climb' manual.

After stops at Gibraltar, Port Said and Karachi, the *Circassia* arrived at Bombay (modern day Mumbai) on March 5th and the usual fun and games with baggage began. When they unloaded the ship, two hundred boxes of equipment were missing and nowhere to be seen. Eventually they were discovered, stowed away in the ship's paint locker, and packed into a sealed goods wagon with the rest of their supplies. Norman Hardie and Tom Mackinnon drew the short straw, agreeing to accompany their cargo on a five-day trip from Bombay to Siliguri in the north of India, using slow local trains.

George Band had a much more comfortable time of it, spending a night at the Grand Hotel in Bombay, before joining Charles Evans for a lecture on Everest at a local club. Then he too began a long, though infinitely less stressful train trip to Calcutta where he met Trevor Braham, the Himalayan club representative who had accompanied John Kempe on his Kangchenjunga trip in 1954. At local institution, Thacker and Spink's bookshop, George chanced upon a copy of SM Goswami's *Everest, Is it Conquered?*, an early conspiracy tract, which claimed that much of the 1953 British Everest expedition film had been shot in a Bombay film studio and that Everest had not been climbed at all.

Charles Evans, meanwhile, had to visit Delhi to deal with some bureaucracy before he too flew up to Calcutta. He begged a ride in an Indian Air Force Dakota, and as he gleefully recalled in his diary, was allowed to briefly take the controls. At Siliguri he met George Band and together they travelled up to the Hendersons' tea plantation at Rungneet in Darjeeling, their base for the next week, carefully dodging the crowds who were filling the air with red powder to celebrate the Hindu Holi festival.

The Hendersons welcomed Charles Evans and his teammates like old friends. Jill Henderson was a vital link between British climbers and the local Sherpa community. In 1953 she had played an instrumental role in persuading Tenzing Norgay to take part in the British Everest expedition, against his initial instincts. There was one crucial piece of diplomacy that she would not be able to help Charles with though this time around, something which no previous pretender to Kangchenjunga's summit had ever had to face:

getting approval from the Sikkimese government to make an attempt on Kangchenjunga.

In the 1920s and 30s Nepal had always been the problem. Its government had jealously guarded its independence and displayed a pathological fear of outsiders, allowing no-one to visit Everest from the Nepali side and only reluctantly giving permission to previous Kangchenjunga expeditions, usually at the last moment. Sikkim, a British protectorate since had 1890, had always been much more compliant.

Two recent events however had redrawn the political map of the whole subcontinent. In 1947 Britain had withdrawn from the jewel in its imperial crown, creating the independent nations of India and Pakistan. Two years later, in 1949, China had invaded Tibet which had been independent for the last 36 years. For the smaller Himalayan states – Nepal, Sikkim and Bhutan – the new political order represented both challenges and opportunities.

During the days of the British Empire, Nepal had been regarded by the British as a 'buffer state' between Imperial China and British India. Now its rulers looked warily to both the north and south, anxious not to be swallowed up by the recently formed People's Republic of China or newly independent India. Their solution was to open up Nepal's borders to the outside world and for the first time actively encourage tourism and closer links to Europe and America.

For Bhutan and Sikkim, the situation was different. Though it had never formally been part of the Empire, during the 1920s and 30s Sikkim particular had been closely aligned to its southern neighbour with strong infrastructural and economic links. When Britain withdrew in 1947, Sikkim could have become completely independent, but within a few years it had elected to become an Indian protectorate, with an Indian Chief minister, or Dewan, and eventually an Indian garrison. Bhutan had also become an Indian protectorate but its ties to India were looser.

All of this might sound like obscure political history, but it had a very significant impact on mountaineering. The Sikkimese had not objected, officially at least, to any of the previous Kangchenjunga expeditions but in the early 1950s they became much more assertive.

For the last four centuries Sikkim had been a determinedly Buddhist nation, ruled by a "Chogoyal" or priest king, descended from a Tibetan Lama. Whereas the world's other two big mountains, K2 and Everest, did not feature highly in local religious cosmology, Kangchenjunga was considered a sacred mountain. It was the "Five Treasuries of the Snow", the home of Sikkim's presiding deity and the general feeling amongst Sikkim's clergy and its populace was that it should not be disturbed by climbing expeditions.

For Charles Evans, this was a real problem which had the potential to derail his expedition entirely. In theory because he was planning to attempt Kangchenjunga from the Nepali side he didn't also need permission from Sikkim, but British diplomats made it very clear to him that both countries had to approve. There had been letters flying back and forward from London to Delhi and Gangtok, the Sikkimese capital, for several months but nothing had been resolved. The only way to get a definite answer was for Charles to go to the royal palace and meet the Sikkimese Chogoyal in person, but even that would not guarantee success.

So on March 9th Charles and Norman Hardie jumped in a jeep and headed for the border. As they made their way north, the landscape changed little: tea plantations, rough tracks and undulating ground. Charles dropped Norman Hardie off at Kalimpong, still an important Sikkimese trading centre, and carried on to Gangtok for his appointment at the Royal palace.

After a long sweaty journey, punctuated by problems with his jeep, Charles desperately needed to rest but he was so concerned about his mission that he went straight to meet Rustomji, the Dewan or Indian chief-minister, only to be told that some weeks earlier a rather unhelpful British diplomat, George Middleton, had promised that when it came to Kangchenjunga there was "no suggestion of an attempt on the mountain."

Charles tried to persuade the chief-minister that though they were indeed intending to make an attempt on the mountain, they would do everything in their power to respect Sikkimese religious sensibilities. After a late stroll illuminated by a full moon, Charles went to bed feeling distinctly nervous.

Next morning it was time to pay an official visit to the palace where he attempted to thrash out an agreement with Rustomji and his highness the Chogoyal. The palace looked splendidly exotic but the elderly ruler remained unhappy about the British expedition and tried to get Charles to agree to a ceiling altitude, above which the climbers would not go. This, Charles felt, was too much of a restriction, for his reconnaissance expedition and for any further attempts. After much discussion, they came up with a solution which Charles hoped would respect local wishes without being too restrictive: there would be no formal limit, but they would agree not to set foot on the very highest point.

After taking dozens of photographs of Gangtok, Charles set off on the tedious journey home, enlivened only by the arrest of his driver for failing to stop at an Indian checkpoint. Back at Rungneet, he briefed the others on his trip. No-one objected to Charles' compromise but the tone of the written agreement showed that he had quite not overcome Sikkim's reservations:

> As arrangements for reconnaissance in the region of Kangchenjunga have already proceeded so far, the Sikkimese Durbar, would not stand in the way, provided the following conditions are observed to ensure against violation of the sanctity of the mountain:
> 1. The party proceeds only so far as may be necessary to survey and ascertain the approaches
> 2. The party will not under any circumstances ascend the peak or its immediate environment
> 3. The present expedition shall not be regarded as a precedent for any future attempt on Kangchenjunga.
>
> Provided an undertaking is given by the Government of India and the UK High Commission that the above conditions will be duly observed the Sikkimese Durbar will not press their objection to the conduct of the present reconnaissance despite their strong feelings regarding any climbing expedition operating the environment of what is regarded by them as the abode of their protective deity.

Quite what Charles would have done if the Sikkimese had refused outright is unclear. The British had not sought an agreement with the Tibetan or Chinese authorities when in 1953 they climbed Everest from the Nepali side, so Charles might have been able to ignore the Sikkimese government, but it was much better to have their agreement albeit with restrictions.

Clearly if John Hunt did come back in the following year, he would have to go through the same tortuous negotiations. All the more reason for Charles to turn his reconnaissance into a full-blown attempt.

CHAPTER SEVEN
Dogged as Done It

Setting out from Rungneet, Jill Henderson on left

It was a great moment.

After all the tension of his trip to Gangtok and the tortuous negotiations with the Sikkimese government, the arrival of Dawa Tenzing and his gang of tough looking Sherpas was just the boost that Charles Evans needed.

Joe Brown noticed how he greeted them "like a long lost family" and was himself quickly caught up in commotion. "They were just like a gang of kids, the excitement was so intense, they were just hugging everyone, it was terrific. They weren't like Sherpas now, who are more likely gillies in Scotland and are better dressed than climbers, they were really 'jungly' with pigtails, they were just fun all the time. It wasn't put on, they were just enjoying life in way that you don't see now, they were marvellous."

The head Sherpa, or sirdar, Dawa Tenzing was an old friend of Charles' and a legendary figure. Dawa was not quite certain of his age but his climbing pedigree stretched all the way from his first portering job on Everest in 1924 up to the 1953 expedition. In a citation for his logbook, John Hunt described him a "porter of the old school, courteous, utterly dependable, solicitous regarding the sahib. He undertook the most arduous work throughout the expedition and was proud of it."

Charles Evans was on more informal terms, regarding Dawa as both a valued team member and a genuine friend. They had first met on the Everest training expedition to Cho Oyu in 1952 and had spent a lot of time together over the last two summers. In 1954, it had been Charles who had recommended Dawa his first job as a sirdar on the New Zealand Barun Valley expedition. He had proved to be very effective both as a climber and a manager of his sometimes unruly Sherpas and was liked by everyone on the team. With Dawa's arrival, Charles was able to relax for a moment, confident that he had a strong and experienced band of Sherpas to support his climbers, most of whom were new to the Himalayas.

A few days later, they were lucky enough to catch their first sight of Kangchenjunga from Rungneet. Like everyone else, Joe Brown was hugely impressed when it appeared from behind a wall of boiling cloud. He noticed a strange atmospheric phenomenon which made Kangchenjunga appear to float in the sky and bear down on top of them. For Charles Evans, the scale of the mountain was as intimidating as it was awesome. As he confided to his diary:

> This is a frightening mountain and in black moods the difficulties, political, organizational, financial, seem great but it is 'dogged as does it', and we are getting along pretty well. It seems also dangerous- sometimes irrationally terrifying- the first sight from Rungneet when you are almost up against it at last.

There wasn't time for too much reflection though, they still had plenty of work to do. In addition to the Sherpas brought by Dawa, they needed to hire 300 local men to carry the six tons of supplies which had just arrived, crammed into five lorries and a shooting brake. Once the local customs officer had checked everything, it had to be broken down into porter friendly 50 lb loads. The heaviest items were the oxygen bottles but the bulk of expedition's stores was food. George Band, the team quartermaster, held a food conference or 'bhat', with Thondup the cook and Dawa Tenzing and proudly showed off all the cooking utensils he had amassed.

To provide light relief from the tedium of all the un-packing and re-packing, there were lunches and official functions as well as personal visits. One of the Henderson's neighbours turned up to show off his extraordinary pet: a huge 20 lb armadillo. George Band was amazed by its human-like its feet and its ability to hang upside down for hours on end. The

Sherpas for their part were equally impressed by George's red check shirt which had come from New Zealand. They advised everyone to marry a Kiwi to ensure a life-long supply.

When Charles paid a social call on Darjeeling's most famous resident Sherpa, Tenzing Norgay, he found someone who was not quite so relaxed as the new arrivals. After his triumph on Everest in 1953, Tenzing had become one of the best known men in India but he was uncomfortable with fame. He had a large new house in the centre of town but was constantly harassed by both advertisers wanting to get product endorsements and relatives and neighbours, calling upon him for financial support. Tenzing told Charles that he was only happy when climbing but he had not gone on any expeditions since Everest and had no current plans to do so. At no point did anyone suggest that Tenzing should accompany them to Kangchenjunga. After all the press controversies at the end of the Everest expedition, which had pitted Tenzing against the British team, it is unlikely that he would have agreed.

Charles and his climbers did visit the newly formed Himalayan Mountaineering Institute where Tenzing worked as the chief climbing instructor. Its mission, according to Indian prime-minister Nehru, was "to create 1000 Tenzings". George Band and Charles Evans also went to tea with the famous pre-war sirdar Ang Tharkay. Apart from Tenzing, he was the best known Sherpa in Europe but though he had enjoyed many adventures with the British mountaineer Eric Shipton and had been the sirdar on Maurice Herzog's Annapurna expedition, Ang Tharkay had given up mountaineering altogether to settle down to life as a farmer. He told George Band that he didn't miss it at all.

When expedition doctor, John Clegg, examined Dawa's band of Sherpas he was surprised at their seemingly poor physiques but Joe Brown immediately recognised how tough and smart they were. Following the practice of the time, each climber was asked to pick a 'personal Sherpa' who in addition to working as a high-altitude porter would look after their 'sahib' on the approach march. George Band chose Tashi from Khumjung, a "bright fellow" according to his diary, and Joe Brown chose Ang Temba. When Joe looked as his logbook he realised that Ang Temba had been to 24,000 ft several times, far higher than he had ever been.

Finally, on March 14th, after a lot of very noisy wrangling, the first of two groups of porters were ready to leave but it was too much to ask for everything to go smoothly. They were loading up a fleet of lorries when the local police arrived and decided to arrest all the drivers, claiming they did not have permits to carry passengers. It took lot of arguing before they finally managed to get away.

For the first 25 miles there was a passable track, but neither their drivers nor the conditions were in top condition. Team doctor, John Clegg recorded in his diary how they crashed not once but twice before they reached the end of the line, a small clearing at 8,000 ft on the Singalila Ridge.

On the first day they marched through the village of Kalipokri, Nepali for 'black pool', but the hailstorm that greeted them had nothing holiday-like about it.

Ahead of them lay some 70 miles of rough tracks and pathways which constantly rose and fell as they zig-zagged across the grain of the country. Charles estimated that it would take about two weeks to reach Base Camp but as ever it all depended on the condition of the high passes.

The 'sahibs' walked in plimsolls, carrying brollies to ward off the rain and very occasionally the sun. Few of their porters had footwear of any kind. They broke into small groups, moving in spurts as they humped their loads from rest stop to rest stop. Unlike John Hunt in 1953, Charles had not planned any specific acclimatisation ascents so they took the approach at a leisurely pace, hoping to gradually adapt to the thin air of high altitude.

The bad weather persisted but the terrain was relatively easy going, except for the occasional dangerous-looking bridge. As Charles Evans joked to George Band, "We half expected to surprise a party of picnickers from Guildford". When they left the Singalila ridge and descended into Nepal, the foliage became denser with endless clumps of rhododendron bushes, not yet in bloom but striking nonetheless.

Their days followed a simple pattern: they would get up early, drink mugs full of tea then walk for several miles before stopping for a large breakfast. Then they would cover a few more miles, make camp in mid-afternoon and rest until supper, reading, completing their diaries or just taking it easy. Whenever they encountered villages, they would supplement their tinned rations with local food. The team cook, Thondup, enjoyed piling their plates high, though his cuisine was sometimes a little odd. As George Band recorded in his diary on March 17th, evening tea consisted of tomato soup, tuna, mashed potatoes with fried onions, peas, carrots and cauliflower in white sauce. For pudding they had tinned damsons and blackcurrant stew but new boy Neil Mather, wasn't in the best position to appreciate it. He suffered from diarrhoea for the first ten days of the approach march. George

Band sympathised, remembering his own epic bout of 'squitters' on Everest in 1953, which lasted for almost a month.

The biggest settlement they passed through was Khebang, just over the border. The local villagers came out in force, dressed in their Sunday best to welcome the British expedition with garlands and floral archways. It was one of the few villages with a school, a sign of the changes that were already happening in Nepal as it opened itself to the world. Westerners however were still a curiosity. As they sat in the centre of the village eating their dinner, the inhabitants crowded round to watch them eat. In return, Norman Hardie took out a portable tape recorder and captured the local girls singing while the expedition doctor John Clegg set up an informal clinic. The local school-master organised a more formal concert and insisted they tell him all about the expedition. Later on, he even sent a note to Base Camp asking if he could visit, though ultimately he never made the trip.

Unlike Everest where the early stages of the expedition had been soured by confrontations between a few of the Sherpas and John Hunt, Charles' team enjoyed a much more relaxed relationship. There was plenty of horseplay and dirty jokes on both sides, with constant banter about 'likpa dorjes', Sherpa slang for 'cock'. As George Band recorded in his diary, one of his team mates had brought along a sex manual. It was constantly being moved from backpack to backpack, in the hope that some unfortunate individual would have to empty their bag in front of a customs officer, and have the offending item displayed to all.

Few of the Sherpas spoke much English, but if they didn't know how to say something, there was usually a way around it. When young Tashi needed a tin of flea powder from John

Clegg but didn't know the correct word, he asked the other Sherpas to take off their shirts and trousers to provide him with a flea. As well as buying village food, the Sherpas were adept at searching out homemade alcohol, both rakshi, the local firewater, and chang, the local beer.

Unfortunately, the Darjeeling porters were equally good at scavenging alcohol, but they were more difficult to work with than the Solu Khumbu Sherpas. The British team paid the going rate supplemented with boxes of 'Battleaxe' cigarettes as baksheesh, but there was still constant grumbling. One day George Band heard a porter singing as he rested against a rock, repeating the same lines over and over again. When he asked for the lyrics to be translated, the message was succinct:

> The sahibs are feasting like Rajahs over there; here I am all alone in my poor corner but there is no baksheesh coming my way.

On March 21st, at the village of Yamphodin, a week into the trek, the inevitable happened: a large group of their Darjeeling porters went on strike. Egged on by lurid tales of the difficult passes yet to come, they dumped their loads and refused to continue unless their wages increased. Charles tried hard to persuade them to continue but in the end seventy men turned their backs on the expedition and headed home. It was a considerable irritation, which would require a few day's relaying of supplies, but Charles was not unduly worried. Porter strikes were such a regular feature of Kangchenjunga expeditions that they were considered an occupational hazard.

Two days later they reached Tseram, the last small settlement before Kangchenjunga, and set up their tents at

Decherol, the ruined monastery haunted by the ghost of the mysterious American climber Edgar Farmer. 'Yalung Camp', as it became known, was an attractive spot, a broad shelf at 13,000 ft, around an acre in size, surrounding by soaring peaks. Two hundred yards further up the valley they could see the terminal moraine of the vast Yalung glacier, which extended for almost twelve miles from its the base at the foot of Kangchenjunga. Close to their camp there were rhododendron bushes and dense clumps of fir trees and juniper bushes, but the glacier itself was brutal looking and intimidating, fringed with steep moraine slopes covered in dirty looking rocks.

While the Sherpas worked hard to amass a huge pile of firewood, Charles paid off the majority of the Darjeeling porters. For the moment he hung on to forty of his best carriers, mostly Sherpas and Sherpanis (female Sherpas), intending that they should supplement Dawa Tenzing's high altitude crew and stay with the expedition until Base Camp proper was fully stocked.

On the night of March 24th, Charles held a joint birthday celebration for Tony Streather and John Jackson, toasting them with rum punch and handing out large slices of the fruitcake that had been presented to them by Edwin Herbert, the president of the Alpine club. Next day, they got to work.

Charles' hope was that with a stronger party and more equipment they would be able to go much further than John Kempe. He had had plenty of time to read Kempe's report and was under no illusions that Kangchenjunga would be easy but was determined that at the very least they would find a way through the two icefalls and reach the Great Shelf. Before anything could happen though, first they would have to spend a couple of weeks carrying a mass of supplies and equipment to Base Camp.

Charles split the team into three parties each with its own mission. While he and the big Scottish climber, Tom Mackinnon, would explore the Yalung glacier to find a porter route to the foot of the mountain, George Band would head for Ghunsa, the nearest big village, to buy fresh food and ground barley for their Sherpas. Norman Hardie and Joe Brown meanwhile would accompany Charles for the first few days, before peeling off to make a detailed topographical survey of the South West Face. They had photographs and route descriptions from Kempe's team, but Charles needed accurate altitudes for the Great Shelf and the other main features.

They left camp full of optimism but within a few days Charles realised that the Yalung glacier was much more difficult that he had expected and that getting all their supplies and equipment to Base Camp was going to be a major operation. The ground was very uneven and almost every afternoon there was a snowstorm which covered the rocks and boulders with a thick layer of snow, in some places thigh deep.

It would be impossible for any porter to get all the way from Yalung Camp to Base Camp in one day, so they scouted out three stopping points along the route: 'Moraine Camp', a "dreary, wild remote place' according to Charles, about six miles up the glacier, 'Crack Camp' the site of a huge, notably weathered boulder two miles further up, and finally 'Corner Camp', at a point where the Yalung glacier twisted to face north east. It was roughly a day's march between each group of tents.

Joe Brown had spent the previous summer in the Alps but had no other high altitude experience. Straight away

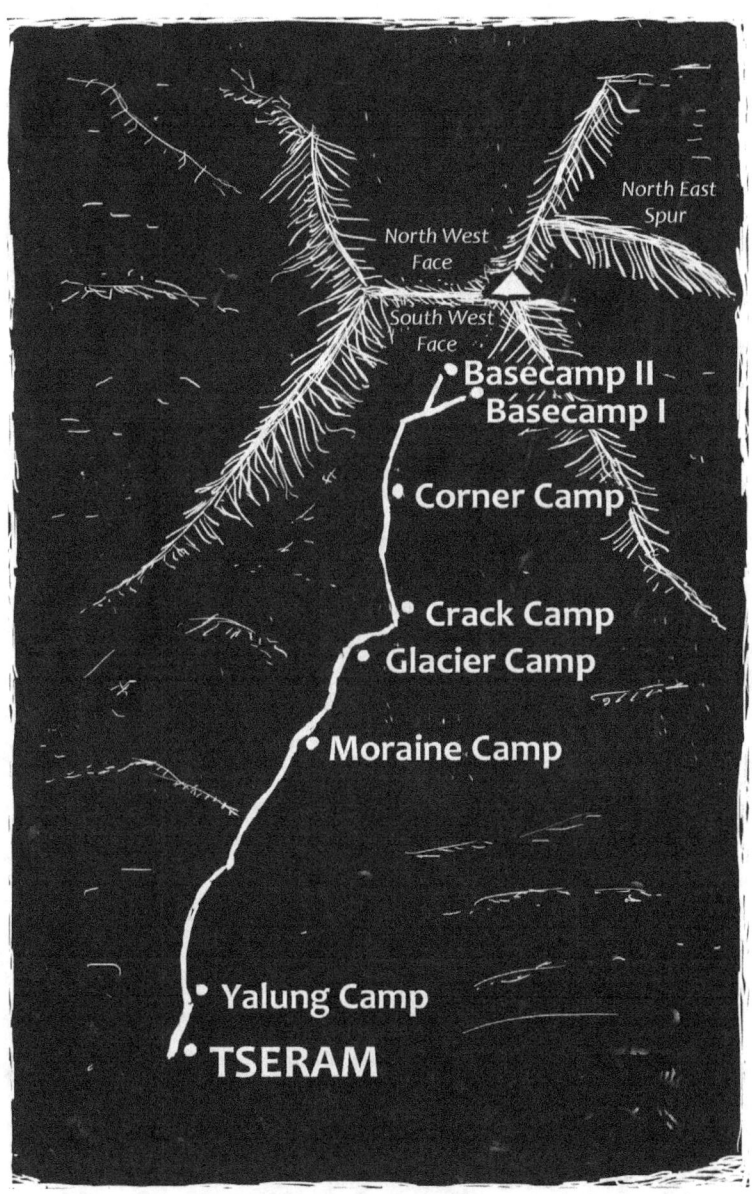

Camps on the Yalung Glacier

he noticed how hard it was to work in the thin air, becoming breathless just going from one tent to the next. At one stage during a particularly hard carry, he fell asleep on the glacier – mid-crossing. In spite of occasionally feeling utterly exhausted, Joe retained his exuberant good humour and even found himself doing some recreational climbing at Crack Camp.

On March 28th, after three days of slog, they reached the site for Corner Camp and for the first time were able to see the South West Face virtually in its entirety. Even two miles away, it was a frightening sight, 10,0000 ft of icefalls and avalanche prone snow bearing down on them. Charles had hoped that the ordinary porters would be able to carry as far as Base Camp but looking ahead it was obvious that only his fully equipped high-altitude Sherpas would be able to cross the heavily crevassed ground in front. His diary entry for the next day gave a vivid insight into how difficult the conditions were:

> 5.30. Absolutely fucked, scorching hot, indescribably wearisome slogging, face burning, face and mouth sticky with hard breathing in the cold air.

The weather continued to deteriorate with heavy snows accompanied by high winds, so powerful sometimes that no-one could leave their tent. One morning, Charles was enjoying 'pit-time' in his sleeping bag when suddenly he heard a loud noise outside followed by a shout from Norman Hardie. Running out in his gym shoes, Charles spotted the team's large 80 lb dome tent, being blown across the icy wastes as if it weighed nothing. Two Sherpas had been sleeping inside it, but rather than join in the chase, they had poked their heads out of their sleeping bags and promptly retreated.

Eventually Charles and Joe Brown retrieved the missing tent from an icy hollow. They carried it back to camp where they made their displeasure with the sleepy-headed Sherpas abundantly clear. The next day, with little chance of improvement in sight, Charles retreated back to Yalung Camp, leaving Norman Hardie to finish the survey.

While Charles' team had been struggling manfully, young George Band was having a much more relaxed time on what he dubbed his 'Himalayan shopping trip'. He'd gone to Ghunsa aiming to buy up to a ton of tsampa and 'atta', stone-ground flour, for their Sherpas but unlike John Kempe who had come away from the village disappointed, George had no problem in securing all the provisions he needed.

He had visited the Himalayas and the Karakoram twice in the last three years but George was still surprised at how friendly and hospitable most people were. He noticed immediately how the Sherpas who accompanied him would take over any houses where they were offered food or lodging, literally jumping up and down on beds to test their comfort and commandeering whatever cooking implements were available.

The toilet pits at Ghunsa, George noted, were stocked with rhododendron leaves which he found 'surprisingly fragrant' but he wasn't quite so happy with other aspects of local hygiene. As he wryly noted in an article for the *Times*, when they were offered straws and pots of chang beer at one house, "Conscious of the sahib's love of cleanliness the hostess sluiced the bamboo straws vigorously with water, then dried them off by drawing them through her armpit".

The village head man was willing to provide the expedition with all the tsampa it needed along with potatoes and eggs, but he warned George that he needed a few days to air the grain. George couldn't object but was rather disturbed to watch several cows and chickens wandering about in the drying area. Rather than wait around and get more even anxious, George decided to head back to the others with a promise that their food would be carried over in a few days.

Back at Yalung Camp, he was pleased to be able to report a successful mission, though he was not quite so happy with the flea-bites or the cold that he had returned with. George retired to his tent to read Dostoevsky's *Crime and Punishment* while Charles took stock of the expedition supply dump and debriefed Norman Hardie, who had also just returned from his surveying trip.

Their introductory week had gone reasonably, though not spectacularly, well. Norman Hardie's survey revealed that the Great Shelf extended from 23,000 ft to 25,000 ft, a little higher than they had expected, but that the top of Kempe's buttress was only 19,500 ft, about a thousand feet lower than they had thought. So far no-one had got higher than 18,000 ft but as far as Charles was concerned, for the moment it was high enough.

In the coming weeks, he planned to build a ladder of camps up the mountain until he was in position to put at least one pair of climbers on the summit. Unlike Aleister Crowley and Jacot-Guillarmod fifty years earlier, Charles knew it would not be quick or easy. Two years earlier on Everest, it had taken over six weeks to get from Base Camp to the summit and if anything, this expedition would probably take even longer.

Charles was pleased though with the way his team were performing. Unlike Everest where there had been a certain amount of what he called "competitive marching" on the way in, everyone seemed to be very relaxed and easy with each other. He was particularly happy with young Joe Brown, his most controversial choice, who was both hard working and fun to be around, keeping everyone amused with his jokes and rude Mancunian expressions.

The Sherpa Team, Dawa Tenzing on far right

Logistically, everything was on track. The earlier porter strike had not had any serious ramifications, and when he did a rough audit on April 4th, Charles was very pleased to see that 150 loads had already gone up the glacier to a cache at Corner Camp. When the Ghunsa men arrived with George Band's recent purchases, Charles was confident that he had enough provisions for a long stay and was charmed by the latest arrivals who he described in his diary as 'the hairiest, ruggedest, most carefree gang of toughs I've seen yet'. Their exuberance, however, wasn't enough to keep entirely at bay the dark moods that occasionally enveloped him.

Though outwardly calm and confident, Charles was worried about what he had taken on, asking himself repeatedly whether he was up to the job, or "fuck all use" as he feared in his worst moments. There had been no major disasters in the first week, but the more he saw of the mountain, the more he worried they might get nowhere. As he wrote in a letter to his friend Ken Pearson on April 4th:

> Base camp a long way up (4 days) a most inhospitable glacier. Lots of cliffs avalanching and the route as far as I've seen it yet, hardly worth a second look, between you and me

When he talked to his sirdar, Dawa Tenzing, he got little encouragement. "The Kangchenjunga gods aren't nice gods," Dawa declared laconically, "and the upper part of the route – it's not good."

Charles kept his fears to himself, trying to live up to his personal mantra, 'dogged as done it'. Judging from the personal diaries of the other team members, no-one sensed how worried he was but on April 6th, his anxieties were reinforced when they received their first consignment of mail from Darjeeling. The newspapers and personal letters were very welcome, and there were even Easter eggs from the Hendersons at Rungneet, but the mail runners also brought some less good news from Delhi.

When he had stopped there a month earlier, Charles had contacted the Indian Air Force about getting some aerial reconnaissance shots of Kangchenjunga. They had duly obliged but their photographs were not really what Charles wanted to see. The west ridge, which he was hoping to join high up appeared to be a very dangerous looking knife edge, and there didn't seem to be any possibility of traversing out either side if they encountered serious obstacles. When Charles showed the photographs to the rest of the team, they were equally despondent, prompting him to call what should have been an enjoyable evening "the lowest of the expedition as far as my spirits go."

There was nothing to be gained from wallowing in misery though and before he could think about the problems high above, Charles had many other lower altitude tasks to complete, the first and most important being to properly establish Base Camp. On April 12th, he and George Band and two Sherpas finally moved in, pitching a pair of tents on flattish area at the foot the mountain which, judging by all the tins of kerosene they found scattered around, had also been used by Kempe in the previous year.

It was a spectacular spot, an icy platform a few hundred yards from the South West Face, protected from avalanches by a series of low ridges to the right and left. It needed to be, because as they soon discovered, both Kangchenjunga and nearby Talung peak were distinctly unstable. As soon as they were comfortably ensconced, George Band began recording the avalanches with a notch on their tent pole. By the following day with the snow continuing to fall, he had marked up 48, more than one large avalanche every half an hour.

As they waited for the weather to improve, they spent their time reading and talking about the future. George had moved on from *Crime and Punishment* and was enjoying Apsley Cherry-Garrard's *The Worst Journey in the World*, one of the greatest misery memoirs in the history of exploration which made their current predicament look relatively minor.

When they weren't reading, Charles returned to a recurrent theme of his last few years: the relative merits of a professional career versus the rough and tumble of expedition life. Both Charles and George agreed that they preferred the latter, as the avalanches continued to thunder down the nearby slopes.

The next day the weather improved, enabling them to make their first foray onto the mountain. As John Kempe had discovered a year earlier, the only feasible way to reach the upper part of the South West Face was to either find a safe way up the Lower Icefall or to climb the steep rock buttress on its right hand side, and then re-join the icefall much higher up. Either way, they would have to ascend almost 2000 ft. Their first attempt to climb Kempe's buttress did not go well. Even though they had come equipped with photographs and route descriptions, Charles and George could not find a safe place to begin the climb and after a few failed attempts on a particularly difficult rock chimney, they temporarily called a halt and retreated back first to Base Camp and then all the way down to Corner Camp, another two and a half miles down the glacier.

After getting on the radio to check progress elsewhere, Charles decided that next day, he would send George Band and Norman Hardie to take another crack at it. As Kempe had discovered, the hardest sections of the rock buttress were at the top and the bottom, but Norman was keen to do some climbing after his week on survey duties. The second time around, George and Norman did manage get a good foothold on Kempe's Buttress but it was harder going than they had expected. When Norman called down on the night of April 19th, he reported that they had just spent a seven-hour day on the mountain but still hadn't been able to get much further than the previous year's party. They would need more time, he said, to fix lines and put up rope-ladders.

With his reconnaissance threatening to turn into a fiasco, Charles felt compelled to go up himself on the following day, this time with a full complement of five climbers and twenty Sherpas. His aim was to follow the route that George and Norman had pioneered, cross over at the top of the icefall and establish their first high camp. When, however, Charles eventually caught up with them, Norman and George sounded more tentative than positive. Yes it was possible, they said, to get from Kempe's Buttress over onto the icefall, but that still left about 500 ft of very dangerous and uncertain snow and ice to overcome. Nothing they had found so far suggested that this approach would ever serve as a repeatable porter route. It was not what Charles wanted to hear but he couldn't really argue with their assessment. He had spent enough time in Everest's Khumbu icefall to know how dangerous this kind of terrain was, and if anything this looked even more lethal.

There was one small piece of good news though, and potentially a significant one. From a high vantage point, Norman and George had spotted a snow gully much further to the west which ran down from a prominent bulge of rock they christened 'the Hump'. Kempe had not mentioned it in his report and it had not looked viable in the aerial photographs, but as they now realised if they could reach the gully, they might be able to bypass the Lower Icefall altogether. Changing route would mean writing off several days' worth of work but better to make a decisive change at this point than to persevere on a course that no-one had any confidence in. First though, they would have to find out whether the snow gully could be reached. If it couldn't, all bets were off.

Charles gave the order to move everything several hundred yards to the west. Their new Base Camp would be on the same site as Pache's grave, one of the main camps on Crowley and Jacot-Guillarmod's 1905 expedition. John Kempe had been sceptical about this part of the mountain but five weeks in and Charles was running out of options. Unless their luck turned, John Hunt wouldn't be returning in 1956—not because Charles had succeeded in climbing Kangchenjunga, but because he had failed to get anywhere near.

CHAPTER EIGHT
The Great Shelf

Base Camp 2, near the site of Pache's grave

If a lammergeier vulture had spread its huge wings and flown past Kangchenjunga on the morning of April 23rd 1955, it might have seen a few tiny dots clambering across the icy wastes at the head of the Yalung glacier, moving slowly as if burdened down. Heading further west it would have passed within sight of the huge peak of Jannu before the mountains gradually started to shrink in height. Twenty miles later the terrain would have begun to rise again as the bird came within sight of Everest and its sister mountains Lhotse and Nuptse, but before that, the lammergeier would have encountered Makalu, another 8000m peak with a very sharply defined summit and at its base, another group of tiny dots moving across the snow: the French 1955 Makalu expedition.

In the 1920s and 30s France had been very slow to get involved in Himalayan mountaineering but with Maurice Herzog's ascent of Annapurna in 1950, it had become the first country to claim an 8000m peak, the holy grail of high altitude climbing. After the humiliations of WW2, France was desperately in need of good news stories and mountaineering was seen as one way to inspire nation's youth and boost France's international profile. At the end of Herzog's best-selling expedition account, he had written, "There are other Annapurnas in the lives of men" but, in the early 1950s at least, the Federation Française de la Montagne was more interested in mountains than metaphors.

Initially, after Annapurna there had been plans for a follow up expedition to Everest but Hillary and Tenzing's first ascent made that seem a less attractive proposition. Instead, the Federation turned its attention to Makalu in the Barun Valley. At 27,790 ft it was the fifth highest mountain in the world. Like Everest, it straddled the border between Nepal and Tibet in a region that had barely been visited by Westerners until the early 1950s.

The British mountaineer, Eric Shipton, had first got close to Makalu in 1952 and Edmund Hillary had photographed it from the summit of Everest a year later, but Makalu wasn't attempted until 1954 when a team from California reached 23,200 ft before being forced back by terrible weather. In the same season, Ed Hillary's New Zealand expedition to the Barun Valley made a similarly unsuccessful attempt on one of Makalu's subsidiary summits, leaving the way open for a French team to apply for a permit for in the spring of 1955, at the same time as Charles Evan's men were attempting Kangchenjunga.

Though the British played down any sense of a race, there was no doubt that the French team was looking for national glory, not just personal fulfilment. If France could become the first country to bag not one but two 8000m peaks, it would put them in the forefront of Himalayan climbing, and if they could do it ahead of their great European rivals, victory on Makalu would be even sweeter.

The leader of the French expedition, Jean Franco, was a very experienced climber and an instructor at the French National Mountaineering School with special responsibility for developing Himalayan climbing. He was very systematic in his approach to equipping and selecting personnel and had plenty of money to get things right.

In advance of the main attempt, Franco had gone out in the autumn of 1954 to reconnoitre the mountain. He dismissed the American route up Makalu's south east ridge as too difficult, but had come back convinced that Ed Hillary's preferred approach, up Makalu's North East ridge, looked like a good option. Back home, Franco put together a crack team of French climbers, most of which were professional mountain guides, and spent the next few months training in the Alps. Unlike Charles Evans, who had found some British mountaineers reluctant to commit to both the reconnaissance and the main expedition, Franco was able to persuade two of France's leading mountaineers, Lionel Terray and Jean Couzy, to take part in both elements.

The French team travelled in style. While the British endured a long journey by ship, they flew from Orly airport near Paris to Calcutta before chartering three Dakotas to take them on to Biratnagar, a brand new Nepali airfield that was not yet in general use. They had the usual hiccoughs with porter strikes, lost equipment and, for one particularly anxious moment, a missing expedition cashbox, but by April 4th 1955, just three weeks after leaving France, they were firmly ensconced at Base Camp. Unlike Charles Evans, who had no time for acclimatisation climbs, Jean Franco had allocated a whole month for training ascents on nearby peaks, while his Sherpas got on with establishing and stocking the first two camps on Makalu.

As well as brand new light-weight oxygen sets, they had brought sufficient canisters for everyone on the French team to both climb and sleep on oxygen, once they got above 23,000 ft. They did have problems early on with throat and chest infections, but because of the work that had been done on the previous year's reconnaissance, the French had none of the stress of route finding that Charles Evans had to endure. To make life even better, the weather on Makalu gradually improved as the expedition proceeded. It did get very windy higher up, but this had a positive effect, removing loose snow from the rocks.

When Jean Franco and his team left Base Camp on April 23rd 1955, aiming to move the centre of operations 2000 ft higher up the mountain, everything seemed to be on schedule and on track. The same couldn't quite be said for the British team.

The Great Shelf

One month in, the 1955 Kangchenjunga Reconnaissance had made little progress. Charles Evans had ruled out an approach via Kempe's Buttress but had not yet found a workable alternative. The monsoon was expected in about four weeks, so there really wasn't much time left.

On the morning of April 23rd, Charles' first problem was rather more mundane but equally pressing. He had woken up to discover that his front teeth were missing and for one dreadful moment thought that he might have swallowed them in his sleep. This was not the first time a British mountaineer had endured dental problems. A few years earlier when Charles was on Annapurna, expedition leader Bill Tilman had mislaid his false teeth, and shortly after Everest, the New Zealand climber George Lowe had lost his dentures on a post expedition trip to an outward-bound centre. Fortunately Charles was luckier. He found the dental plate in his sleeping bag and was able to have his breakfast with a full set.

As Charles knew only too well, time was running out. If snow conditions were bad now, when the monsoon arrived they would become infinitely worse. Two months after leaving Britain, one month after setting up Yalung Camp and they were still not much further up the mountain than Kempe's party of the previous year. Everything now depended on that narrow gully that Norman Hardie had spotted a few days earlier. If they could find a safe way to reach it and bypass the Lower Icefall, they still had a chance to make progress, but if it proved to be another blind alley, they would be going home empty handed.

Pache's grave was the obvious place to set up their new Base Camp but it remained an eerie spot. The snow had melted to reveal a commemorative plaque recording the date of Alexis

Pache's death. Scattered around were old tin cans and, as the expedition doctor John Clegg later discovered, Pommery champagne corks. It was however a much more comfortable spot than their previous Base Camp. There were no dangerous looking crevasses and there was even some scrubby looking grass and moss. As Charles wrote in his diary it was also "incomparably safer than the icefall we were in yesterday."

George Band and Norman Hardie were the first occupants. Having failed to find a good route via Kempe's buttress, they were determined to reach the top of the Lower Icefall one way or the other. The weather showed little sign of improvement, with heavy snowfalls and poor visibility but they persevered and set up a new camp, just below the Hump.

The real breakthrough came on April 28th when Charles came up to Camp 1 with Joe Brown and a couple of Sherpas. Following what would become a familiar pattern, the morning was so misty that initially they couldn't see George and Norman, though they could hear them working high above. When they eventually found them, Norman had good news at last : they had got to the top of the Hump, worked their way down the gully on the other side and crossed over on to the Lower Icefall where it briefly flattened out into a small plateau. Their hunch about the snow gully had proven to be correct. At last Charles had some positive developments to report in his expedition dispatches.

The small plateau was the perfect site for Camp 2 so Charles and the Sherpas headed up to pitch a tent. Then suddenly, there was a deafening roar from above. An enormous avalanche was hurtling down Kangchenjunga and it sounded like it was heading straight for them. They braced themselves to be covered in snow or swept away but nothing happened.

After hearing a second and then a third avalanche and remaining unscathed, they concluded that it must be a safe spot and finished putting up the tent. Charles and Joe stayed up, while George and Norman went down with the Sherpas, happy with what they had achieved.

Next day Charles woke up feeling terrible. His throat was sore, his voice was weak and if he ate anything he felt like vomiting. The only positive thing was that the plateau was as safe as they had hoped. It hadn't been visible on their aerial photos so they had not been sure quite what to expect but a brief reconnaissance revealed it to be a small glacier about half a mile long and a quarter of a mile wide, which seemed relatively crevasse free.

At the far end, the Upper Icefall began. It was another tangled mass of icy blocks flowing down in fits and starts from the Great Shelf but it didn't look quite as dangerous as the Lower Icefall. The main challenge was its covering of heavy snow. As Charles and Joe climbed upwards, they had to plough their way through thigh-deep drifts. When after a few hours they had reached just 22,000 ft, Charles called a halt and they slogged back to their tent, aiming to come back on the following morning to choose a site for Camp 3, several hundred feet higher up.

It was not to be.

Before they left Britain, Charles had arranged to have regular weather forecasts for the region broadcast on All India Radio. That night they heard that a depression was centred on Kangchenjunga and there was likely to be a lot more snow. The forecast was not wrong. When they woke up next morning their tent was half submerged.

They didn't have sufficient kerosene or food to sit the bad weather out and the conditions made it impossible to get any higher, so Charles and Joe decided to retreat for the moment. Their first obstacle was the 400 ft gully that stretched from the plateau back up to the top of the Hump. It was so choked that the only way to make any progress was for Joe to literally crawl upwards on all fours, pressing the snow down to create steps for Charles. After a huge effort they managed to get to the top without setting off any significant avalanches but when they tried to descend the steep slope on the other side, they found themselves in an even more dangerous position.

The slope was slightly convex, bulging outwards as it descended, making it even more avalanche prone. Joe went in front and gingerly began to work his way down, when suddenly he heard a sharp crack. Charles didn't notice but a few minutes later there was another crack, followed by strange hissing noise. The slope was about to avalanche, taking them with it.

Back in 1905, a slip had started the avalanche that killed the Swiss cavalryman Alexis Pache. Jules Jacot-Guillarmod had only just survived by swimming through the snow. Now for a brief moment it looked as if they might also be carried away on a river of white. For Joe it was the most dangerous moment on the expedition: "We just turned and ran up hill, and that's hard to do and you end up with such an oxygen debt, you can't talk... the mood change was incredible, we went from being in control, from thinking everything is alright, to suddenly thinking, 'we're trapped'."

After their close encounter, they slowly retreated to Camp 2, stopping with exhaustion every ten steps but grateful to have survived. Inside their tent, Charles continued to work his way through a history of the mutiny on the Bounty, while Joe got stuck in to George Band's copy of *The Worst Journey in the World*. "Who'd want to go to the Antarctic after he'd read this?" he asked, but both men were now starting to get nervous about their own predicament. Over the radio Charles heard that Norman Hardie had tried to reach them that morning with supplies but had turned back after triggering an avalanche lower down. Charles warned Norman not to try again until the snow had consolidated and got ready to spend an anxious night.

The next morning, Charles was unable to keep any food down. He'd spent much of the night coughing. Joe still had a hearty appetite but neither man was looking forward to spending another day of enforced 'pit-time' in their sleeping bags with very little chance that anyone would come up to relieve them. As Charles confided to his diary, they really were now starting to feel cut off, so it was all the more surprising when at around 1.00 p.m. they heard a shout from outside.

"What about giving us a fucking hand?" called Norman Hardie. He had come up with Tony Streather and two Sherpas, Aila and Kunde Ang Dawa. They looked exhausted but they had brought both food and fuel, and had even succeeded in fixing a rope ladder to the difficult slope at the apex of the Hump. From now on it would be both easier and safer to ascend and descend.

Charles' black mood lifted immediately. Yesterday, as he admitted to his diary, he had experienced intense fear but now he was hopeful that at last things were going his way. Norman and Tony started straight back down, but the two

Sherpas stayed up and before long were tidying Charles and Joe's tent and boiling water for supper.

There was no more snow that night and with the previous falls starting to consolidate, next morning they made swift work, climbing beyond their previous high point and starting on the steep ice cliffs that blocked their way. The blizzards came back later, but it didn't stop first Tom Mackinnon and then Tony Streather arriving with more supplies.

After weeks of frustration, the expedition had moved up a gear. Norman Hardie's sterling work on the route between Camp 1 and Camp 2, meant that whatever the weather it was possible for supplies and reinforcements to come up the mountain. On May 4th, Charles made another significant breakthrough, finding a way through the Upper Icefall to set up Camp 3, at 21,800 ft. It was a wild looking spot, a small ledge under a huge ice cliff, regularly battered by the wind but seemingly protected from avalanches. Crucially, it was big enough to hold four or five tents and would serve as Advance Base for the weeks to come, a high-altitude depot where they could build up a large cache of supplies.

The next big task would be to try to reach the Great Shelf, the base for an attempt on the summit. Charles' confidence was growing but his physical health seemed to be slowly but inexorably declining. He couldn't shake off his sore throat and had developed a severe cough. The higher he went, the harder he found it to keep any food down. Whether the cause was the altitude or the stress he wasn't sure, but either way Charles decided to descend to Base Camp for a rest and was soon joined by Norman Hardie and George Band.

Though it could hardly be called luxurious, Base Camp was considerably more comfortable than any out-post higher up.

It was home to both Thondup, the expedition cook and John Clegg, the team doctor.

Clegg was an anatomist at Liverpool University. Occasionally when he had a free moment, he would collect plant and insect specimens but there was usually something to do. So far the most serious medical case was a Sherpani who unbeknownst to everyone had joined the expedition pregnant. Sadly, she miscarried a few weeks after they reached Tseram and had to return home with her husband. Other than that, Clegg had held impromptu surgeries as they passed through villages on the approach march and had dealt with haemorrhoids, cuts and a host of minor problems from the climbers and the Sherpas.

He had no serious worries about Charles' health but he did notice how 'flea-bitten' and tired his leader seemed when he came down. Several other members of the team had also developed colds and coughs but the large tin of throat pastilles specially taken for such an eventuality, had been scoffed by the Sherpas, who mistakenly thought they were sweets.

Clegg decided it was time to brew his own cough medicine, *Mistura Kangchenjunga Fortis,* a potent cocktail of aspirin, ether, chloral hydrate and Dover's powders- a traditional British blend of opium and south American herbs that had been used to treat colds since the eighteenth century. Reactions were mixed: Norman Hardie swore in disgust, John Jackson praised it for its high ether content and the Sherpa Pasang Dorje pronounced wisely that indeed it had "something extra".

Charles' days at Base Camp went quickly. He had a bath, listened to Newcastle United take on Manchester City in the 1955 FA Cup Final on the BBC World Service and caught up with both his dispatches for the *Times* and his personal correspondence. They were in a better position than they had been for weeks, and after a few days of rest, he felt refreshed and ready to go. George Band admitted that he was slightly unnerved by the fact that their current route took them close to the site of the 1905 accident, but Charles wasn't worried. He made a note to search out *The Great Beast*, John Symonds' biography of Aleister Crowley, when they finally got back home.

For the next stage they would be using oxygen for the first time on the expedition, though not the open circuit sets that Charles preferred. Tom Bourdillon, his former partner on Everest, had developed an updated closed circuit set and asked if they could test it in the field. Unlike the simpler open-circuit models, which enabled a climber to breathe a mixture of ambient air and bottled oxygen, closed circuit sets had much tighter face masks and were designed in such a way that a climber's out-breath was sent back through a soda lime canister, which converted most of the exhaled carbon dioxide back into oxygen. In theory closed circuit sets were much more efficient but in practice they were bulky and tended to overheat and, as Charles had discovered on Everest, were more prone to faults than the open circuit variety. Charles remained wary but the only way to find out if Tom really had come up with a significantly improved design was to try a set out.

On the morning of May 9th, he and Norman left Base Camp, climbing steadily. Their sets worked perfectly and two days later they reached Camp 3. Charles was pleased to see how well the Sherpas were going and was very impressed by the pile of supplies they had amassed and the large cave they had hacked out of the ice. He was less happy though with the return of his nausea, which seemed to be altitude related. He managed to eat something on the night of the 11th, but promptly vomited it up over his sleeping bag first thing next morning. To add to his discomfort, it was freezing cold. Camp 3 lay in the shadow of the ice-cliffs above and didn't warm up until late in the day. It was very tough getting away early, but one upside of the closed circuit system was that it slightly warmed the incoming oxygen as it re-cycled it.

Charles and Norman took the lead while their two Sherpas, Urkien and Annullu, followed close behind, climbing under their own steam and carrying large rucksacks. Ahead lay the jagged ice-cliffs and wayward seracs of the Upper Icefall but compared to lower down it was relatively straightforward climbing. They moved quickly and methodically, chopping steps and fixing ropes whenever necessary, impressed by the boost that the oxygen gave them even if they did find the sets uncomfortable and slightly awkward to wear.

Then suddenly, as a bitter reminder of the events on Everest, Charles was stopped in his tracks, feeling as if he later wrote "as if a firm hand had been clamped over my mouth and nose". The rubberised lining of his mask had come free and wrapped itself around his face. Charles was halfway up a particularly steep ice slope but he had no option but to tear his mask off with one hand while clinging on to his ice axe for dear life with the other. Then with a huge effort he hauled himself up to a ledge and lay panting for a few minutes before he yanked the lining out altogether and then carried on going.

A few hours later they reached the top of the icefall but were prevented from going any further by a series of deep crevasses. Anallu and Urkien were exhausted and keen to descend as soon as possible, so they helped Charles pitch a small tent and then turned around to head back down. Camp 4 was at around 23,500 ft. In the distance, Everest was just visible, poking above the clouds.

Their oxygen test had yielded mixed results. Neither Charles nor Norman liked the wearing them; they were too bulky to be comfortable and as in 1953, Charles found the tight mask claustrophobic. He hated the feeling of being in a bubble, cut off from the world. On the other hand, apart from the detached lining, the sets had worked well and helped get them very high very quickly. They used so little gas, there was even enough left for them to sleep on oxygen for a few hours.

Unfortunately the technical glitches got worse the following morning. Charles wanted to get going early but when they put their oxygen sets on, they discovered that the valves were frozen tight. Norman managed to loosen them but their oxygen cylinders also needed warming up. The only option was take the bottles inside their sleeping bags and clasp them between their legs, like some kind of inverse hot water bottle.

It was a miserable start but, breaking with its usual pattern, the weather improved as the day went on, and without too much trouble they managed to find a route through the crevasses in front of them, using a large collapsed serac as a snow bridge. After a short climb up a snowy corridor surrounded by further seracs, they finally reached the Great Shelf, the huge feature visible from Darjeeling 50 miles away, which ran the whole way across the South West Face.

After spending so many weeks trying to plot a course through the chaotic jumble of the Upper and Lower Icefalls, they were surprised to encounter what looked to Charles like a vast, slightly twisted football pitch. It was covered in snow but seemed to be free of all the obstacles they had encountered so far. Charles had studied photographs of the Great Shelf many times, but it felt unreal to actually be standing on it, staring up at the gigantic features he had previously only seen from far away.

The most important of these was a long narrow couloir they had nicknamed "the Gangway", which began three hundred feet above the Great Shelf and terminated very close to the West ridge. Many weeks earlier, they had identified it as the most likely route to the summit and close up it looked even more promising.

At 11.45 a.m. they reached a broad ledge at the foot of the Gangway and for the first time took off their cumbersome oxygen sets. The view was astonishing. Below them stretched a sea of cloud and then far away in the distance the top of Makalu, the goal of Jean Franco's French team. Closer at hand, they could see the tips of two of the most striking mountains in the Eastern Himalayas, Jannu and Kabru. As Charles wrote in his diary, it was a scene he had dreamt about for many months:

> We sat on a little ice shelf feeling like aviators – goggled and masked – looking down over Kabru to a line of cloud over India. A very happy and triumphant moment for Norm and me.

A few hours later, they were back at Camp 3, radioing down to tell the others the good news. Charles was so pleased that he fished out a bottle of brandy from their luxuries box and toasted their success.

In theory, Charles had fulfilled his mission. They had systematically reconnoitred the options on the South West Face and found a route to the Great Shelf. All that remained was for John Hunt and Tom Bourdillon to return in 1956 to finish the job. That of course was never really Charles Evans' plan. Within two weeks, possibly less, the monsoon would arrive and they would undoubtedly be forced off Kangchenjunga but that still left enough time to make a concerted bid for the top.

Two days later on May 14th, Charles gathered the troops at Base Camp and outlined his timetable for the following week. He told them he foresaw two more high camps: a large well-stocked position on the Great Shelf, and a single tent higher up, from which two pairs would make successive bids for the summit, one day apart. Then came the moment that everyone was waiting for: the announcement of who would make the first attempt.

It was a crucial moment in the expedition. If Charles got it right, they would pull off an extraordinary coup. If he got wrong they would still have achieved their mission, but they would undoubtedly all go home feeling decidedly flat. So who would carry the torch for the 1955 Kangchenjunga team? Now on his sixth Himalayan expedition, Charles was one of the world's foremost high altitude climbers. His deputy Norman Hardie assumed that he would be the lead climber of the first pair and hoped to be his partner, but Charles saw things entirely differently. He chose Norman and Tony Streather as the second summit team, following in the boot-prints of George Band and Joe Brown.

It was an extraordinary moment for both men: Joe Brown, the baby of the team, who prior to the expedition had only once climbed outside of Britain, and George Band, the Cambridge graduate who had showed so much promise but achieved so little on Everest in 1953. They would be the spearhead of the British team and Charles would only make an attempt himself if the first two pairs failed. Norman wasn't at all sure and tried to change Charles' mind over the following days but he stuck to his decision. He had spent enough time with both Joe and George to know that they were up to the job. They were the team's best two rock climbers and the higher they got on Kangchenjunga, the more those skills would be needed.

The whole team celebrated that night with a ration of "Mummery's Blood", a potent mixture of rum and treacle, but the hard work was far from over. As Charles knew from personal experience on Everest, the position of the final camp was crucial. The higher they could place it, the more likely that one of his pairs would reach the summit. Before that could happen though, the Sherpas and other members of the team would have to make a Herculean effort to carry sufficient oxygen and supplies up to Camp 5 on the Great Shelf to establish a fully stocked Advance Base. Only then could they even think about positioning the final camp.

The first task, leading the 'big carry', would fall to the big Glaswegian, Tom Mackinnon, assisted by John Jackson and eleven of their strongest Sherpas. They would leave Base Camp on May 15th, collect almost 400 lbs of stores from Camp 3, and climb up via Camp 4 until they reached the Great Shelf where they would dump everything before descending on the same day all the way to Camp 3. Charles Evans and Neil Mather would follow a day later with the first summit pair, George and Joe. They would spend one night on the Great Shelf and then on the following morning help George Band and Joe Brown set up their last camp. Then Charles and Neil would descend to Camp 5 and wait on the Great Shelf in case of any setbacks or emergencies. It was a simple enough plan but they had neither the time nor the oxygen to deal with any significant setbacks.

If everything went perfectly, the first pair would head for the summit on May 22nd, followed a day later by the second team, Norman Hardie and Tony Streather – if a second attempt was necessary. John Clegg, the expedition doctor, would remain at the foot of the mountain manning the radio, poised to despatch runners with to the nearest telegraph station if it all went according to plan. If the first two attempts did not succeed, there wasn't really enough oxygen to mount a third but Charles was determined to try anyway with Dawa Tenzing or one of the other Sherpas.

Over on Makalu, the French team were at a much more advanced stage. By May 14th, Jean Franco's two lead climbers, Lionel Terray and Jean Couzy, were already at 25,600 ft, poised to make the first summit bid. The weather was perfect and the forecast was good for the following few days.

On the next morning, while most of the British team were still at Base Camp, Terray and Couzy left their high camp and made a very rapid ascent to the summit. Then, even more remarkably, they descended all the way back down to Advance Base by early evening on the same day. When their team-mates asked them how it had gone, Couzy replied that it had been like "a fine morning's climb in the Alps." Over the next two days a further six Frenchmen were aiming to get to the top, but for the moment all they could do was smile.

If that evening, the giant lammergeier had made its way back from Makalu to Kangchenjunga, it just might have seen Charles Evans, standing outside the tents of Base Camp, hands in pockets, pipe in mouth, staring up towards the summit wondering what would happen next, as the wind blew snow over Alexis Pache's grave, a potent reminder of the risks that they were all about to take.

CHAPTER NINE
The Big Carry

The Great Shelf

Six foot tall, fourteen stone, aged 42: Tom Mackinnon did not have the profile of a typical Himalayan climber. Born in Glasgow in 1914, he was a pharmacist by trade, running a chain of chemist's shops established by his father. Tom started climbing in his twenties, first in Scotland and then, at the end of the 1930s, venturing further afield to Norway and later the Alps. After the war, his ambitions grew, with trips to the Garwhal mountains of India in 1950 and then Nepal in 1952.

Tom was not a leader of men or someone with a blazing desire to climb new routes but he was a very solid and experienced mountaineer whose easy-going temperament made him an ideal candidate for a long arduous expedition. So far he had not made any outstanding contributions to the Kangchenjunga expedition, but as both he and Charles knew, what happened next would be crucial to the success or failure of the expedition.

Tom and his partner, John Jackson, would be using oxygen sets but the Sherpas would have to climb under their own steam and each carry around 30 lbs of supplies and equipment to the Great Shelf. Though Charles and Norman had found the route and picked the site for Camp 5, they hadn't had time to fix ropes or mark out the trail with flags, so Tom would have to be especially careful between Camps 4 and 5.

On the afternoon of May 15th he and his team set off, initially with empty packs. Most of the gear had been cached at Camp 3 so the first few days were easy. They spent a night at Camp 1 and then Camp 2 and then loaded up at Camp 3. After that it all became much harder.

Tom and John Jackson were very impressed by the boost their oxygen sets gave them but there was a problem. Two and a half months into the expedition, they had both lost a lot of weight. Instead of fitting snugly, their oxygen masks were loose, leaking warm air into their snow goggles. As they climbed from Camp 3 to Camp 4 on May 18th, Jackson had made the fatal mistake of removing his goggles when they

The Big Carry

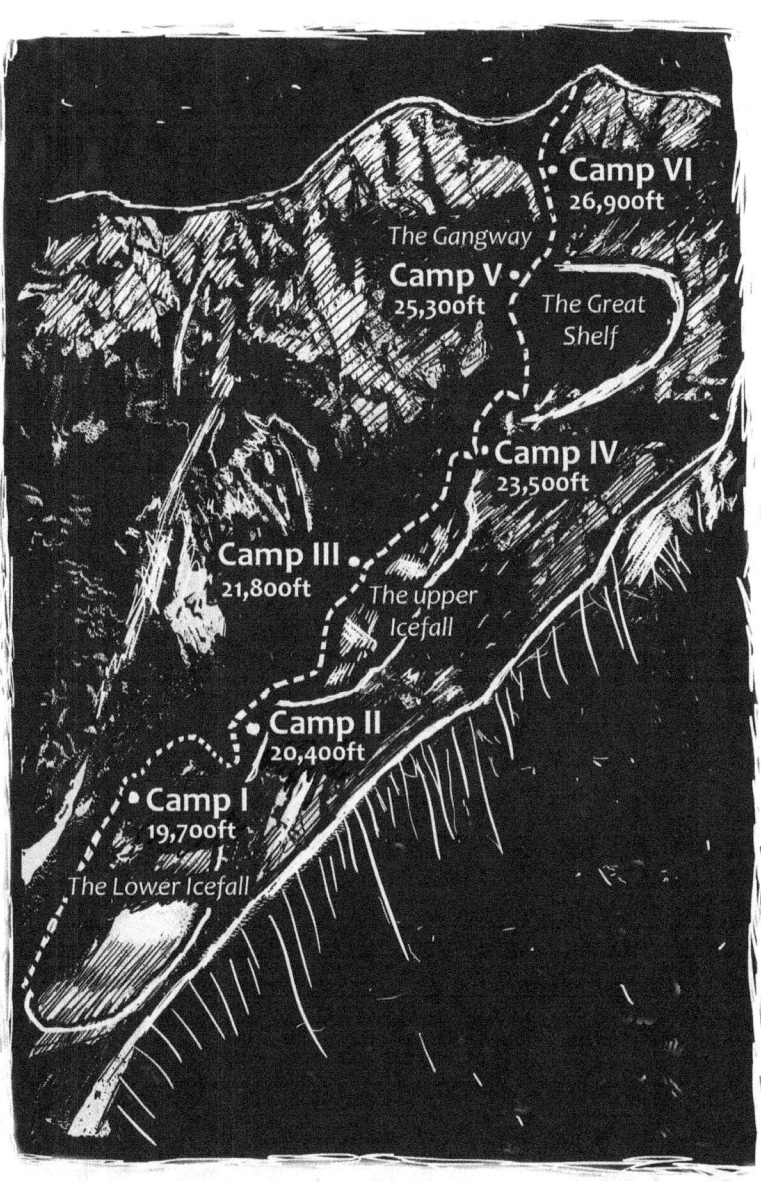

Camps on the South West Face

misted up. He didn't notice anything at the time but when he reached camp that evening, he had developed full blown snow blindness, a temporary but excruciating condition. John had tossed and turned his way through the night and had woken up on the following morning, barely able to see. He insisted that he would carry on but it was obvious that he would not be able to lead one of the Sherpa parties, making Tom entirely responsible for the route-finding.

To add to Tom's woes, the Sherpas had spent the morning of May 19th reorganising their loads to make them lighter but in doing so had inadvertently abandoned several crucial bits of kit on the snow. Tom understood their desire to travel light but there was no point in getting to Camp 5 without a full set of tent poles or a complete stove, even if it might save weight in the short term. All Tom could do was order the Sherpas to re-pack most of the abandoned gear, and load up his own rucksack with anything they couldn't carry.

Seventeen hundred feet below, at Camp 3 Charles Evans was anxiously staring at the sky as he prepared to move up the mountain with Neil Mather and the first summit pair. A few days earlier he had written in his diary: "The time of my planning and organising is over. My hardest time to come... Hope to Christ I can do it, physically."

Charles was no longer plagued by the self-doubts that had marked the beginning of the expedition but increasingly he found it impossible to keep food down and could not shake off his cough. Joe Brown and George Band still had very hearty appetites but Charles vomited up almost everything he ate, and the higher he went, the worse it got.

To make matters worse, the weather seemed to be deteriorating yet again. The sky was heavy with dark clouds and snow was already starting to fall. Charles was in radio contact with Base Camp, but because of the mountain's topography he could not speak directly to Tom Mackinnon. As the wind howled Charles got ready to move up, hoping that the 'big carry' was already underway. If it wasn't, they were all going to be in for a very uncomfortable night. because there weren't enough tents higher up to house the whole team.

Back at Camp 4, the repacking still hadn't quite finished. John Jackson was still in agony with his eyes but he knew that if he stayed in his tent it would send out a terrible signal to the Sherpas. Even though he could barely see in front of him, he insisted on taking part and humping 30 lbs of supplies.

At 10.20 a.m., about an hour after Charles Evans left Camp 3, the 'Big Carry' got underway. The Sherpas were arranged on three ropes: Tom leading the first party with the Sherpas Phurchita and Changjup in charge of the second and third. John Jackson was in the middle party, short roped to Phurchita. It was a hard, hard slog with the Sherpas having to stop every twelve steps on the steepest sections. At one stage a Sherpa vomited in front of John Jackson out of sheer exhaustion but fortunately John could neither see, nor smell, anything.

All went steadily until just below the Great Shelf when Changjup's load came free while he was helping another Sherpa. His sack rolled the slope, disgorging its contents as it went. Rather than carrying on, Changjup, immediately untied and headed down to retrieve it before Tom Mackinnon realised what was going on. It was a delay that no-one needed.

For most of the morning, Tom was out in front step cutting. The thick snow that covered the Great Shelf made the going harder and harder but having started out late, he set a relentless pace. If they couldn't get to Camp 5 by early afternoon, they would not be able to descend a full 3500 ft back to Camp 3.

Tom's oxygen gave out in the middle of the Great Shelf but he wouldn't let himself slow down .

John Jackson was equally aware of his responsibility but when they reached the steep slope below Camp 5 it was too dangerous to continue. He untied from Phurchita and waited patiently while the others climbed up to Tom and the first party of Sherpas. They had pitched a tent at Camp 5 and were piling up their loads inside. As soon as they were done they hurried on down but when the third party reached the bottom of the slope, they were so tired they couldn't reach the tent. Instead Tom Mackinnon let them bury their supplies in shallow snow holes half-way up the final slope. Then finally, when everything had been safely organised, Tom turned round and began the long gruelling descent.

The first men reached Camp 4 by 4.30 p.m. only to find Charles Evans's party comfortably settled. They were followed soon after by another three Sherpas and an utterly exhausted and still very blind John Jackson. Even though he wanted to continue descending, Charles insisted that John stayed put. The Sherpas looked equally tired but there was no alternative but to send them down. As a precaution Charles put Annullu, an Everest veteran who was one of their strongest Sherpas, in the lead.

By 5.00 p.m. Charles was getting anxious. There was still no sign of Tom Mackinnon and the last Sherpa, Pemi Dorje. As the minutes ticked by and the sun sank down towards the horizon, Charles began to fear the worst. As every mountaineer knew, a lot of accidents happen on the descent. It sounded as if Tom had exhausted himself, so where was he now? Lying in a crevasse somewhere?

In fact it was Pemi Dorje, who was having real difficulties. He was one of their youngest recruits and initially had not been chosen to work at high altitude. Pemi had done so well though on all the early carries across the Yalung glacier to Base Camp that Joe Brown had recommended him for promotion. Over the last few days however, he had been moving very slowly and looking ever more tired. Though he managed to carry his load as far as Camp 5, on the way down Pemi had fallen into a crevasse. Tom Mackinnon hauled him out, but when Pemi tottered into Camp 4 and promptly collapsed in the snow, it was clear that he was far from recovered and would not be able to descend that night.

Tom Mackinnon looked equally beat but it didn't stop him from talking excitedly about going back on the following day to help Charles finish the job. As he warmed up, Tom told them how tough it had been for Sherpas climbing so high without oxygen and how it had been "touch and go" as to whether they would get Camp 5 established at all. His narrative wasn't quite coherent but Charles was immensely relieved to have him back.

He was not quite so happy with the latest weather report radioed up by John Clegg. The temperature was rising and the wind was about to change direction. Whether this presaged the early arrival of the monsoon no-one was sure but more snow was expected. That night no-one slept well, the overcrowding compounding their worries.

Next morning, they woke up to be greeted by a raging blizzard. There was no question of Tom or John Jackson being able to descend or of anyone going up. All they could do was periodically venture out of their tents to clear the drifts of snow that built up on the outside. Charles tried to shoot some footage for the expedition film but it was a virtual white out for most of the day, so they just lay in their sleeping bags and as Neil Mather recorded in his diary, talked about "a diversity of subjects from British and Alpine climbing huts, to women".

By the following morning the weather had only marginally improved, but it was so uncomfortable at Camp 4 that Tom Mackinnon and John Jackson decided to go down, taking Pemi Dorje with them. For Charles these were desperate, miserable days. His nausea had returned and even the usually stoic Dawa Tenzing had declared how trapped and depressed he felt. To assuage the Gods and pray for good weather, the Sherpas burnt an offering over a stove but the skies remained distinctly ominous.

Sixty five miles away on Makalu, Jean Franco and his French team also noticed the high clouds and also wondered if the monsoon was about to break. If so it would hinder their march out but they were in ebullient form. Over the last couple of days eight members of their team had reached the top, their only regret was that it had not been a little more challenging. News of their success was already on its way back to France, where it would be hailed by French President, René Coty, as a "magnificent feat which fills our countrymen with pride".

Finally on May 22nd, after two days of enforced idleness, Charles woke up to clear skies. To the south, Darjeeling was just visible, and one Sherpa even spotted Everest in the far distance. George Band started his diary entry with a "Hurrah!" but having endured so much heavy snow, it was impossible to make an early start. The insides of their tents were a shambles of soggy sleeping bags and damp duvet jackets and trousers. Outside, it was just as chaotic, with ropes, ice axes and oxygen bottles encased in hard packed snow.

Everything had to be literally dug out by hand. Much to Charles' consternation, they discovered they only had one rope, the other having gone down with Tom Mackinnon and John Jackson. Their only option was to send Dawa Tenzing down to collect a spare coil that had been left below, while Charles and Joe Brown got ready to head up to Camp 5.

It took almost five hours from the moment Charles woke up to the moment he left camp, leading the first of two parties. The heavy snowfall of previous days had obliterated the tracks made by Tom and his Sherpas. As they trudged upwards through knee-deep snow, the wind blew relentlessly, tearing into their faces and forcing them to take ever more frequent stops. By late morning they had barely reached the upper slopes of the Great Shelf.

Then, suddenly, someone spotted the corner of a box, poking up above the snow. It was Changjup's load, which he had managed to retrieve but hadn't been able to carry all the way to Camp 5. Joe Brown went over and took out the most important food packets and then added them to his pack.

Charles was aware of Changjup's problems but he was totally thrown by what he saw a few hundred feet higher up. Sticking out at crazy angles was a chaos of oxygen bottles, tents parts, cooking equipment and supplies. The precious loads that the Sherpas had struggled with three days earlier and which Tom Mackinnon had organised so carefully must have been caught in an avalanche and come tumbling down.

For a few moments Charles was too numb to take it all in but instinctively he began collecting things and shoving them into his already overloaded rucksack. The others followed suite but the extra weight slowed them down even more. Halfway up the steep slope that led from the Great Shelf to Camp 5, Charles and Joe felt their oxygen run out, leaving them gasping for air. They were both very aware of the need to conserve as much oxygen as possible and had not intended to start on second cylinders, but with 200 ft of very steep climbing to go, Charles had no choice but to begin a second bottle.

Then almost seven hours after they set off, Charles and Joe reached the small plateau chosen for Camp 5. Nine days earlier Charles had climbed to the same point with Norman Hardie and revelled in the view. Now as he stared down was filled with horror. Tom had told him that he had pitched one tent and left a second one inside but Charles could see nothing but pure virgin snow. Had the same avalanche that smashed into Tom Mackinnon's supply cache also swept away the tent and everything within it? The thought was too appalling to contemplate. It would have undoubtedly meant the end of the expedition. Then suddenly Joe Brown spotted something poking out above the snow: the tip of a tent pole. At 25,300 ft it was impossible to do anything frantically, but Charles was desperate to see what had been preserved inside it.

By the time the second party reached them it was long past 4.00 p.m. Their faces were blue with anoxia, long icicles hanging from their noses. There wasn't a moment to lose though before the sun went down and their freezing cold camp site became even less hospitable. Immediately everyone began digging the tent out with their ice-axes, trying to be as careful as possible not to accidentally rip the fabric. As they had noticed earlier that morning, the snow had consolidated and was very hard to break into but eventually they were able to excavate the first tent and pitch the second.

Charles' biggest worry was the fate of the oxygen cylinders. Without them, there would be no summit attempts; but there was no sign of them. Eventually Joe Brown managed to locate ten bottles but there were still several unaccounted for. With the sun going down and the temperature dropping rapidly, Charles had no choice however but to halt the search and pitch their tents for the night. The wind continued to howl and screech, making the job even harder. At one point a strong gust ripped a row of pegs out of the ground and sent two tents sailing into the air like crazy kites, leaving Charles Evans to hold on for grim life by the guy ropes. It was a surreal moment but eventually they were manhandled down and made secure. Inside, they slowly warmed up, changing as Charles wrote "from cold exhausted creatures near our last gasp.... to some semblance of warmth and rest."

The wind did not abate and after a long difficult night, Charles woke up to find their camp half submerged in snow. The oxygen bottles and ration boxes they had left outside to anchors the guy ropes were almost completely buried. Just three hundred feet above them was the beginning of the 'Gangway', the snowy corridor they hoped would take George and Joe to the top of the South West Face, but if they couldn't retrieve their gear, it might as well have been a thousand feet higher.

It was still very cold, the sky overcast. Though they were up at 5.00 a.m., by 10.00 a.m. no-one was ready to move so Charles decided that it would be better to take another rest day, rather than forcing his exhausted men to push on up. They would spend their time hunting for more supplies and reorganising their loads, aiming to make an early start on the following morning. It was a wise move. As the day progressed, they found more and more stuff; most remarkably they managed to retrieve a radio set that had been carried away in the avalanche but was still in working order.

Charles remained in a melancholy mood. After the tremendous excitement of his first visit to Great Shelf nine days earlier, the pleasure seemed to have gone out of the expedition. All that was left was struggle and grind. Several oxygen bottles were still missing and though he was pleased to see how well George Band and Joe Brown had coped with all the difficulties, he felt too numb to share their excitement.

As the day wore on, conditions improved until by late afternoon they were able to sit outside their tents and take in the view. Down below Camp 4 was just visible, but there didn't seem to be any movement around them and when they shouted they got no response. Better news came over the radio from John Clegg at Base Camp, who was able to report that the Indian Meteorological Office was now predicting three days of fine weather.

There wasn't any sign of improvement at dawn on the following day but Charles was determined to go on anyway. Over the course of the expedition he had kept notes on how long it took to do basic tasks at different camps, in order to assess the effect of altitude. This morning, he noted that it took two hours to melt enough snow to give everyone a drink, five minutes to put on each boot and just under four hours before everyone was ready to leave, an improvement on the previous days but remarkably slow all the same.

With the tents still in shadow, it was so cold that the valves on their oxygen sets were frozen stiff and needed to be soaked in warm water before they would open. Even though he was wearing two pairs of silk gloves, George Band noticed how blisters formed on his fingertips as soon as he touched anything metal.

When they eventually got away, Charles and Neil Mather took the lead, aiming to do all the step cutting so that Joe Brown and George Band would have an easy day. Ultimately, however, it was Dawa Tenzing who did most of the work. He insisted on leading and rapidly chopped steps from the bottom of the Gangway high up past the mid-point.

Charles wasn't sure exactly where they were heading but he hoped to find a flattish area big enough for a two-man tent. The Gangway was getting ever steeper but as on Everest two years earlier when Hillary and Tenzing had struggled to find a good site for their final camp, so on Kangchenjunga. Charles began to despair that they would ever find anywhere suitable.

In the end their only option was to dig a small platform in the snow, but at 26,900 ft, with their oxygen cylinders exhausted, it was impossible to work quickly. The only spare bottle had been ear-marked for George and Joe's sleeping oxygen, so no-one wanted to start on it. It was all looking very grim, when George Band noticed something astonishing. Tashi, one of the Sherpas, appeared to have a cylinder that was still at least a third full.

It turned out that he had been climbing for several hours, oblivious to the fact that after stopping for a rest a few hundred feet lower down, he had forgotten to turn his oxygen set back on. It was a comical moment but this was no time for laughter. George Band immediately donned Tashi's set and began hacking into the icy slope. Two hours later he reached bare rock and had to stop. They now had a perfectly cut ledge but there was a problem.

The platform was four and a half foot wide but their tent was six inches wider – part of it would overhang, making for a very uncomfortable night for one man. There was nothing anyone on the support party could do though, so after pushing the remaining gear inside the tent, Charles and Neil wished their teammates both good luck and began the slow climb down to Camp 5. Though they were descending, it was utterly exhausting.

At 5.30 p.m. Charles' party finally reached Camp 5 and was greeted by Norman Hardie and Tony Streather who had come up to prepare for the second summit attempt. Norman had endured a difficult few days, suffering from bronchitis but as soon as he saw Charles and Neil and their two Sherpas, he rushed out to help them, plying them with warm drinks. Charles in particular looked so done in that Norman immediately offered him his oxygen mask and insisted that he sit still for a few minutes. In his hypoxic state, Charles was overcome with emotion, his eyes welling up with tears as he watched Tashi and Dawa collapse in the snow, utterly spent. They had given their all.

Up at Camp 6, Joe and George were melting ice and getting ready for a well-earned meal to set them up the challenge of their summit day. With the stove purring away, they were relieved to be inside a relatively warm tent but anxious to be in such an exposed position. With nothing to protect their tent from the wind, they felt extremely vulnerable so they roped up and attached themselves to a spike of rock outside.

Their meal that night was suitably calorific with asparagus soup, tinned ox tongue and potatoes, washed down with mugs of powdered lemon juice, and cocoa. Joe smoked five cigarettes and wished he'd brought a whole packet. Years later he would regret it: "I've thought since what a horrible thing to do, to inflict it on George (*a non-smoker*), because he was in the tent too, and I've thought 'what a bastard'".

After dinner they chatted about their life back home and the climbs they'd enjoyed and until the moment came when they had to decide who would sleep on the side of the tent closest the slope and who would bed down on the overhanging side. Joe took out two matchsticks. Whoever drew the shortest was in for an uncomfortable night. Six foot two George made his choice – and immediately regretted it.

Down at Camp 5, Charles Evans was shivering in his tent with Neil Mather. Unlike George and Joe, they didn't have the luxury of sleeping oxygen and were feeling cold and uncomfortable. Then suddenly a thought crossed Charles Evans' mind and before he knew it, he was nudging Neil and shouting.

"We've done it! They're up there. We've done it!"

Neil let out a whoop of joy and before long Norman Hardie was calling from the next tent, demanding to know what was up.

"We're just feeling good about ourselves," Charles replied.

"And so you should," Norman came straight back. "You have every right to be."

After eight incredibly tough weeks, the Kangchenjunga reconnaissance expedition was within striking distance of the summit of the world's highest unclimbed mountain. In spite of all his earlier doubts, they had succeeded to an extent that no-one could have imagined when they left Liverpool all those weeks earlier. Charles had found a route to the Great

Shelf, conquered his self-doubt, forced his body to carry on when all it wanted to do was retreat. Like a true leader, right at the end he taken a back seat and handed over the responsibility for the success of the expedition to the best men for the job.

Now it was all up to George and Joe, the two youngest members of the team. If they got it right, they would be hailed as heroes, but if Joe Brown in particular failed to live up to his promise, as Charles noted in his diary, "All Manchester would hound him out."

CHAPTER TEN
High Achievers

The Summit Cone

"There was a young climber called Brown
Whose farts brought him world-wide renown
He swallowed a thistle to make his arse whistle
Hoping to bring the thing down."

They were an archetypal 'odd couple'. George Band was tall, blond and bespectacled, a recent graduate of Cambridge University who amused himself on the expedition writing nonsense verse. Joe Brown was short, dark and wiry, a general builder from Manchester who had left school at fourteen and never looked back. Like George he was quick witted with a storehouse of Northern expressions, which he rolled out much to the entertainment of the other climbers. "It smelt worse than an Arab wrestler's jockstrap," was one of his most pungent.

If it hadn't been for Kangchenjunga they would probably have never met, but here they were at 26,900 ft, poised to make history. In its own way their partnership was a symbol of the 1950s, a new era of social mobility where working class boys could make good and upper-class boys could no longer automatically assume pole position. Their respective routes into climbing however, had been very different.

George was a typical Oxbridge man who could have taken part in any of the British expeditions of the 1920s or 30s. The son of a Presbyterian missionary, he was born in Taiwan in 1929 and educated at a British public school. He began climbing at Cambridge in 1950, joining the University Mountaineering Club and eventually becoming its President.

He did his first serious mountaineering in the Alps with his university friends and then got a very lucky break in 1952 when he was invited to join the forthcoming Everest expedition. In theory, aged just 23, he should have been too young to take part but John Hunt had liked him straight away, and had been particularly impressed when George presented a recent trip to the Alps in the form of a 'military appreciation', or planning exercise.

Everest, however, had not gone as planned. After an impressive start, George had developed a gastric infection, which had put him out of action for the second half of the expedition. Only right at the end, when Hillary and Tenzing were on their way down from the summit was he fit enough to climb really high.

A year later, George had returned to South East Asia with a Cambridge University expedition, aiming to climb Rakaposhi, the huge peak that towers above Pakistan's Hunza valley. Once again it was not quite the experience he had envisaged. His young team did well initially but was forced to turn back 4,700 ft from the summit because of terrible snow conditions.

When Charles Evans offered him a place on the 1955 Kangchenjunga expedition, George was still uncertain about his future. After Cambridge he had supported himself between his travels through writing and lecturing, while fending off his parents' questions about settling down and getting a proper job. How long he could continue going on big expeditions every year was increasingly up for debate.

Joe Brown, by contrast, had already worked for ten years as a general builder, only stopping for a brief stint of National Service. Climbing was a hobby, a place to escape to at the weekend with his friends from the *Valkyrie Club* and the *Rock and Ice*. He quickly discovered that he was very good at it but until Charles Evans invited him to join the Kangchenjunga expedition, he would never have believed that one day he would be part of a national team on a major expedition to the Himalayas.

At the beginning he'd been worried about not having as much travelling money as the others and not being familiar with the complex dining etiquette on the ship out to India.

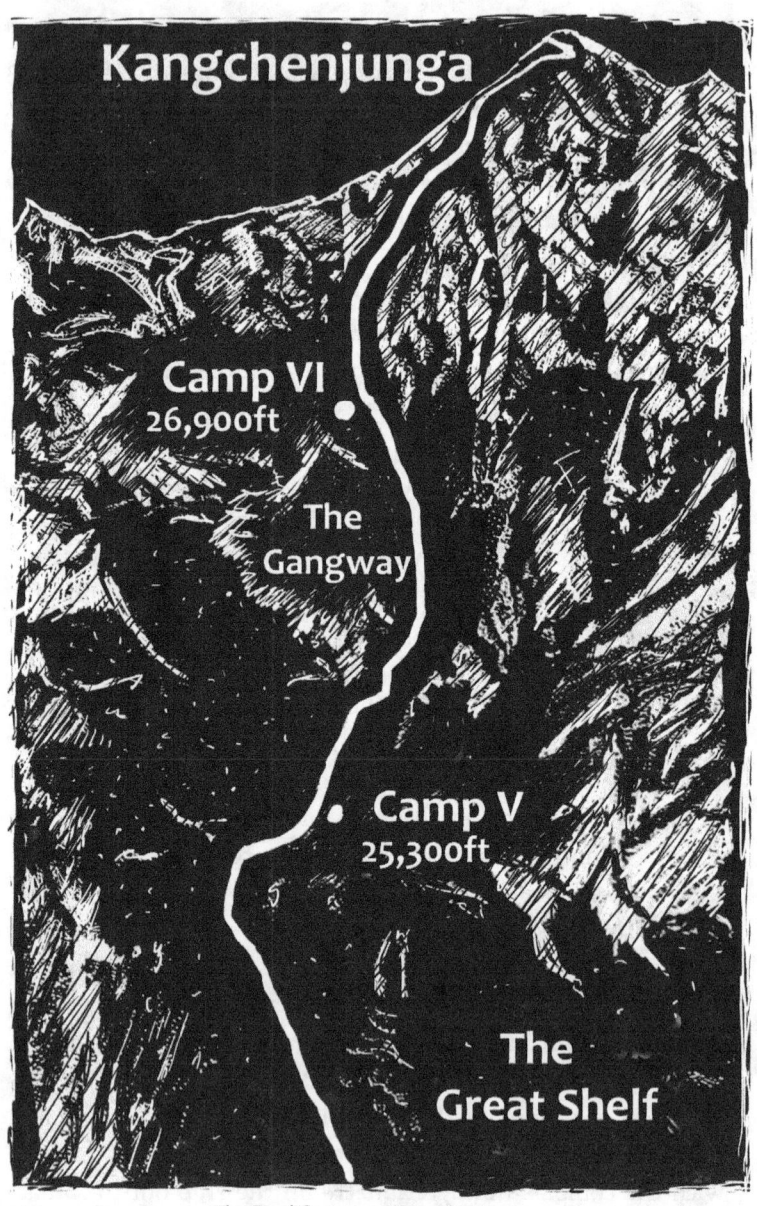

The Final Camps on Kangchenjunga

When they reached Darjeeling, his accent and his manner of speaking had marked him out as being different from the others. George Band joked in his diary that even the Sherpas noticed it: "Sherpas doubt whether Joe is British. He talks a different language."

Joe smoked a lot and always seemed to be hungry. Other climbers were wary of yak meat but he would ask for extra steaks. At one breakfast at Camp 2, he managed to get through half a pound of cheese, half a bottle of ketchup and a couple of Mars bars. He threw it all up half an hour later, but his appetite was undimmed.

Back in Britain there had been some who warned Charles that taking Joe was too much of a gamble. Norman Hardie, his deputy, had his doubts about Joe's ability on snow and ice and tried to persuade Charles that he should really be the other member of the first summit team, but Charles paid no heed. Though he liked and respected Norman, he was convinced that Joe and George would work well together and that they should be his first summit pair.

So the stage was set for an epic moment in the history of British mountaineering. If George and Joe could get to the top, they would not only become the first men to stand on the summit of the world's third highest mountain, but they would also become the first all-British pair to conquer an 8000m peak. George Band would be able to shake off any lingering sense that he hadn't quite fulfilled his potential on Everest and Joe would prove all the doubters wrong and signal that he really was an outstanding all-round mountaineer. For the moment though, at 5.00 a.m. on the freezing cold morning of May 25th 1955, Joe and George's first big challenge was much more basic: to get out of bed.

As Jean Franco and the French climbers on Makalu had found, even at a very low flow rate, oxygen significantly enhanced sleep but in spite of this, they had still spent the night swaddled in every item of clothing they possessed. George had even kept his heavyweight high-altitude boots on for fear that he would suffer the same fate as Ed Hillary, who had woken up on the morning of his summit attempt in May 1953 with a pair of boots that were frozen solid. Before he could put them on, Ed literally had to cook them over the stove.

George had not enjoyed a restful night. He had been continually tormented by small flurries of snow, which skittered down from above, spilling over the edge of the tent. As he lay there half-awake half-asleep, nightmare visions of avalanches were punctuated by slightly more conscious bouts of worrying about the task ahead and the responsibility and privilege of being in the first pair. George knew that Norman Hardie and Tony Streather were just a day behind but there was no certainty that the severe weather would not return. It was crucial that he and Joe should get up and down safely but Charles had warned them not push their luck and risk turning the second attempt into a rescue mission.

George's deliberations were brought to an abrupt halt when the oxygen ran out. Immediately they both woke up with a start and prepared to ease themselves out of their sleeping bags. Several minutes later, Joe went outside for his morning ablutions and then got to work melting snow over their Primus stove. George meanwhile, gave the oxygen sets a once over, cursing the blisters on his finger-tips.

Outside, the sky was clear, and Joe was glad to report that in spite of George's nightmares there didn't seem to be much new snow. Nothing happened quickly at high altitude, though. It took three hours, two pints of tea and several Digestive biscuits, before they were ready to leave.

Their plan was to continue up the Gangway, the same narrow channel spotted by Aleister Crowley fifty years earlier but rather than take it all the way up to the crest of the West Ridge, they were going to come off early and traverse across the face towards the summit following a line of snow patches visible from below. The West Ridge might have seemed a more direct route, but they could see through their binoculars that it was broken up by a series of rock towers, and mindful of all the weeks that it had taken Paul Bauer to navigate the North East Spur, they wisely opted to join the ridge as close as possible to the summit.

Each of them would carry a single 1600-litre oxygen cylinder, which at an average flow rate of 4 litres per minute, should last for almost seven hours. Fully charged a cylinder weighed 16 lbs, when exhausted 11 lbs 3 oz. The rest of the apparatus came in at 7 lb. As discussed with Charles and Norman, their notional 'turn-around time', the point at which they had to abandon their attempt if they wanted to safely descend, was at around 1.00 p.m. After that they were to head back down all the way to Camp 5, leaving Norman and Tony Streather to take over their positions in the small two-man tent at Camp 6. It was a neat, sensible plan but as Charles Evans had warned them, there were plenty of things that could go wrong before the cup met the lip.

Further down the mountain, all eyes were strained upwards. John Clegg was on radio and binocular duty at Base Camp, under strict instructions to keep a careful watch over the slopes leading up to the summit and give Charles Evans regular updates on what he could see. Clegg's more pressing problem was Pemi Dorje, the ill Sherpa. After his exertions on the 'big carry' a few days earlier, Pemi had seemed to improve but over the last twenty-four hours his condition had deteriorated. His pupils were different sizes and no longer seemed sensitive to light, his limbs were twitchy and his knee reflexes no longer responded. John Clegg thought it might be the aftermath of a minor stroke but he couldn't be sure.

At Camp 5, Charles Evans was utterly focused on what was happening above. As team leader his responsibility was to stay in reserve with his sirdar, Dawa Tenzing. If anything went wrong on one of the summit attempts, they were poised to go up and help. Not that Charles was in such good shape himself. His stomach had not improved and before long he was vomiting up both his breakfast and his previous night's dinner.

Once he had cleaned himself up, Charles' first task was to see off Norman Hardie and Tony Streather. That morning they would leave for the top camp supported by two Sherpas, Urkien and Ila Tenzing. Fearing that the first pair had not taken quite enough oxygen for their summit bid, Norman and Tony had decided to carry up two extra bottles each. Having just endured a nasty attack of bronchitis, a fully recovered Norman was raring to go. He kept on telling Charles that the success of the expedition was down to his leadership and repeating that he too should make a summit attempt. Though Charles might have been flattered, he was not persuaded.

By the time Norman and Tony left Camp 5, the first summit pair, George Band and Joe Brown, were already well on their way. The snow on the Gangway was so crisp and firm that it was tempting to crampon their way up but thinking ahead to the return trip when they might be much more tired, they were careful to cut steps. Joe had broken his axe earlier in the expedition so he had borrowed one from John Clegg. Though he had less step-cutting experienced than George Band, Joe found it easier to cope with the altitude and gradually moved into the lead.

On they climbed, gradually warming up with the effort. Joe tried to remember the Indian Air-Force photographs sent to Charles Evans several weeks earlier. It was crucial that he and George should come off the Gangway at the right moment but with oxygen leaking from his mask and his goggles constantly fogging up, it wasn't easy to see properly. At around 10.30 a.m. the clouds had cleared enough for John Clegg to spot Joe and George veering off right towards a snowy couloir. "Why have they come off so early?" he wondered.

In their desire to get up quickly, George and Joe had left the Gangway prematurely. Only when they were stopped by a sheer 100 ft wall of rock did they realise their error and turn back. Ultimately their mistake cost them about an hour and a half of precious time, and more importantly, precious oxygen. The only way to make up for it was to reduce the flow rate to two litres per minute and push on without any rest stops. As they got higher and higher, the ground grew steeper and more uneven, making it unsafe to move in tandem. Instead they took turns to do the lead climbing, while the other man took a firm belay.

Below them, the clouds came and went, frequently obscuring John Clegg's view from Base Camp. When he spoke to Charles Evans at midday he had nothing to report on the summit attempt and only had bad news about Pemi Dorje. The young Sherpa was by then semi-conscious and felt strangely dry to the touch. To add to Clegg's worries, another Sherpa, Ut Tsering, was coughing up droplets of blood. Whether this was severe bronchitis, or the sign of something much worse, it was too early to tell.

Though it was overcast at Base Camp, above the cloud layer the skies were clear. Norman Hardie and Tony Streather arrived as planned at Camp 6 with their two Sherpas, only to find the tent collapsed. It had been anchored down by George and Joes' ice-axes but obviously they had been needed elsewhere. By the time Norman had re-pitched it and melted enough snow for a hot drink, he expected to be able to see George and Joe descending the Gangway, but he saw nothing and grew increasingly anxious. Would they stick to their turnaround time and return early enough to descend to Camp 5? Would George and Joe get all the way to the top or would he and Tony have to finish the job?

Fortunately, after their earlier error, things were going well for George and Joe. They had by then left the Gangway for the second time and moved onto the mixed terrain of the West Face. Joe instinctively gravitated towards the rock while George stuck to the snow whenever possible. Frequently though, there wasn't a choice.

Since they arrived at Base Camp they had spent nearly all their time on snow and ice but now, close to the summit, they were being forced to do some serious rock climbing. At sea-level, it would have been an enjoyable challenge, but getting around difficult rock corners at almost 27,700 ft was a lot more frightening. When things got really difficult, Joe hammered in a piton for protection but there was no mistaking, things were now much more demanding.

The last test before they reached the crest of the west ridge was a 120 ft gully, raked at an angle of sixty degrees. The only way up, was to break it into two separate pitches. With George finding it hard to climb at a low flow rate, Joe spent most of the time in the lead until finally they both came out onto the crest and were able to stop for their first break of the day.

After almost six hours of continuous hard work, George was exhausted. The bridge of his nose was sore from the chafing of his mask, and no matter how much he swallowed he couldn't quite get rid of the clots of phlegm that collected on the roof of his mouth. Joe seemed to be faring slightly better. As a much lighter man, he coped more easily with the altitude. The problem was his eyes.

Like John Jackson a few days earlier, Joe had lost so much weight that his oxygen mask didn't fit properly and was leaking into his goggles. George had warned Joe not to be tempted to take them off, even when they were climbing on dark rock, but Joe hadn't always heeded his advice. So far he had suffered no obvious ill effects but it was inevitable that he would develop snow blindness.

For all their aches and pains though, they were both thrilled to be on the West Ridge, protected from the wind in their small hollow. They tentatively took off their masks and found that if they didn't move, they were able to breathe quite happily. For five minutes, they sat relishing the view, swigging back lukewarm lemon juice and gobbling down a handful of toffees and few chunks of Kendal mint cake. It was 2.00 p.m., an hour past their turn around time. By George's calculation they had barely two hours of oxygen left. "We've got to be on our way down by 3.00 p.m. or we'll end up spending the night out," George warned Joe.

"We better get going then," was Joe's succinct reply.

Back down at base-camp John Clegg was facing a different kind of crisis. Even though he had given Pemi Dorje penicillin and inserted a nasal catheter to deliver oxygen directly into his lungs, he appeared to be getting weaker and weaker and with just a basic medical kit, John Clegg's options were limited. Whenever there was a break in the clouds, he would leave his patient for a moment to scan the summit area with the big Base-Camp binoculars but as he told Charles by radio at 2.05 p.m., he could see still nothing.

For Charles, it was an extremely tense day, numbed only by the heavy-headed dullness that came with spending so much time spent at high altitude. He could neither help John Clegg at Base Camp, nor do anything to assist the men above. The summit slopes were visible from Camp 4 and occasionally from Base Camp, but he could see nothing from his station at Camp 5. He just had to sit tight and wait.

At that very moment it was perhaps merciful that Charles could not see what was happening higher up. Kangchenjunga had saved its best for last. After a relatively straightforward traverse, keeping just below the ridge crest to avoid the wind, George and Joe had been stopped in their tracks by a sheer wall of golden brown rock, riven by a series of deep vertical cracks.

Like Hillary and Tenzing who two years earlier had been faced with a very dangerous and difficult rock step just below the summit of Everest, so George and Joe had encountered the trickiest bit of climbing at the climax of their attempt. They couldn't see a way around the rock wall and with little oxygen remaining, there was no question of retracing their steps. Joe Brown looked up and thought hard. It was his moment of truth. If he made the correct decision, he would prove his absolute right to be on the expedition. If he got it wrong, they would never see the summit they had worked so hard to reach.

Back home in the Peak District, Joe had become an expert in 'hand jamming', a demanding technique in which a climber deliberately locks one hand within a crack in a rock-face, and then uses their free hand feet to lever their way upwards. Apart from early on in this expedition when he had done some recreational bouldering at 'Crack Camp' on the Yalung glacier, those skills had not been needed. Now, staring upwards, he could see no other way of climbing the final rock-face.

With George paying out the rope from below, Joe cranked up his oxygen set to six litres per minute, three times the flow rate he had been using for the last few hours. He wedged one fist into the crack and began to force his way upward, hold after hold, foot after foot until he was forced to stop at an overhang just below the top.

The fate of their summit attempt hung on Joe's next move. They were long past their turnaround time and with Joe's oxygen was bound to run out soon. In normal circumstances tackling overhanging rocks was part of the challenge of climbing, but at 28,000 ft on Kangchenjunga with 20 lbs of oxygen set on his back, Joe was extremely exposed. If he slipped now, George had a good belay, but they were on the steepest rock they had encountered so far and there was no guarantee he could hold his partner.

Joe reached his hand over the rock and with a final heave pulled himself up and over. Moments later he shouted down: "George we're there!"

They had done it. In spite of the problems earlier in the day, in spite of the bad weather, the avalanches and the oncoming monsoon, they had reached their goal.

Joe took the rope in as George adjusted his oxygen set and quickly climbed the last pitch. As he ruefully admitted to diary that evening, in a final piece of 'lifemanship', he chose to run his apparatus at 5 litres per minute, 1 litre less than Joe. All thoughts of rivalry ended though when he finally stood at the top. Fifty years after Aleister Crowley's first attempt, twenty-six years after Paul Bauer's legendary battles on the North East Spur, at 2.45 p.m. on Wednesday May 25th 1955, Kangchenjunga had finally been climbed.

As George took in the view he noticed how the summit platform sloped gently upwards towards a rocky promontory at the southern end and where a five-foot-high snow cone marked the absolute apex. Following the agreement Charles Evans had made all those weeks earlier in Gangtok, they left it untouched. "I had not the slightest inclination to stand on the top of it" Joe Brown remembered in 2017. "We didn't have a flag, nobody on Kangchenjunga did. The feeling you got on the top was not 'wow we've done it', it was 'We don't have to do anymore'. It wasn't like a fantastic piece of rock climbing where you wish it would go on forever. With high altitude climbing, when you get to the top you think: "That's great. Done it.""

Below them lay a sea of billowing clouds at around 20,000 ft, stretching all the way from India in the south to Tibet in the north. The only summits visible were the true Himalayan giants, Everest and Lhotse and a little closer Makalu, the 27,800 ft peak that unbeknownst to them, Jean Franco's French team had climbed ten days earlier. It was the reverse of the view that had greeted Hillary and Tenzing at the summit of Everest back in 1953.

"Let's get this photo business over," said Joe. They took a portrait shot of the other for the press and then George began to take a panorama of photographs, revelling in the scenery around him. Then at 3.00 pm, after just fifteen minutes on the summit they prepared to go down. Within two hours the sun would set and it would grow dark. More pressingly, they had very little oxygen left.

The quickest way to get down the steep pitch below the summit would have been to abseil but rather than risk a complicated manoeuvre, they decided to retrace their steps. Just before they left, George remembered that he had promised to bring back a rock from the summit, so he grabbed a lump of gneiss, a souvenir that would later be broken up and shared around the team.

An hour later just after 4.00 p.m., Joe's oxygen ran out, followed twenty minutes later by George's. At last they could discard their heavy sets but the end of their oxygen had an immediate effect. George was hit by a wave of exhaustion and dizziness. He stepped on some loose snow which with a 'whoosh 'gave way, sending him sliding down the mountain. In 1905 a small slip had put an end to the Crowley expedition and four men's lives, in 1931 Hermann Schaller had been torn off the North East Spur when his porter Pasang lost his footing. For a split second it looked as if the 1955 expedition would be the latest to be punished by the Demon of Kangchenjunga, but then George flipped over onto his stomach and dug his ice axe in hard. Quickly he came to a stop and lay breathless, Joe Brown standing above him with a wry smile. "It makes me tired just to watch you do that," was his only comment.

At Camp 6, Norman Hardie and Tony Streather were still scanning the Gangway high above them, hoping to spot George and Joe on the way down. If everything had gone according to plan, they should have already reached Camp 6 and been well on their way down to Charles Evans 1,600 ft below. With no sign of them, increasingly Norman was convinced that something had gone seriously wrong.

Camp 6 was a small two-man tent, equipped with just two sleeping bags. If George and Joe turned up late and were unable to descend, they would all be in for a very uncomfortable night. If they didn't turn up at all, Norman and Tony's summit bid would become a rescue attempt. There was no alternative but to send down their two Sherpas Urkien and Ila Tenzing. So far on the expedition, for safety's sake, their Sherpas had almost always been escorted by at least one team member when moving between camps, but Urkien and Ila Tenzing were amongst their most experienced men, and at that moment it was impossible to play it any other way.

By 5.30 p.m., the tent was in shadow, causing the temperature to drop rapidly. Norman squeezed into his sleeping bag, but in spite of his gnawing hunger, he had no appetite for food. What if there had been accident? Would there be enough oxygen for Charles Evans to help them? Unlike the French Makalu expedition, they didn't have any spare capacity. The weather remained calm, but Norman could hear nothing from above.

He wasn't the only one who was worried. At Base Camp, a much more serious crisis was unfolding. Pemi Dorje had stopped responding to oral penicillin, so John Clegg had rigged up an improvised intravenous drip. He had just about enough equipment with him but it wasn't easy to keep thing's sterile and as he admitted in his diary, it was all a little 'Heath Robinson'.

Clegg had discussed Pemi's condition over the radio with Charles. He suspected that it might be some kind of thrombosis, but in the early 1950s high altitude physiology was still in its infancy and neither man had ever seen anything like this. Today Pemi would probably have been diagnosed as suffering from cerebral oedema, treated with corticosteroids and diuretics and evacuated from the mountain as quickly as possible, but in 1955 there were no helicopters capable of flying safely to 18,000 ft and drugs like Dexamethasone had not been developed.

It was a strange climax to the expedition for Charles. High up at Camp 5 on the Great Shelf, he could take no direct part in the dramas that were unfolding at the top and bottom of the mountain. All he could do was man the radio and hope that his faith in George and Joe would be repaid and that Pemi would recover. At 5.15 p.m. Ila Tenzing and Urkien arrived at Camp 5 but they were on their own and had no news of the first summit pair. Shortly afterwards John Jackson radioed up from Camp 4. He could see the upper slopes of the mountain clearly but had not spotted anyone coming down.

Charles left his tent and called up a few times, more in hope than expectation. There was no response. Then at around 7.00 p.m. Ila Tenzing thought he heard a shout from above. He grabbed a torch and went out with Charles. Perhaps the first pair were on their way down to Camp 5 as planned? They tried shouting up again and thought they got a reply but after several minutes waiting in the bitter cold Charles concluded that it was a false alarm.

In fact, George and Joe were making slow but steady progress down the mountain and had indeed occasionally been shouting to their comrades below. After George's slip, they had taken things very carefully, not that they had the energy to do anything fast. Their main concern was not to miss Camp 6 in the darkness but fortunately Norman and Tony heard their shouts and came out of their tent with torches to help guide them back.

When they finally lurched into the tent at Camp 6, George and Joe were utterly exhausted. They could barely move until they had drunk a mug of hot lemon juice, but George was still able to come up with a witty quip. "Well we've knocked a *second* bastard off," he said to Norman Hardie, echoing Ed Hillary's famous remark to George Lowe after climbing Everest.

Inside the tent, it was as uncomfortable as could be imagined. The only way to accommodate all four men in was for each to back into a corner and then sit with their feet projecting into the middle. As they drank mug after mug of soup, George told the tale of their day, recounting how they had come off early and lost an hour and half and how later on they had encountered the most difficult climbing right at the top.

As the tent warmed up, George's frost-nipped fingers became incredibly painful but Joe Brown was in an even worse state. Like John Jackson a few days earlier, he was suffering from full blown snow blindness. The backs of his eyes began to prickle and before long the tears were pouring down. "It really does feel like someone has pulled your eyelids back and stuffed them with red hot ash," he remembered years later.

Eventually it was time to turn in but sleep didn't come easily. There were no bags for George and Joe, never mind extra oxygen. The priority was to give Norman and Tony as good a night as possible, so once again George lay down on the overhanging section of the tent and clung on for dear life, hoping that the creaks coming from the canvas below weren't a sign that the stitching was about to give way. Joe, meanwhile, spent the night rolling around on the ice-cold tent floor in agony. It was not quite the victors' celebration they might have wished for.

In spite of being hooked up to an oxygen bottle, Norman Hardie couldn't get to sleep either. Even though the expedition had already succeeded beyond everyone's expectations, he was determined that he and Tony would also reach the top. The British team would never the match the French, who had got eight climbers onto the summit of Makalu, but getting two pairs to the top would be a real achievement.

On the following morning everyone tried to get off as quickly as possible. Joe's snow blindness was no better and his balance was shot but George Band was able to guide him down on a tight rope and to their relief, they found well-cut steps leading all the way down to the Great Shelf.

At Camp 5, 1,600 ft below, Charles Evans was still anxiously awaiting news. He'd had another difficult night, waking up with a migraine and a painful cough. Charles had by then more or less given up on food but he still found himself retching on an empty stomach. At 8.00 a.m. John Clegg called up to say that he had just seen two figures descending from Camp 6. One of them looked like Joe Brown and was moving rapidly.

Then an hour later, just before 9.00 a.m. Charles finally spotted George and Joe approaching Camp 5. He and Dawa ran out into the snow, without any crampons or rope.

Running was a misnomer at 26,300 ft, but finally they were close enough to call up.

"Did you do it?" shouted Charles.

"Yes!" was their simple answer.

Once down, they were immediately ushered into Charles' warm tent but before he could hear the full story of their descent, he radioed down to Base Camp and told John Clegg to immediately send off a runner to Darjeeling with a message for the *Times*:

> Please pass mother birthday greetings, May 25th. Five feet short

Months earlier Charles had agreed a series of code phrases with the *Times*, to be used at the climax of the expedition to report whether or not it had been a success. Within a few days it would be decrypted back in London:

> Kangchenjunga has been climbed on May 25, the last five feet were left untrodden.

For Charles, the feeling of relief was immense but as he admitted to his diary, he was too numb to feel any sense of personal triumph:

> It is a great day for me, but one I can hardly appreciate – I'm tired and anoxic so much so that I can't fully enjoy it now. What I do enjoy is sitting on a box here, late evening doing nothing but look at the cloud seas over the Talung gap.... I'm awfully glad Joe and George have done it.

Apart from having one very sick Sherpa at Base Camp, Norman Hardie and Tony Streather were still above, and until they returned safely Charles couldn't relax.

Down at Base Camp, John Clegg was overjoyed to hear the news. After all the tension of the previous day, he could hear the relief in Charles Evans' voice but wondered if the second attempt would be an anti-climax. Was it really necessary to chance their luck for a second time? Norman Hardie and Tony Streather had no such doubts.

Though not quite so visually ill-matched as George and Joe, Noman and Tony were a strong if unlikely pairing. Norman Hardie was a thirty-year-old Kiwi who had decided to make Britain his temporary home a few years earlier. Bespectacled and bearded and rather intense, he worked as a civil engineer but since his youth had been a very keen outdoorsman, enjoying hunting, hiking and more recently, mountaineering.

In 1952 Norman had applied unsuccessfully to join the British Everest expedition but even though he had been turned down, he had graciously agreed to work for expedition leader John Hunt, supervising the endless traffic of supplies and equipment in and out of the Royal Geographical Society. In 1954 he had gone with Ed Hillary and Charles Evans on the New Zealand Barun Valley expedition, and had immediately said yes when Charles Evans invited him to join the Kangchenjunga team.

During the first stages of the expedition, Norman had been very concerned about its ambiguous status as a 'reconnaissance which might turn into an attempt' and had been very worried about the prospect of a new, 'official' team taking over the following year and grabbing all the glory. If he'd had his way, he would have been with George Band or Charles Evans on the first attempt but that was not how it turned out. Norman felt perfectly safe with Tony as a climbing partner and knew how strong he was, but he didn't like the sound of the final rock cliff and in particular the crack that Joe had climbed.

Tony Streather was another member of the Kangchenjunga team who had been considered for Everest but like Norman, he had not been chosen. Not that Tony had been all that surprised. Although he would go on to take part in several of the most well-known Himalayan expeditions of 1950s and 1960s, Tony was always very modest about his achievements, insisting that his stamina and lung capacity were far more important assets than any technical climbing skills.

He had enlisted back in 1945, aged nineteen and had gone on to serve in both the Indian and Pakistani armies, first as an officer in the Rajputana rifles and then the legendary Chitral Scouts. When he posed for the cameras in spring 1955 Tony looked every inch the 'pukka Sahib' with a small clipped moustache and sharply creased khakis. For the last few years he had been stationed in Britain, having transferred to the Gloucestershire regiment, but his years in India had left an indelible mark. He spoke Urdu and several other local languages and in spite of his military bearing, preferred to cajole rather than hector the porters and Sherpas.

A self-confessed 'accidental climber', Tony's initiation into mountaineering had come through work rather sport when in 1950 he had been appointed official liaison and transport officer to a Norwegian expedition to Tirich Mir, at 25,288 ft the highest peak in the Hindu Kush. After several years patrolling the high passes of the North West Frontier, Tony was so well acclimatized to high altitude that he was able to accompany the Norwegians all the way to the summit, insulated by a pair of pyjamas worn under his battle dress.

Tony's ascent of Tirich Mir brought him to the attention of the British Everest Committee who invited him to join a small training expedition to the Alps in the autumn of 1952. The plan was to test out potential team members for their fitness and technical abilities but Tony's limited equipment knowledge quickly became apparent when he was spotted trying to put on his crampons – backwards. Needless to say, he was politely turned down.

Tony had by then caught the mountaineering bug so when shortly afterwards he received a letter asking him to assist an American party making an attempt on K2, he immediately agreed, on the proviso that he could be part of the climbing party. The Americans readily agreed, but the 1953 K2 expedition turned out very differently to Tirich Mir.

After six weeks on one of the toughest mountains in the world, Tony and his new American friends had found themselves pinned down by a ferocious storm which left them trapped in their tents for six days at 25,500 ft. The wind was so relentless that they could hardly cook or boil water to drink. Eventually the youngest member of the team, Art Gilkey, had developed thrombophlebitis in both legs.

The expedition leader, Charles Houston, was a distinguished mountaineer and medical doctor. He realised straight away that Gilkey would die if they didn't take him down to lower altitude but the snow conditions and the steepness of the mountain made this a virtually impossible task.

Together Houston's team struck camp, wrapped Gilkey in a tent and began lowering him down. Then, inevitably, one member of the team slipped and pulled almost everyone else off, Tony Streather, included. Miraculously, the last man on the rope, Pete Schoening, held all the others but when they regrouped, they were in very poor shape.

While they were recovering in a bivouac tent near the accident site, they had left the immobile Art Gilkey carefully pinned to the slope by a pair of ice-axes. When half an hour later, Tony Streather had climbed across to talk to him, he had found nothing but a bare, icy slope. "An avalanche must have come down and taken him away," Tony remembered five decades later, "I went over to the spot where he was and it looked completely different".

Eventually, after climbing down past the blood-stained rocks which marked Gilkey's fall line down the mountain, the battered and bruised American team had made it back to base camp but for everyone involved, K2 was a deeply traumatizing experience. When Tony was invited to join the Kangchenjunga expedition of 1955, he felt compelled to say yes, not just because he wanted to get back into the mountains, but because he needed to test himself. "I had to go," he remembered in 2017, "To prove that I hadn't lost my nerve." So far on Kangchenjunga, Tony had done well, but on the morning of May 26th 1955, he was about to face his hardest test yet.

Initially it all went smoothly. As John Clegg watched from Base Camp, he saw Tony and Norman emerge from their tent and start up the Gangway towards Kangchenjunga's West Ridge. They were tiny figures in his binoculars, but he could see that they were moving quickly.

Unlike the first pair, Tony and Norman had the advantage of climbing a known route. Some of the steps cut on the previous day had to be scraped out or re-cut completely but after a night quizzing George Band, Norman had a very good idea of what to expect and would not make the mistake of coming off the Gangway too early. Unlike George and Joe, Norman and Tony had brought two small extra cylinders, which they hoped would enable them to make both the ascent and the descent on oxygen.

Everything was going according to plan when after about an hour, Tony noticed that a windproof jacket attached to Norman's oxygen set had worked its way loose. He shouted up to warn him but when Norman turned around to take the apparatus off, his main oxygen bottle popped out of its leather straps, fell down onto the ice valve first and then sped down the slope, hissing furiously and narrowly missing Tony Streather below. In a single moment of bad luck, they had lost almost a third of their collective oxygen.

Norman tried to carry on under his own steam, but when Tony noticed that his partner was climbing more and more slowly, he offered up his own large bottle. It was a selfless act but Tony was sure that Norman was better at route finding and step cutting and offered to run his own set at a very low rate, to economise on oxygen.

Like most of the well-known New Zealand climbers of his era, Norman was most comfortable climbing on snow and ice, so sometimes he took a slightly different route from George and Joe. Steadily he climbed on, occasionally glancing down at the camps below. There was a layer of cloud at 20,000 ft but the Great Shelf was visible and at one stage they even thought they spotted George and Joe descending towards Camp 4. The weather was calm and bright and after their earlier mishap with the oxygen bottle, there were no further problems for the next few hours.

At around 12.00 p.m. they reached the final cliff before the summit and stopped below the crack that Joe Brown had first climbed a day earlier. Though Joe had left a rope sling around halfway up to help the second pair, neither man liked the look of the crack. If they were going to do some serious rock climbing, they would have to take their crampons off and put them back on afterwards when they returned to the snow. All that would take a lot of time and oxygen and, apart from on K2, Tony had little experience on this kind of difficult, technical terrain.

Having got this far there was no question of turning around, so tentatively Norman started to climb a gully that lead up to the crack. After losing his larger cannister, he didn't have enough oxygen to risk increasing the flow rate. The sight of Joe's rope sling, silhouetted against the hard blue sky, only made the task ahead look even more intimidating.

Then out of the corner of his eye Norman noticed something – a gully which appeared to curve off behind the rock pitch. Joe hadn't mentioned it and the idea that they might be able to avoid the final pitch altogether seemed too good to be true, but Norman felt compelled to investigate. Sure enough, to his utter amazement, when Norman followed it round, he discovered that that the gully did indeed go all the way to the final ridge where it met some tracks in the snow left by George and Joe a day earlier. Norman shouted down and within a few minutes Tony had followed him all the way to the top.

It was an amazing turn of good fortune, allowing them to reach the summit at 12.15 p.m., around two and a half hours earlier than the first pair. The 'last big problem' of Kangchenjunga turned out not to be anything of the sort. As Joe Brown would joke years later, his difficult route up the crack in the cliff face would probably never be repeated because ultimately it was so unnecessary.

Norman and Tony revelled in their good fortune. Whereas the first pair had just a quarter of an hour, they were able to spend almost a whole hour on top. First they paused to drink a flask of lemon juice and eat a few snacks and then they indulged in an orgy of photographs. Like George and Joe they were very interested to peer down onto the north ridge and trace Bauer's route up the North East spur. Norman studied it closely and was very glad that they had not taken that route.

In the distance they could see Everest, the mountain both men had missed out on two years earlier. K2 was too far away for Tony to spot, but Norman could see Makalu, whose secondary summit he had attempted with Ed Hillary back in 1954. Had the French conquered it, he wondered, or would he be coming back in the following year?

First though, he and Norman would have to get down safely.

Tony swapped oxygen cylinders, taking Norman's smaller bottle, and at around 1.10 p.m., they began their descent. Initially it all went well, but then Norman noticed that Tony was moving erratically and seemed to be struggling. When he caught up, he saw immediately that Tony's snow goggles were almost completely fogged and much more alarmingly, that the oxygen cylinder he had put on a short while earlier was exhausted. Norman had checked everything the night before and it had been fine so it must have been slowly leaking throughout the day.

It was very bad luck: one oxygen cylinder lost, another leaky. There was no option though but to continue on regardless. Occasionally Tony stopped to rest and take a few breaths of oxygen from Norman's mask, but for the most part he struggled down under his own steam. On the really difficult sections Norman kept Tony on a short rope or hammered in a piton for extra protection. Fortunately there were no further dramas and eight and a half hours after they had left Camp 6, they returned to their tent, exhausted, starving and above all, parched.

Though in theory they still had almost enough time to get down to Charles at the camp below, neither man wanted to do anything other than melt snow for tea and warm their frozen limbs. Without George and Joe, they had much more room in the tent but no-one would get a comfortable night's sleep.

Down at Camp 5, Charles Evans had spent the day waiting anxiously for news but as the hours rolled on he was forced to assume that Norman and Tony must have decided to stay high for an extra night. He had no idea whether or not they had reached the summit, but at least they had been spotted by Tom Mackinnon coming down from the summit.

The atmosphere on the mountain was tense. In the late afternoon, John Clegg had called up to tell Charles that Pemi Dorje had died. From mid-morning onwards, his condition had steadily worsened until he was gasping for air, his pupils dilated, "obviously dying" as John Clegg recorded starkly in his diary. At 1.35 p.m. Pemi Dorje had taken his last breath.

The other Sherpas greeted events with a sense of grim inevitability. They were all glad that the expedition was over and suspected the ascent of Kangchenjunga was linked with Pemi's death. They asked John Clegg if he had died at the same moment Tony and Norman reached the summit. One of the porters, a former monk called Changjup, put it bluntly, "Kangchenjunga finish, Pemi finish".

The British climbers felt awful. Joe Brown had picked Pemi Dorje out early and championed him as a strong Sherpa who was good enough to join the high-altitude team. "It was the one thing on the expedition that caused me a bit of sadness. If we had known as much as we do today about altitude sickness, we would have just got him onto a stretcher and rushed him down and he would have recovered. But he died."

When Charles Evans broke the news to Dawa Tenzing, the veteran Sherpa burst into tears. Pemi Dorje was his brother-in-law, married to his younger sister, but he hadn't been able to protect him. For Charles it was an awful moment which, he wrote, "cast a gloom on our success". So far it had been a remarkably accident free expedition, so the idea that one of the Sherpas should die at Base Camp, so close to the end of the expedition seemed particularly cruel.

Next morning, Charles woke early and was out at 7.00 a.m., hoping to see Norman and Tony on their way down to the Great Shelf. He spotted no-one and retreated to his sleeping bag to keep warm. John Clegg radioed up to say that after a General Election in Britain, Anthony Eden had been elected prime minister. More interestingly, he added, there were now rumours that the French had climbed Makalu. As for Norman and Tony, for once John Clegg had good news from above: he had seen them descending from Camp 6. At last, Charles' final two charges were on their way down.

At 9.30 a.m. Charles emerged from his tent for the second time, hoping to record their arrival on his 16mm camera. He climbed the slope above camp and then sat perched on the edge of a crevasse, watching Norman and Tony far above as they descended a narrow gully. They were moving painfully slowly, so he waited for several minutes before calling down to Dawa Tenzing to come up with a flask of hot juice.

Throughout the expedition, Dawa had been a stalwart, but he had been shaken by the death of Pemi Dorje, and like everyone else was showing signs of real exhaustion. He laboured his way up to Charles and sat down in the snow next to him, silently waiting, his face tired and drawn.

When Norman and Tony were finally in earshot, Charles called out: "Did you get up, you buggers?"

"Yes," replied Norman, "Who won the election?"

Charles couldn't answer. His eyes were welling up with tears again as he thought about all the hard work that both the climbers and the Sherpas had done. After 50 years and five attempts, he had led the first expedition to the summit of the world's third highest mountain. His job was done.

CHAPTER ELEVEN
The Long Journey Home

Charles Evans

As soon as Norman and Tony had rested and eaten a little, everyone started down the mountain. There was no time to lose. Thick banks of monsoon cloud were building up on the horizon and the temperature was rising. All over Kangchenjunga crevasses were opening up and paths that had been used for weeks were becoming impassable. As the ice softened, the Upper Icefall became even more treacherous. The aluminium ladder which had for weeks acted as a bridge over the huge crevasse above Camp 1 now only just straddled the gap and had to be crossed very gingerly.

It was imperative to get off the mountain as quickly as possible but as Charles discovered, several days of high-altitude anxiety and enforced inactivity was not the best preparation for a rapid descent. He made it from Camp 5 to Camp 3 on the same day but though Dawa carried on down, Charles could go no further.

There were compensations though. After weeks of carefully restricting their diet in case they had to stay longer, at last they could gorge on the expedition's luxury box. At Camp 3, Charles found half a bottle of Drambuie, which had been opened a day earlier by Tom Mackinnon. Even more delicious, there was a round of Cheddar cheese and a box of ships' biscuits.

Down at Base Camp, the mood was much more sombre. The death of Pemi Dorje had hit everyone hard and until Dawa returned, the Sherpas were unsure whether to cremate or bury him. Having raced ahead of the others, he arrived late in the afternoon of May 27th. As George Band recorded in his diary that night, he was utterly distraught, "genuinely overcome" to see the body of his dead relative.

Initially Dawa asked the other Sherpas to gather firewood for a funeral pyre but on the following morning he had a change of heart and decided they should dig a grave instead. Fifty years after Alexis Pache's body had been carried down the mountain and buried nearby, the Sherpas said their final prayers and scattered handfuls of rice over Pemi Dorje's grave before placing a huge flat stone on top. That afternoon they carved his name on to the rock, along with the date of his death and the Sherpa's famous mantra: 'Om Mani Padme Hum', 'Hail the Jewel in the Lotus Flower.'

By the afternoon of May 28th, everyone was down at Base Camp but the end of the expedition was a bittersweet moment. Everything had gone so much better than anyone could have expected but at the climax one member of their team had died. They had escaped the monsoon, avoided avalanches and survived storms, but could do nothing about Pemi Dorje's mysterious illness. No-one was in a mood to celebrate but they couldn't leave the mountain without marking the moment.

Charles delved into the expedition stores and emerged with two bottles of 1947 Veuve Clicquot. Thondup, their endlessly inventive cook, rustled up a special end of expedition meal with yak steaks and peas for the main course and a 'chuck it all in' pudding consisting of stewed pears, tinned damsons and custard. As the evening wore on, the toasts began. They first raised a mug to Alf Bridge, the expedition's indefatigable secretary and then to the Hendersons, the stalwarts of the Himalayan club – and suppliers of the champagne. Then finally they toasted Kangchenjunga itself.

Before they retired, Charles Evans made a brief speech congratulating everyone for their achievement. He began by reminding them that when he took up John Hunt's offer to lead the reconnaissance, his main stipulation was that he would have sole choice over team selection. That had been the key to the expedition's success, he went on to say, not because he had chosen the most famous or highly-regarded climbers but because he had selected a group of men who would work well together.

In an article written for the *Times*, Charles went further, emphasising that it was the camaraderie and team spirit displayed by both climbers and Sherpas which ultimately made the difference between success and failure:

> The biggest mountains are not climbed because of the quality of the equipment, or of the oxygen sets, or of the planning. Vital as those things are, they are only tools for men who have one goal, and who are so far masters of themselves that they can subdue their strong individualities in order to attain that goal. It was what we tried to do, under cover of a great deal of laughter, and while having an enormous amount of fun.

The following day's hangovers gave them a perfect excuse to lie in their tents and catch up on letters from home, a large consignment of which had arrived just as they were about to leave the mountain. As usual there were copies of *The Times* but though they read them avidly, their sponsoring paper's Kangchenjunga news was always particularly out of sync with the expedition itself. Their most recent newspaper, published on May 12th, featured an article written on April 7th by George Band about his 'Himalayan Shopping Trip' to Ghunsa.

Joe Brown's news was not so frivolous. His girlfriend Val, a keen climber, had been knocked off her motorbike while returning to Manchester from the Lake District and was laid up in hospital with a fractured skull and a broken jaw. Her injuries weren't life threatening but she was expected to be off work for six months. Charles immediately agreed to let Joe fly back home rather than take the boat when they reached India.

May 29th was also the anniversary of Hillary and Tenzing's first ascent of Everest. Though Charles and George were otherwise occupied, several members of the 1953 team were enjoying a re-union on the Isle of Skye. At least two were planning to join John Hunt in 1956 for the 'main' Kangchenjunga expedition, though there would obviously be a big question mark over that now.

Charles Evans' thoughts, however, were on more pressing issues. He sent one of the Sherpas, Tashi, to Ghunsa to notify the headman that porters were needed to carry their equipment out and that he wanted to leave as soon as possible. In the mean-time, Charles decided that it would be more comfortable to shift everyone down to Moraine Camp at the edge of the Yalung glacier where if they were lucky there would be firewood and maybe even some grass to pitch their tents.

Charles had already decided to abandon a certain amount of equipment high on the mountain. There was no point in risking lives to bring down tents and sleeping bags, no matter how valuable they were. The expedition had come provisioned with 5,000 cigarettes, but there were only two smokers on the team, Joe Brown and John Jackson, so dozens of packets were untouched. Joe put together a stash to take home, but he distributed the others to the Sherpas, who were more than glad to swap their coarse Battle-axe cigarettes for Europe's finest.

On May 30th, after paying their final respects to Pemi Dorje and taking a few last photographs, they said goodbye to Base Camp. Just before they left, there was a report on the radio confirming that the monsoon had officially arrived but there was still nothing about their ascent of Kangchenjunga. Clearly the runner they had sent down on May 26th had not yet reached a telegraph station. In 1953, James Morris, the *Times'* journalist embedded in the Everest team, had managed to get the word out in less than two days, but this time round the headline writers would have to wait longer.

For the next week they took it easy as they waited for the Ghunsa porters to turn up. It was, Charles later wrote, like a 'holiday camp'. They pitched all their tents and tarpaulins and spent much of their time simply lounging around filling in their diaries and chatting. Someone dug out the expedition's rugby ball but they were all too exhausted and breathless to play for more than few minutes.

Gradually the team began to break up. Tom MacKinnon was first to leave, called back to Scotland for work. Neil Mather mooted the idea of a 30-day overland walk to Kathmandu, before the others persuaded him to take a more modest trip to the nearby Kambachen Valley. Similarly, the expedition doctor, John Clegg, talked about making a strenuous ascent of a high pass, the Tiptu La, but in the end opted to spend a few leisurely weeks fishing in Kashmir. The de-mob happy Sherpas raced down to Tseram and came back with several jars of rakshi, the local fire water, to get the party started.

Every night they built a huge camp fire and danced around it, while the sahibs discussed future plans. George Band and Joe Brown talked about a trip to K2 while Charles Evans said he was interested in revisiting Annapurna, the mountain that had defeated him a few years earlier. More immediately, he asked Dawa Tenzing and Changjup if they wanted to return with him on an all expenses trip to England. It wasn't hard to get them to say yes.

For the most part Kangchenjunga stayed hidden behind a layer of cloud, but on their first evening off the mountain, the veil was briefly lifted. For the first time in weeks, Charles was relaxed and eating properly, but as he revealed to his diary, the sight of Kangchenjunga towering above them brought back a hint of the old anxieties:

> We saw the summit – as though a sinister giant was plucking with his fingers a hole through which to point at us. Foreboding, sinister it would be, were we not leaving. Through the hole we could see the Gangway, looking smooth and glistening in the moonlight and impossibly steep.

The Sherpas were glad that the expedition was over but they had not forgotten Pemi Dorje. Tashi made a visit the nearest monastery at Ghunsa to offer donations from both the Sherpas and the sahibs. "Otherwise," he warned, "We shall all suffer."

On June 2nd, eight days after Joe and George reached the summit, *All India Radio* finally reported the first ascent. As many newspapers subsequently noted, the news had come in almost two years to the hour after the public announcement that Everest had been climbed, on Coronation day 1953. The first radio report contained no details of who had actually made the first ascent, but as the newsreader noted, it had been reported in the British press that Kangchenjunga was harder than Everest. In a sign of the growing equality of the age, the same radio bulletin added that the first all women Himalayan expedition, organised by the Ladies Scottish Climbing Club, had just climbed a 22,000 ft peak in the Jugal Himalaya.

The first press report had been published in the *Times* that morning. The grand old man of British newspapers still reserved its front page for advertisements with the exception of a small box in top right hand corner which contained important news headlines. In this case it read quite simply "Kangchenjunga Climbed". Inside an editorial revealed that a telegram had just been received from Charles Evans but it had given no details, other than the fact that the expedition had stopped 5ft from the top of the absolute summit, following their agreement with the Sikkimese government.

That day, Kangchenjunga made headlines all around the world. The *New York Times* hailed the British 'conquest', *Le Monde* noted how the British victory had come less than two weeks after French success on Makalu and the *Times of India* praised the "human courage, endurance and teamwork that have dared and wrested invulnerability from the snowy peak". With the identity of the summit teams still unreleased, most papers concentrated on Charles Evans, noting how he'd had such a near miss on Everest in 1953 and praising his team for achieving much more on Kangchenjunga than anyone had expected. A lot of the press commented on their decision not to actually set foot on the highest point of the mountain. The *Press and Sun Bulletin* of New York had the wittiest line, commenting that "the greatest restraint since the man who ate only one salted peanut is shown by the English climbers who stopped five feet short of the summit of Kangchenjunga."

Reuters, the press agency, quickly began hunting down the other participants in the drama. They found John Hunt at Sligachan on Skye, still enjoying his Everest reunion. He was very generous with his praise, even though Charles' success meant that he was unlikely to fulfil his own long-held ambition to climb Kangchenjunga. "It was," he told the Reuters correspondent, "a most brilliant performance", adding that "the ascent of Kangchenjunga has always been reckoned to be the most difficult feat in mountaineering, at any rate as far as the highest peaks in the world are concerned".

Charles' old friend and team-mate, Ed Hillary, was tracked down to Melbourne. "I have been anxiously awaiting news of the expedition for some time," he said rather formally. "Kangchenjunga is a most formidable mountain and their victory is a very notable one." Asked whether he had any plans to return to the Himalayas now that both Kangchenjunga and Makalu had been climbed, Ed was evasive, though he did add that for the next few years, his "interests" would be in Antarctica.

On the following day, *The Times* published a fuller editorial in which they paid tribute to the Kangchenjunga team and reminded readers of John Hunt's statement that climbing Kangchenjunga was "the greatest feat in mountaineering". Further north, local British newspapers in Manchester and Lancashire, were full of praise for Joe Brown and Neil Mather. The twin towns of Bury and Ramsbottom both laid claim to Neil as their favourite son. His father, who ran a cinema in Bury, told one reporter how he had received regular letters from Nepal but had been surprised to hear of their success. "We never expected it," he added, "because the mountain is said to be worse to climb than Everest."

The *Manchester Evening News* was particularly thrilled with the British success, labelling local hero Joe Brown as "a small man with big ideas". His climbing pals in the *Rock and Ice* club commented that he was "as safe as the Bank of England on a mountain" while his big sister gave a classic sibling comment:

> As a kid Joe was always falling down and hurting himself. Twice I've had to rush him to the Royal Infirmary. He's always wanted to climb things.

Back at Moraine Camp, the British team were amused to hear the weather forecaster from *All India Radio* add his own impromptu congratulations during his meteorological bulletin on June 3rd, but by then their principle interest was making a swift return to Darjeeling. On the following day the Ghunsa porters arrived and began packaging up what remained of their supplies and equipment. Three months earlier, Charles had hired some three hundred porters for the approach march but for the return trip they were able to make do with just sixty.

Some of the tents and equipment were staying in Nepal with Norman Hardie. He had decided to make the longest supplementary trip of all, spending two months in the Solu-Khumbu region of Eastern Nepal, with three of their Sherpas – Urkien, Ila Tenzing and Gyalgen – and then making a further trip to Everest Base Camp with his wife Enid and a friend from Britain. In return for surveying the area around Chamlang, a smaller peak close to Makalu, the Mount Everest Foundation had agreed to cover one third of his expenses. Norman was planning to travel cheaply though. There would be no tinned lambs tongues or damson stew for him. Instead he was planning to live on Sherpa food, supplemented with boiled bamboo shoots, wild mushrooms and ferns. His only luxury would be a bag of coffee.

Before Norman said his goodbyes, on the night of June 5th they held their final leaving party, celebrating their departure from Kangchenjunga by jamming open the valves of two Butane cannisters and lighting the gas as it shot out. Having consumed a large amount of Rakshi, everyone was very pleased to watch the flames soar into the air.

The next morning, they got off in the pouring rain. The monsoon was well and truly upon them, inundating the landscape and converting their umbrellas from sun shields into rain barriers. There was no particular hurry, so they allowed their porters to race off in front, while the Sherpas and sahibs following at a more leisurely pace. It was a decision Charles soon came to regret when late in the afternoon of the second day, he realised that they were hopelessly lost and to make things worse, separated from all the tents and food.

Thondup the expedition cook had been in the lead, but his route finding had proved inferior to his cuisine. He had ploughed on, only finally admitting to his mistake when they found themselves at the bottom of a dark valley filled with shoulder high rhododendron bushes. It was too late to retrace their steps so they spent a wet and miserable night sheltering from the rain under a large overhanging boulder. Save for a small sack of rice, they had nothing to eat and though the Sherpas somehow magicked up a set of sleeping bags, they were soon wet through.

Charles was not pleased. After spending the next day trying and failing to catch up with the main column, he ordered the unfortunate Thondup to get going at 3.00 a.m. on the following morning, find the porters and get them to stop. When they finally caught up later that afternoon, the Ghunsa men roared with laughter. The idea that the great sahibs and their Sherpas had got so lost that they were actually heading back into Nepal, was too good a joke not to savour.

The rain continued as they crossed the border into Sikkim and trekked up to the Singalila ridge. It was famous as Charles noted for the incredible views either side, but they saw nothing other than mist and rain. In compensation, as they drew closer to Darjeeling, they were met by mail runners, carrying telegrams and messages congratulating them on their success. There were missives from friends, work colleagues and family, and rather more grandly, a short message from Prince Phillip, the expedition patron, hailing their "magnificent achievement" and praising them for showing so much respect for other people's feelings by stopping short of the summit.

Their first direct contact with the press came on June 12th at the village of Sandakphu, a few days before Darjeeling, where they met Peter Jackson, the Reuter's correspondent. Jackson's subsequent interview, with its revelation that Joe Brown and George Band were the first men to reach the summit, was widely syndicated around the world

The summit pair, however, were modest about their achievement. "It wasn't difficult climbing," said Joe, in a tone of voice that didn't seem quite his own, "but it was hellish hard work. You wanted to get up and down on oxygen, in fact it ran out about one and a quarter hours after we left the top and even before that, we had been going at a low flow-rate. We were jolly lucky to get good weather and at times I was even feeling hot." George Band upped the drama a little, telling how they'd had to rush down the mountain at the end, fearing the light would go before they reached camp. For his part, Charles Evans stuck to the 'group effort' theme insisting that everyone had played a vital role and "it just happened" that the final climb fell to George and Joe. When asked which was more difficult, Everest or Kangchenjunga, Charles refused to be drawn.

The following morning, while Peter Jackson's story was being run back to Darjeeling, they carried on to Tanglu where they met a much bigger reception. Ever solicitous, their Darjeeling hosts the Hendersons had come out with John Jackson's wife Eileen and a horde of photographers. A smiling Tenzing Norgay was there too along with his niece and the good wishes of Darjeeling's Sherpa community.

"Anyone for a beer?" called Jill Henderson and before long they were sitting down to a lavish picnic with all the trimmings. The French Makalu team were still in town and eager to meet them but lunch was long and lazy. Then once everyone had eaten and drunk their fill, they piled into a waiting line of Land Rovers and headed off back to the Henderson's plantation at Rungneet where baths, clean clothes and yet more beer awaited them.

En route they met the French climber Jean Couzy and later that evening the whole of French team arrived for another impromptu party. As they regaled Charles' men with tales of how they had almost all reached the summit, Joe Brown noticed a few of his teammates wondering aloud why they weren't also allowed a crack at the summit of Kangchenjunga, but the prevailing emotion was relief and celebration rather than regret.

Over the next few days there were visits from the local barber and receptions at the Sherpa climbers' association and the local Darjeeling Planters' club. The only sour note came in an article published in an Indian newspaper, the *Hindustani Times*, a title with a long history of anti-British coverage. Under the headline "British betray Sherpas – Wouldn't allow Sherpas to the summit" they alleged that there had been a lot of tension on the expedition.

Nothing could have been further from the truth, but the claim followed a series of press controversies that began in 1953 with reports of ill feeling between Tenzing Norgay and the British team on Everest and continued in 1954 with allegations in Pakistani newspapers that the Italian team which climbed K2 had prevented their Hunza porters from reaching the summit.

Tenzing Norgay took Charles Evans to one side and told him that everyone knew it was nonsense, and that such accusations "smelled of politics". He was angry enough to make a public speech in which he insisted that the British and the Sherpas would continue to work together harmoniously for many years to come. Tenzing's intervention killed the controversy but none of the climbers were really bothered by it. They knew that they'd shared a great experience with the Sherpas and no trumped up story in the press was going to change that. In order to seal their friendship, the Sherpas and climbers held yet another party, this time collectively knocking back twenty bottles of rakshi.

Then finally it was time for the expedition to break up. Most of the team was booked in for a return trip on the *SS Circassia* in early July, leaving them with a fortnight for sight-seeing and tourism. John Clegg headed off for his fishing trip to Kashmir but didn't manage to get any further than Delhi, where he was laid low for ten days with a severe attack of dysentery. George Band was more fortunate. He and Neil Mather flew to Kathmandu where they spent several days being feted at cocktail parties and dinners. They were even invited to attend a royal wedding.

As for Joe Brown, he left Darjeeling for England on June 16th. His first stop was Calcutta where he had to get a plane ticket and an export certificate for his gear and equipment. The British embassy laid on a limousine but the Indian customs' officers were much more interested in talking about Kangchenjunga than issuing him with the correct paper-work so it took two days before everything was square.

When he finally reached London, Joe had customs problems of a different kind. His luggage included a neatly packaged parcel of one thousand expedition cigarettes. An official asked if he had anything to declare. "No," said Joe, while the customs man rested his clip board on the consignment of contraband.

Back in Manchester, Joe met a gaggle of reporters waiting outside his girlfriend Val's house but when he went to see his pals at the *Rock and Ice* club, there was no great welcome for the first British climber to scale an 8000m peak. "No man is a hero in his own house. The *Rock and Ice* were like brothers, how would you expect them to react? They're British, the most you'd get was 'well done lad'. I got no free drinks."

Charles Evans carried on to Calcutta where he had lectures to give and functions to attend. A few members of the Indian press were still trying to rekindle the controversy over his decision not to select a Sherpa for one of the summit teams, but at a press conference on July 2nd Charles was having none of it:

> You might as well ask why I did not go to the top myself. I thought I could help the expedition by sitting at a particular place. I thought the Sherpas could help more by doing a particular job and other people by doing their jobs.

When the questions moved on and Charles was asked whether he agreed that a climber's sex drive diminished at high altitude, he concurred but was not forthcoming with any detail.

A few days later, Charles left India, arriving in London on July 7th with Changjup and Dawa Tenzing. John Hunt was there to greet him as well as a posse of dignitaries from the Alpine Club and the Royal Geographical Society. Next day they were photographed at the RGS, poring over a scale model of Kangchenjunga. After that Dawa and Changjup were taken around the sights of London, though they weren't impressed with everything they saw. Changjup was amazed by sound of the London Underground and Dawa admired the city's parks and duckponds, but as Charles noted, he was underwhelmed by Buckingham palace. "It is rather small and very plain," he said.

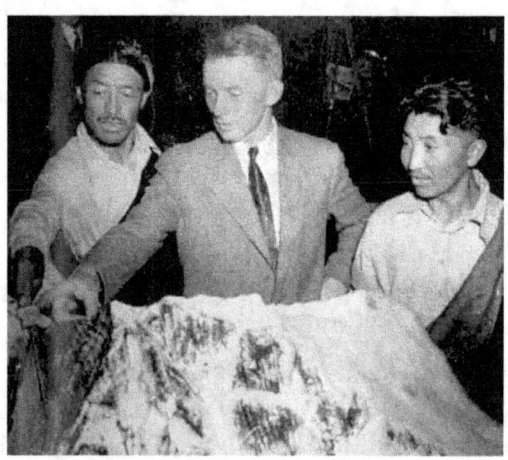

Dawa Tenzing, Charles Evans, Changjup at the RGS

In the weeks that followed the two Sherpas went as far afield as North Wales and the Peak District as different members of the team took turns to show them around Britain.

Charles Evans and Norman Hardie had briefly entertained the fantasy of building a Sherpa style house in North Wales, complete with barrels to brew chang and marwa, but when it came to it Charles did not press his visitors to help achieve his grand design. Instead Dawa and Changjup visited car factories and town halls and enjoyed themselves thoroughly.

Months later Norman Hardie bumped into the two Sherpas in the Solu Khumbu, sporting Trilby hats given to them by well-wishers in Scotland. When he asked what else they would like to have brought back from England, Dawa replied straight away: "A good English cow". Changjup however was having none of it. "Don't be silly," he said, "How would you get it on the plane?"

On July 27th the remaining members of the team sailed into Liverpool. By then the original party of nine had been reduced to six but the Alpine club held a reception for friends and dignitaries and photographers from regional newspapers came on board to snap up their local heroes.

Three weeks later Neil Mather, George Band and Tony Streather joined Charles Evans for a special programme broadcast on BBC TV, produced by a young David Attenborough. John Hunt played the role of studio host celebrating "a great British achievement and an outstanding British mountaineering feat." Over the course of an hour of prime-time television, he steered Charles and other 'gallant' members of his team around a large model of Kangchenjunga, interrogating them on the most difficult and most memorable parts of the climb.

That autumn the Kangchenjunga team went on tour, telling their story in lecture theatres all over the country. As with Everest, there was a concerted drive to emphasise how team-work had played a crucial role in getting them to the top but this didn't always lead to the most dramatic presentations. As a reviewer for the *Manchester Guardian* wrote after seeing a lecture by George Band and Neil Mather:

> Perhaps on account of the modesty of the lecturers who played so large a part in the ascent, one did not quite catch the sense of strain and excitement proper to climbing the third highest mountain in the world and one reputed to be of exceptional technical difficulty.

On October 19th Charles Evans was awarded the Livingstone medal by the Scottish Royal Geographical Society for outstanding leadership. Two weeks later John Hunt announced that his planned expedition to Kangchenjunga would not be taking place. Instead he would be leaving the army to begin an entirely new career as the first director of the Duke of Edinburgh scheme.

Though there had been plenty of headlines around the world ultimately, for all its difficulty, the first ascent of Kangchenjunga never matched the attention paid to Everest, two years earlier. Back in June 1953, news of the British team's success shared the front pages with the Coronation of Queen Elizabeth II, the two events supercharging each other's significance. The most strident newspapers had described Everest as the symbol of a 'new Elizabethan age' in which Britain would prosper and once more show its greatness to the rest of the world but that British renaissance had never quite materialised. Rationing had only just ended and the British economy was in the doldrums. News of Kangchenjunga's first ascent shared the front page with stories about railway and dock strikes that were then paralysing whole sectors of the economy. The election of Anthony Eden as the new Prime

Minister after the retirement of Winston Churchill signalled the end of an era but there wasn't the same heady optimism that had characterised the early 1950s.

For the press and general public, mountaineering was no longer regarded with quite such awe. As Ed Hillary hinted earlier in the summer, his attention and much of the world's was turning towards Antarctica and the epic Commonwealth Transarctic expedition that would run for three years between 1955 and 1958. The same period also saw the opening of the Space Race, a new and even more dangerous field of exploration.

Kangchenjunga was the last of the world's big three mountains to be climbed. It marked the end of an era in which mountaineering was seen as a major national endeavour. Over the next decade there would be first ascents of all the remaining 8000m peaks, mainly by European climbers and their Sherpas, but these victories would be celebrated in specialist magazines and journals, not on the front pages of national newspapers.

The epic of Kangchenjunga which had begun in 1899 with Douglas Freshfield's tour of the mountain had come to a fittingly British climax, but it wasn't quite the end of the story. In the decades that followed, mountaineers from all over the world would succeed in settling old scores, climbing the other faces of the mountain and achieving a new set of 'firsts' that the 1955 team would never have thought possible. As for Charles Evans and his party, some would go on to great things but for others, their lives would not pan out quite how they expected.

CHAPTER TWELVE
And Then

In June 1953 after news came back of the first ascent of Everest, the celebrated British mountaineer Eric Shipton quipped that at last everyone could get on the with the 'real climbing' and forget their obsession with the world's highest mountain. There were hundreds of unclimbed peaks in the Himalayas, he pointed out, so why was everyone so fixated on just one mountain?

Shipton's comment could have equally applied to Kangchenjunga. After five major expeditions and many lives lost, the 'Five Treasuries of the Snow' had finally been climbed, so perhaps it was time to leave the mountain gods in peace and move on to other challenges. In the case of Kangchenjunga, this seemed particularly appropriate because it was surrounded by so many untried satellite peaks. That was not however how things turned out.

If the 1950s was the 'Golden Age of Himalayan Climbing' when almost all the world's major peaks were first ascended, the 1970s was a kind of renaissance period in which a new generation of mountaineers returned to the Himalayas and the Karakoram to re-engage with those big mountains using new techniques on new routes.

In the case of Kangchenjunga, the next expedition didn't take place until 1973, a full eighteen years after the first ascent, when a Japanese team attempted to reach the west summit. Unlike Everest and K2, Kangchenjunga has multiple peaks so there was still the possibility of claiming a 'first'. At 27,904 ft the West summit was barely 200 ft lower than the main summit but it proved too much for the Japanese. Two climbers succeeded in reaching the top but both died on the descent, one hit by a rock, the other collapsing at around 26,250 ft. It was a grim reminder that Kangchenjunga was a very dangerous mountain, but it didn't stop further attempts. Two years later, nine members of a powerful Austro-German team followed the same route to the West summit and all returned alive.

As well as tackling the subsidiary summits, the other big challenge was to reach the main peak via the routes that defeated the climbers of the 1930s. The German Paul Bauer had won international acclaim for his 1929 and 1931 expeditions to the North East Spur but though he had fought hard, on neither expedition had his team managed to get above 25,262 ft. In 1977 an Indian army expedition decided that it would try to succeed where the Germans had failed.

When they arrived at the Spur in early March, they found ropes and crampons abandoned by Bauer's men almost fifty years earlier. More tragically, history seemed to repeat itself when a young Indian climber, Sukvinder Singh, fell to his death very close to the spot where Hermann Schaller and Pasang had died in 1931. This was distinctly un-nerving for everyone but they carried on and on May 31st, Major Prem

Chand and Naik Nima Dorje Sherpa battled their way through strong winds to reach the summit just before three o'clock in the afternoon. When news reached expedition leader Narinder Kumar lower down the mountain, he immediately dispatched a radio telegram to India's Chief of Staff proudly announcing, "Your boys have done it."

The second great piece of unfinished business was the Northwest face, the route recommended by Douglas Freshfield in 1899 when he made his epic tour around the mountain. Günter Dyhrenfurth's party failed spectacularly in 1930 but in 1979 a small Anglo-French team decided to take up the challenge. The era of big siege style expeditions was drawing to a close. Instead, a new generation of climbers aimed to move quickly and lightly, applying 'Alpine style' techniques to high altitude mountaineering.

The three British climbers and one Frenchman who reached Pangpema Base Camp in April 1979, had just two Sherpas and a very small support staff. They did almost all their own load carrying and most radical of all, were committed to climbing without oxygen. A year earlier Reinhold Messner and Peter Habeler had made the first ascent of Everest without any bottled oxygen, kicking off a new phase in elite climbing.

The other major technical development was in ice climbing equipment. When Frank Smythe toiled away on Kangchenjunga in 1930, he was equipped with a long wooden ice-axe and very basic crampons. The only way up the ice cliffs at the base of the mountain was to cut a staircase of steps. By the mid-seventies short ice-axes and front point crampons had revolutionised climbing techniques, enabling mountaineers to avoid the tedious process of step cutting altogether and actually enjoy ice-climbing.

It took several weeks and two abortive attempts but on May 16th 1979, Doug Scott, Pete Boardman and Joe Tasker finally reached the summit and enjoyed an amazing sunset over the surrounding mountains. It was a fantastic achievement, a triumph of grit, tenacity and technical skill which showed just how far high altitude mountaineering had come.

In subsequent years, Kangchenjunga followed the same pattern set on Everest and K2 with an extended series of 'firsts' for different categories of climbing. In 1983 the French climber Pierre Beghin made the first solo ascent climbing the 1955 route without oxygen in just three days. Three years later, in 1986, two Polish climbers, Jerzy Kukuczka and Krzysztof Wielicki, made the first winter ascent and in 1989 a Soviet team succeeded in making the first traverse of all Kangchenjunga's summits. The first woman to climb the mountain was the British mountaineer Ginette Harrison, who reached the summit in 1998.

She was the fourth woman to attempt Kangchenjunga and the only one to get down alive. In 1992 Wanda Rutkiewicz, then considered the world's leading female climber, had died high up on the mountain sheltering just below the summit. She wasn't the only elite climber though to perish on Kangchenjunga. Over recent decades several international stars have lost their lives on its slopes, further reinforcing its reputation as an incredibly dangerous mountain.

While it remains highly regarded in climbing circles, Kangchenjunga no longer has the public profile that it enjoyed in the early 1930s. It remains an essential challenge for elite climbers trying to ascend all fourteen 8000m peaks but it has never been targeted by the commercial climbing industry, which more than ever is focussed on Everest. In spite of all the photographs of long lines of climbers on the Lhotse Face, or even worse the overcrowding close to the summit, Everest continues to be the only mountain with real name recognition among the general public. John Hunt's assertion that Kangchenjunga is by far the harder mountain, and therefore a much greater prize, no longer resonates.

Like Kangchenjunga itself, the early climbers who risked their lives on its slopes have been largely relegated to the bookshelves of history. Ironically, Aleister Crowley, its first would-be conqueror, is the exception but his fame, or notoriety, has less to do with mountaineering and more to do with his other activities. Immediately after his attempt of 1905, he briefly tried to drum up interest in the United States for another Himalayan adventure, but found no backers and gave up in frustration. After that Crowley occasionally climbed for pleasure in the Alps and ascended various holy mountains in North Africa but the main focus of his life and travels became the occult.

He founded a new religion called Thelema whose guiding moral laws were revealed to him by a messenger from the ancient Egyptian God Horus. "Do what thou wilt" was its central principle, its rituals included plenty of 'sex magick' and drug taking. Over three decades he wrote dozens of books and articles devoted to Thelema as well as poetry, fiction and his 'auto-hagiography'.

Like his climbing mentor, Oscar Eckenstein, in his later years Crowley was dogged by lung problems. He became addicted to heroin after it was prescribed to treat his asthma and spent years trying to break free of its grip. When the fortune inherited from his father was spent, Crowley's became increasingly itinerant though he never quite ran out of wealthy supporters willing to supplement his small but erratic income from writing. His activities often brought him into conflict with British newspapers, in particular *John Bull* who denounced him as "one of the most shameless degenerates who ever boasted of his British birth". Declaring him "a man we'd like to hang," they claimed that when food ran out on one of his expeditions he had chopped up and eaten two of his porters.

Lawsuits frequently ensued, some of which he won but the largest of which left him bankrupt. In one of the strangest incidents in a very strange life, he even staged his own suicide at a famously jagged rock formation near Lisbon called the *Boca do Inferno*, the gates of Hell. He hoped to raise money by selling the rights to *My Hymen*, the scandalous tale of his elopement with his most recent lover, Hanni, but the publishers weren't fooled and turned the book down.

When he died of acute bronchitis in 1946, Crowley was living at a modest boarding house in Hastings but as his biographer and literary executor John Symonds noted, he was still smoking expensive cigars and drinking fine brandy. The British press did not report his passing kindly, the *Daily Express* declaring, "Black Magician Crowley Dies. Wickedest Man in Britain". This wasn't quite the end of his story.

In the 1960s Crowley was rediscovered by a new generation. His predilection for sex and drugs and his interest in Eastern mysticism turned him into a counter cultural hero whose face appeared on the cover of *Sgt Pepper's Lonely Hearts Club Band*. Rock and Roll's fascination with Crowley outlived the Beatles. Ozzy Osbourne wrote songs about him and the British R'n'B singer Graham Bond at one point claimed to be his illegitimate son. For many years, Jimmy Page, the guitarist with

Led Zeppelin, owned Boleskine Manor, Crowley's house next to Loch ness, as well as Equinox, an esoteric bookshop named in his honour.

As for his achievements as a mountaineer, in many ways Crowley was strangely prescient. He correctly predicted that both Everest and K2 would be climbed via their South East ridges and his rejection of long siege-like expeditions in favour of what he called 'rushing a mountain' anticipated 'Alpine Style' high Himalayan climbing. In an article from 2008, the leading British climber Mick Fowler went as far as to describe one of Crowley's very early British ascents - Ethelreda's Pinnacle at Beachy Head – as "one of the most serious and technically difficult climbs in Britain at the time", but in general Crowley's obsession with climbing is still regarded as a curiosity, something which doesn't quite fit with the more sensational aspects of his character.

His co-leader in 1905, Jules Jacot-Guillarmod, did not return to the Himalayas or go on any major expeditions but he did carry on climbing in the Alps and continued to play an active role in the Swiss Alpine Club and various geographical societies. There's no evidence that he ever encountered Crowley after Kangchenjunga but when he came to write his account of the events of 1905, he was less aggressive and more conciliatory than might have been expected.

True to character, Jacot-Guillarmod led a more conventional life than his former partner. He married in 1907 and had three daughters. After showing an early interest in mental illness, he went on to own and run a specialist psychiatric clinic near to Lausanne. He did not entirely lose his taste for travel and adventure though. In 1919, working partly for Swiss Red Cross, Jacot-Guillarmod made a nine-month round-the-world trip, which took him from Russia to the United States, Japan and China. Six years later in the summer of 1925, he fell seriously ill while attempting an overland trip from Cairo to Cape Town. He tried to get back to Switzerland but died on board a French postal ship crossing the Gulf of Aden and was buried in the nearby port, many thousands of miles from his home in Europe.

For many years Jacot-Guillarmod was largely forgotten but in 2013 a major exhibition was held in Lausanne showcasing his expeditions to K2 and Kangchenjunga. His biographer Charlie Buffet was able to draw upon an archive of over 12,000 photographs and diaries that spanned thirty nine years. Jacot-Guillarmod never matched Aleister Crowley for column inches in the press but today his pioneering role in Himalayan climbing and photography has begun to be recognised.

Kangchenjunga's next suitor's reputation is much more problematic. Paul Bauer's attempts in 1929 and 1931 won him world-wide fame but his subsequent involvement with the Nazi government turned him a much less attractive figure. In the mid-1930s Bauer had become the leader of the German mountaineering Association where he vowed to guide climbers "in the spirit of the Nationalist Socialist state" and implement the so-called 'Aryan Paragraph', the Nazi race law which prevented Jews and Slavs from taking part in public life, mountaineering clubs included.

At the beginning of WW2 Bauer re-joined the German army and fought in France and the Caucasus, the mountain range in Russia where twenty years earlier he got his first taste of expedition life. Later he became the commander of the German army's mountaineering school. Like many other officers and officials, when the war ended Bauer was taken before a court to assess his role in the Nazi hierarchy. He maintained that he had never been a committed party member and the court believed him, declaring him a 'fellow traveller' rather than true Nazi. Within a few years he was back at work as a notary in Munich and had re-joined the University mountaineering club.

Bauer's involvement with the Nazis prompted a certain amount of angst at the Alpine Club in London. He had been elected a member in 1933 after his heroic exploits on Kangchenjunga but like several other German climbers his membership had been revoked when war broke out. In the early 1950s the club debated whether to readmit him. In spite of objections from others, including the leading American climber Charles Houston, he was given the benefit of the doubt and re-admitted.

If proof were needed that his reputation had been restored, John Hunt even wrote the forward to Bauer's book *Kangchenjunga Challenge*, which appeared in English for a second time in 1955.

Bauer published three further books and though he did not do any more high altitude climbing, he acted as an advisor on several expeditions including a proposed attempt on Kangchenjunga by a group of Tyrolean mountain guides in the early 1970s. When he died in 1990 at the venerable age of 93, he was widely mourned in the German press.

The only hitch in Bauer's post-war career came in 1957 when he was put forward for the vice presidency of the Alpine Club in its jubilee year. It's hard to know how serious a move this was, but this time round his nomination was successfully blocked – by his old rival, Günter Dyhrenfurth.

Whereas Paul Bauer had thrived under the Nazis, Dyhrenfurth had never enjoyed the same official approval because of his openly anti-Nazi stance. He was forced to resign from his job at the University of Breslau in 1933 after refusing to swear an oath of allegiance to Adolf Hitler and moved to Zurich with his family, to escape Germany's growing anti-Semitism. He did manage to raise the money for a second major expedition, to the Karakoram mountains in 1934, but that was his last.

Hettie Dyhrenfurth became an international celebrity in her own right in the mid-1930s and was even invited to visit the Whitehouse while on her first American tour. She was so disenchanted with Europe that when she returned to the US in 1936 she decided to stay permanently. The Dyhrenfurths were not formally divorced until 12 years later but both eventually re-married.

Günter stayed in Switzerland and continued to be an active mountaineer until 1946 when he was badly injured in a climbing accident. Thereafter his focus changed to writing, becoming an authority on Himalayan mountaineering and an advisor to dozens of expeditions. He died in 1975 at the age of 89; like his nemesis Paul Bauer, he was a great survivor.

As for Charles Evans' 1955 team, among mountaineers, their first ascent is still regarded a model expedition. It didn't have the scale or the same nationalistic fervour of the earlier expeditions of the 1950s – the summit teams didn't even carry a Union Jack – but it epitomised a low key but utterly focussed approach to solving a mountaineering problem.

When he sailed off that February, no-one expected Charles Evans to return in triumph six months later. His team was too small and untested and was modestly equipped compared to the recent Everest and K2 expeditions. At best, Charles was expected to come back having discovered a feasible approach for John Hunt to take in the following year, at worst he would report that the South West Face was no more climbable than Bauer's North East Spur or Dyhrenfurth's route from the North West. Charles of course was remarkably successful and unlike the first ascents of Everest and K2 he managed to get two summit pairs to the top.

The Kangchenjunga Reunion 1990 ©Gowron
Top Row: Tony Streather, Norman Hardie, George Band, John Clegg
Bottom: Neil Mather, John Jackson, Charles Evans, Joe Brown

Afterwards he received much of the kudos. As well as the Livingstone medal, Charles was awarded the Royal Geographical Society's Patron's Gold medal in 1956. His high public profile led him to be offered the prestigious position of Principal of University College of North Wales in 1958.

Thirteen years later he was knighted for his services to education.

For all this, life after Kangchenjunga was far from easy. Charles' job became very uncomfortable in the 1970s when he found himself under sustained attack by Welsh Nationalist students. Ironically, considering that he had grown up an exclusive Welsh speaker, he was denounced as just not Welsh enough. Charles faced down the activists and stayed in post until 1984 but behind the scenes there was a second, more private battle that he stood no chance of winning.

It began in the late 1950s shortly after he married Denise Morin, the daughter of Nea Morin, the pioneering female climber. Charles and Denise spent their honeymoon in the Himalayas, trekking to Everest Base Camp. Back in Britain they climbed together in North Wales, but it wasn't long before Charles began to suffer from strange tingling sensations in his limbs which were eventually diagnosed as the first signs of multiple sclerosis. Within a few years the disease had confined him to a wheelchair.

For someone who had been so physically active and had spent so much of his time outdoors it was a terrible blow but Charles was stoical and tough. He bought a boat and took up sailing, voyaging as far afield as Shetland and Norway. When it finally became too much for him, he helped Denise organise her even more ambitious nautical adventures, which included a nail-biting voyage around Cape Horn. By the end of his life when Charles was confined to a nursing home he would follow her trips on a map at his bed-side and talk to her via short wave radio. When he died in 1995, he was universally acclaimed for his courage and modesty and for the leadership qualities he showed on his Himalayan climbs.

And Then

Dawa Tenzing, Charles' great friend and a key member of the 1955 expedition continued to work as a sirdar for several years. When later in life Dawa hit hard times, the Kangchenjunga team and other friends came together to provide him with a monthly pension. Today several of his descendants work in the Nepali climbing industry.

Norman Hardie, Charles' deputy, lived to the ripe old age of 92 and returned to the Himalayas many times. In 1960 he joined Ed Hillary and Griffith Pugh to help set up the Silver Hut expedition, a pioneering trial to study the impact of spending long periods of time at high altitude. In later life, much of his spare time was spent on voluntary work for the Himalayan Trust, the charitable organisation set up by Hillary to build schools and hospitals in the Solu Khumbu, the Sherpa heartland. Between 1966 and 1988 Norman made no less than fourteen trips to Nepal.

As for his summit partner on Kangchenjunga, Tony Streather, even though he regarded himself as an 'accidental mountaineer', Tony had one of the busiest and most distinguished climbing careers of all the Kangchenjunga team. In 1957 he travelled to Pakistan to attempt Haramosh, a very striking 24,300 ft mountain in the Karakoram, with a small party from Oxford University. Tony signed up as leader, hoping for a nostalgic visit and a chance to see old friends in Pakistan but what started off as a student climbing expedition ended up as a grim ordeal when two of his companions, John Emery and Bernard Jillot, were ripped off the mountain by an avalanche and sent tumbling down into a snow basin below.

Having lost their ice axes and crampons they were unable to get out. Tony climbed down with the other climber Rae

Culbert to rescue them, only for Culbert himself to fall off and drag Tony with him. Over the next five days the four men tried desperately to extricate themselves but ultimately only Tony and John Emery survived. It was a harrowing experience but Tony returned to the Karakoram in 1959 to attempt a near-by peak, Malubiting.

Tony went on no further expeditions in the following decade. It looked as if he had hung up his ice-axe forever but in 1976 he surprised everyone when at the age of 50 he returned to the Himalayas at the helm of a British army expedition. Twenty-four years after he had been tried out and rejected by the organisers of the 1953 Everest expedition, he led a very successful attempt which put two men on the summit. Like Norman Hardie, Tony Streather reached the age of 92 before he died in 2018.

Norman and Tony were of course the second pair to reach the summit of Kangchenjunga. The first team George Band and Joe Brown, unsurprisingly got more attention. At the time, they were both still very young and committed to climbing but it wasn't long before their lives took very different directions.

George Band spent the first year after Kangchenjunga lecturing and writing but in 1957 he got the 'proper job' his parents had always craved, joining Royal Dutch Shell as a petroleum engineer. For the next two years he worked hard but his moment of truth came at the end of the decade when he met a Texan millionaire who offered to fund his next major expedition. George wrote to his bosses asking for extended leave but they weren't keen, so he was forced to choose between his passion and his career. In the end the briefcase prevailed over the rucksack and he spent the next thirty years in the oil industry though he did continue to climb whenever he could. On retirement he devoted much of his time and energy to the Alpine Club and the Royal Geographical Society.

The other team members continued to be involved in the sport. John Jackson spent most of his life teaching outdoor pursuits. He made his last big ascent, Kilimanjaro, in 1990 aged 69. Tom Mackinnon became president of the Scottish Mountaineering Club and a keen yachtsman. John Clegg climbed in Wales with Joe Brown and later led expeditions for Aberdeen University. Neil Mather continued to climb in the UK as an active member of the Rucksack Club.

The climber whose life was probably most changed by Kangchenjunga was George's partner Joe Brown. When he left for the Himalayas in 1955, he was a twenty-four-year-old general builder who never had quite enough money to fund his climbing ambitions. Just twelve years later he was famous enough to write a well-regarded autobiography and was the owner of the first of what would become a small chain of climbing shops.

Joe's first big trip after Kangchenjunga was to the Mustagh Tower in the Karakoram, a 23,862 ft high obelisk shaped peak so unremittingly steep that it was thought impossible to climb. To add extra pressure, shortly after the small British team reached Pakistan in the spring of 1956 they heard news that a very strong party of French alpinists had also just arrived with their hearts set on the same goal. With the British team climbing from the west side and the French from the east, Joe and his partner Ian McNaught Davies found themselves taking huge risks on extremely difficult and exposed slopes. In the end, after some very difficult climbing, they reached the summit five days ahead of their rivals.

Back in Britain, Joe was invited to take part in the first of what would become a long series of television and film projects. He starred with George Band in a BBC documentary about climbing, which also included an appearance by the 80-year-old Geoffrey Winthrop Young. After making a memorably confident TV debut, Joe began working with Tom Stobart, the climbing cameraman who had been responsible for the 1953 Everest film. Over the following couple of years, they made adventure films in the Dolomites, Iran and Jordan while Joe also tried to hold down a job as a climbing instructor at an outdoor pursuits centre.

Then in the early 1960s a new kind of television appeared in which Joe would play a big role: the televised outside broadcast or OB. His first OB, an ascent of the Aiguille du Midi in the Alps, was organised by Eurovision, the European broadcasting organisation responsible for the famous song contest, and included climbers from all over the continent. It was successful enough for the BBC to commission a series of further outside broadcasts including Joe's famous ascent of Old Man of Hoy in 1967 which was watched by close to fifteen million viewers. Seventeen years later in 1984 Joe repeated the climb with his 17-year-old daughter Zoe, who was such a hit with viewers that she went on to become a children's TV presenter in her own right.

In between those televised visits to the Old Man of Hoy, Joe opened two climbing shops in Llanberis and Capel Curig in North Wales and started to manufacture climbing helmets and harnesses. His thriving business didn't stop him, however, from going on further mountaineering expeditions. In the 70s and 80s, he climbed all over the world from South America to Africa to the Himalayas and the Karakoram, and began a part-time career doing safety and stunt work for feature films. His filmography included the third *Rambo* movie, the James Bond film *A View to a Kill*, and he even doubled for Robert de Niro in the 1986 film *The Mission*.

Then in 1990, at the age of 60 Joe went on his last major expedition to Everest's neighbour Cho Oyu before finally deciding that it was time to retire from high altitude mountaineering. After that he continued to climb with friends but stuck to lower peaks in Wales and Europe. He died at his home in Llanberis in 2020, six weeks before the 65th anniversary of his historic climb.

Like the actor Albert Finney, who was born in Salford a few miles away from Joe's childhood home in Ardwick, Joe Brown came to prominence in the era of the working-class hero, the post war years when Britain's artistic and sporting centre of gravity moved northwards. The Beatles ruled the airwaves, Manchester United bossed the football pitch and climbers like Joe Brown and Don Whillans set new standards of rock climbing. Whereas Britain's Himalayan expeditions of the 1920s and 30s had been dominated by public school climbers from Oxbridge and the army, Joe helped open the door to a new generation who didn't let their background or their income get in the way of their ambition.

Kangchenjunga was a key moment in that revolution. When Charles Evans agreed to lead the expedition, he insisted on being given a free hand to choose his own team. His decision to invite Joe, in the face of some opposition from the climbing 'establishment', was generous and forward thinking. Though Charles was himself a public school Oxford educated middle-class professional, his outlook on life was down-to-earth and meritocratic. When it came to selecting the first summit pair, he had no doubt about choosing Joe and George Band, two climbers from contrasting backgrounds, because quite simply he thought them the best men for the job.

In the fifty years after the first ascent, 195 odd climbers reached the summit of Kangchenjunga, just a fraction of the number who climbed Everest in the same period. Today Kangchenjunga is slowly growing as a trekking destination but numbers are tiny when compared to basecamp treks to Annapurna and Everest. With attempts from the Sikkimese side currently banned, it's hard to imagine that Kangchenjunga will ever enjoy the same prominence that it had in the 1930s during the era of Bauer and Dyhrenfurth or the heady days of 1955 when it was front-page news all around the world.

It is difficult to know whether the Demon of Kangchenjunga is pleased to be left alone or would prefer a little more attention, but judging from past experience he or she probably prefers the former. If Kangchenjunga has not become the commercial escalator that Everest is today, perhaps its relative anonymity is not such a bad thing.

Afterword

En route to Kangchenjunga 2017

This book was written over the course of three years in which time I was assisted by numerous people. I'd like the thank all the librarians and archivists who helped me: first and foremost Glyn Hughes and Nigel Buckley at the Alpine Club,

Stefan Ritter at the German Alpine Club and Kelda Roe at the Mountain Heritage Trust.

I'd also like to thank all the friends who read the manuscript at various stages and helped me enormously. In particular I'm hugely grateful to Tim Jordan who as ever gave the book a really thorough and incisive read, but I'd also like to give my sincere thanks to John McAvoy, Steve Brookes, Jerry Lovatt and my son Frank Conefrey. I'd also like to thank Akshaya Mohan my copy editor and Chris Jennings who designed the book and helped me enormously to get it published. As ever, a big hand to Adam T. Burton for his lovely maps.

I'd like to say a particular thank you to the team members who graciously agreed to be interviewed. I talked to Joe Brown, Tony Streather and Denise Evans in 2017 and corresponded with Norman Hardie. I'd also like to say a big thank you to Denise for allowing me to use extracts from her husband Charles' diary and to Phil Streather, who helped me set up the interview with his father and gave me access to his personal archive.

I'd also like to thank Tom Briggs and the staff at Jagged Globe who organised my trek to Kangchenjunga and say a particular thanks to Rob Wymer our guide, our sirdar Kharma, Nara the cook and all the Sherpas and porters who made the trip so comfortable and well organised. A big hello to all of the party : Diana, Jerry, Sue, Edward, Alwyn, Ann, Kate, Edward, David, and the sadly deceased but much loved Ken and Bob.

Last but not least, as ever, my biggest thank you goes out to my children Frank and Phyllis who put up with me during the writing of this book and most especially my darling wife, Stella Bruzzi, who supported me wonderfully throughout. All my love.

Bibliography

Band, *Road to Rakaposhi*, Hodder and Stoughton, London, 1956

Boardman, Pete and Tasker, Joe, *The Boardman Tasker Omnibus*, Baton Wicks, London, 2012

Buffet, Charlie, *Jules Jacot-Guillarmod Pionnier Du K2*, Editions Slatkine, Geneva, 2012

Bauer, Paul, *Himalayan Campaign*, Blackwell, Oxford, 1937

Bauer, Paul, *Himalayan Quest*, Nicholson and Watson, London, 1938

Bauer, Paul, *Kanchenjunga Challenge*, Kimber, London, 1955

Braham, Trevor, *Himalayan Playground*, The In Pinn, Glasgow, 2008

Brown, Joe, *The Hard Years*, Gollancz, London, 1967

Crowley, Aleister, *The Confessions of Aleister Crowley*, Routledge and Kegan Paul, London, 1979

Crowley, Aleister, *The Spirit of Solitude*, Vol 2, Mandrake Press, London, 1929

Crowley, Aleister, *Diary of a Drug Fiend*, William Collins and Sons, London, 1922

Dyhrenfurth, Günter, *Die Internationale Himalaya-Expedition*, Werner Laurie, London, 1955

Dyhrenfurth, Günter, *To the Third Pole*, Werner Laurie, London, 1955

Dyhrenfurth, Hettie, *Memsahib im Himalaja*, Verlag Deutsche Buchwerkstatten, Leipzig 1931

Evans, Charles, *Kangchenjunga, the Untrodden Peak*, Hodder and Stoughton, London, 1955

Evans, Charles, *On Climbing*, Museum Press, London, 1956

Evans, Charles, *A Doctor in the XIVth Army*, Leo Cooper, London,1998

Franco, Jean (trans Denise Morin), *Makalu*, Jonathan Cape, London, 1957

Freshfield, Douglas, *Round Kangchenjunga*, Edward Arnold, London, 1903

Hardie, Norman, *In Highest Nepal*, Allen and Unwin, London 1957

Hardie, Norman, *On My Own Two Feet*, Canterbury University Press, Christchurch, 2006

Hobusch, Harald, *Mountain of Destiny*, Camden House, Rochester, 2016

Hooker, Joseph Dalton, *Himalayan Journals*, John Murray, London, 1854

Hunt, John, *Life is Meeting*, Hodder and Stoughton, London, 1978

Isserman, Maurice and Weaver, Stewart, *Fallen Giants*, Yale University Press, New Haven and London, 2008

Jacot-Guillarmod, Jules, *Six Mois dans l'Himalaya*, W. Sandoz, Neuchatel, 1904

Jackson, John Angelo, *More than Mountains*, Harrap, London., 1955

Jackson, John Angleo, *Adventure Travels in the Himalaya*, Indus, New Delhi, 2005

Kaczynski, Richard, *Perdubado,* North Atlantic Books, Berkeley, 2002

Kumar, Narinder, *Kangchenjunga. First ascent of the North East Spur*, East-West publications, London and the Hague, 1978

Pierse, Simon, *Kangchenjunga*, University of Wales, School of Art Press, 2005

Scott, Doug, *Himalayan Climber*, Baton Wicks, London, 1992

Smythe, Frank, *The Kangchenjunga Adventure*, Gollancz, London, 1930

Smythe, Frank, *The Spirit of the Hills*, Hodder and Stoughton, London, 1935

Smythe, Tony, *My Father Frank*, Baton Wicks, London, 2013

Symonds, John ,*The Great Beast 666,* Pindar Press, London 1977

Thompson, Simon, *Unjustifiable Risk*, Cicerone, Cumbria, 2010

Tucker, John, *Kangchenjunga*, Elek Books, London, 1955

Journals

The Alpine Journal, London:
Bauer, Paul, *The Fight for Kangchenjunga, 1929*, AJ42, 1930

Bauer, Paul, *Kangchenjunga 1931*, AJ44 , 1932

Braham, Trevor, *Kangchenjunga: The 1954 Reconnaissance*, 1996

Hunt, John, *Kangchenjunga Eastern Approaches*, 1996

Side, Douglas, *Towards Kangchenjunga*, AJ60, 1955

Smythe, Frank, *The Assault on Kangchenjunga*, AJ 42, 1930

The American Alpine Journal:
Dyhrenfurth, Norman, *What are the Chances of Climbing Kanchenjunga*, 1948

The Geographical Journal:
Freshfield, Douglas, *The Glaciers of Kangchenjunga*, Vol. 19, No. 4 Apr., 1902

Evans, Charles and Band, George, *Kangchenjunga Climbed*, Vol 122, 1956

The Himalayan Journal:
Bauer, Paul, *The German Attack on Kangchenjunga*, 1929, HJ2, 1930

Bauer, Paul, *The Fight for Kangchenjunga*, HJ 4, 1932

Braham, Trevor, *Kangchenjunga Reconnaissance 1954*, HJ 19

Dyhrenfurth, Günter, *The International Himalayan Expedition*, April 1931, vol III.

Hunt, John and Cook, C.R. *A Winter Visit to the Zemu Glacier*, HJ10, 1938

Longstaff, Tom, *In Memoriam Chettan*, HJ3, 1931

Machnik, Andrzej, *Kangchenjunga climbed in Winter*, HJ43, 1987

Smythe, Frank, *The Problem of Kangchenjunga*, HJ7, 1935

The Mountain World:
Band, George, *Kangchenjunga*, 1956/1957

Franco, Jean, *Makalu, The Happy Mountain*, 1956/1957

Principle Sources

Prologue:
For Douglas Freshfield see *Across Country from Thonon to Trent* for his early climbs, *Round Kangchenjunga* and various articles in the Alpine Journal and the Geographical Journal for his 1899 expedition, and *From a Tramp's Wallet* the biography of Douglas Freshfield by Hervey Fisher. For Vittorio Sella see *Splendid Hills, The Life and Photographs of Vittorio Sella* by Ronald Clarke plus various publications by the Sella Foundation. For the early pictorial history of Kangchenjunga see Simon Pierse's *Kangchenjunga*.

1: A Himalayan Beast
As might be imagined, the problem with the 1905 expedition is that there are widely conflicting versions of what actually happened. For Aleister Crowley's version of the story, see *The Confessions of Aleister Crowley*, his auto-hagiography and archival material within the Yorke collection at the

Warburg Institute in London. Also see John Symonds biography, *The Great Beast 666*, Richard Kaczynski's *Perdurabo* and for details of the 1902 K2 expedition, *The Ghosts of K2*. For Jacot-Guillarmod's version of events see his pamphlet *Au Kangchenjunga* (and the copy of this annotated by Aleister Crowley at the Warburg Institute) and Charlie Buffet's biography *Pioneer du K2*. For contemporary press coverage in the *Pioneer*, the *Journal de Lausanne* and the *Daily Mail*, including reports from Crowley, Jacot Guillarmod, Reymond and De Righi see the 1905 cuttings collection at the Alpine Club in London.

2. and 4. The Struggle for Kangchenjunga and Monsoon Story

For the story of Bauer's expeditions the principle English language sources are *Himalayan Campaign* and a slightly revised later version *Kangchenjunga Challenge*, plus the articles written by Bauer in 1930 and 1932 for the Alpine Journal and the Himalayan Journal and his *Himalayan Quest*. See also contemporary press coverage in the *Times*. For biographical material about Bauer see files held at the German Alpine Club. For background on Bauer and German mountaineering of the period, see Harald Hobusch's *Mountain of Destiny* and Lee Holdt's Phd thesis *Mountains, Mountaineering and Modernity: A cultural history of German and Austrian Mountaineering 1900-1945*.

3. A Mountain God

For the 1930 expedition the principle sources are Frank Smythe's *The Kangchenjunga Adventure*, Hettie Dyhrenfurth's *Memsahb im Himalaja* and Günter Dyhrenfurth's *To the Third*

Pole and *Die Internationale Himalaya Expedition 1930*. Also articles in the Alpine Journal and Himalayan Journal by Smythe, Dyhrenfurth and Wood Johnson plus comprehensive coverage in the Times. For biographical details of Dyhrenfurth before and after the 1930 expedition, see files at the German Alpine Club; for biographical details of Frank Smythe, see Tony Smythe's *My Father Frank*.

5. The Sport of Imbeciles

For the 'Golden Age of Himalayan Climbing', Isserman and Weaver's *Fallen Giants* is a good general introduction plus monographs by Maurice Herzog, John Hunt, and *Everest 1953*. For John Kempe's expedition, see articles in the Alpine Journal, John Kempe's diary at the Alpine Club archive, and John Jackson's More than Mountains, John Tucker's *Kangchenjunga* and Trevor Braham's *Himalayan Playground*.

6-11 The 1955 Reconnaissance

My principle sources for the 1955 British expedition were Charles Evans' *Kangchenjunga, the Untrodden Peak*, plus the diaries of Charles Evans, George Band, Neil Mather and John Clegg and interviews conducted in 2017 with Joe Brown, Tony Streather, Denise Evans and correspondence with Norman Hardie. I also consulted further archival material in the Alpine Club and Mountain Heritage Trust and articles written after the expedition by Charles Evans and George Band in the Alpine Journal, the Himalayan Journal, Mountain World and Sports Illustrated. Again the *Times* provided comprehensive coverage of the expedition throughout. For individual biographical detail see Charles Evans *A Doctor in the XIVth Army* and the missing chapter *Darjeeling and Beyond* later published in the Alpine Journal, Norman Hardie's *On My Own Two Feet*, John Jackson's *Adventure Travels in the Himalaya* and Joe Brown's *The Hard Years*. For details of the Makalu expedition, see Jean Franco's *Makalu* and articles in the Himalayan Journal and Mountain World.

12. And Then

For a good concise history of expeditions post 1955 see Jose Luis Bermudez's *Climbing on Kangchenjunga since 1955* in the Alpine Journal plus further articles in the AJ by Doug Scott, Trevor Braham, Ginette Harrison and George Band. For biographical details of the 1955 team, see list of sources in 6-11 plus Tony Streather's *Valedictory Address to the Alpine Club* in 1992 and various obituaries in the AJ. For details of the Indian expedition of 1977 see Narinder Kumar's *Kangchenjunga, First Ascent of the North East Spur*.

Index

Aiguille du Midi 298
Allwein, Eugene 52, 55, 64, 67-73, 120, 123, 125, 129-137
Annapurna 145, 162, 180, 198, 201, 268, 300
Aufschnaiter, Peter 70-72, 74, 120, 134,

Band, George 1, 163-281, 296
Bauer, Paul 2, 45, 49-76, 78, 81, 82-116 passim, 118-141, 146, 147, 153, 239, 246, 259, 284, 290-292
Beghin, Pierre 286
Beigel, Ernst 52, 67-75, 120
Boardman, Pete 285
Bourdillon, Tom 157-159, 163, 165, 208, 212,
Bridge, Alf 167, 182
Bruce, Charles 85, 87
Brown, Joe 1, 163-281, 297-299
Brown, Val 266, 277

Clegg, John 168 - 249
Caucusus, The 6, 51, 52, 58, 59
Chand, Prem 285

Changjup, 221, 225, 260, 268, 278-279
Chettan 106-113
Couzy, Jean 200, 214, 275,
Crowley, Aleister 13-44, 60, 52-140 passim, 147-152, 239, 287-289

Darjeeling 4, 20, 55
De Righi, Alcesti Rigo 21, 34, 35-42
Dorje, Naik Nima 285
Dorje, Pemi 222, 240, 241, 244, 258- 269
Dych Tau, 51
Dyhrenfurth, Günther 2, 82-116, 119, 121, 122, 140, 146, 153, 285, 291, 292, 293, 300
Dyhrenfurth, Hettie 82, 83, 86, 88, 89, 107, 110, 114, 115, 292
Dyhrenfurth Norman 147

Eckenstein, Oscar 16, 17, 19, 28, 43, 287
Elbrus 6
Evans, Charles 155-281, 292-295
Everest 3, 44, 53

Farmer, E.E. 77-81, 83, 84, 91, 94, 100, 118, 151, 180, 185
Franco, Jean 199-200, 211-212, 224, 238, 246,
Freshfield, Douglas 5-9, 14, 16, 17,19, 20, 51, 58, 59, 60, 62, 64, 88, 92, 96, 98, 281, 285

Ghunsa 9
Graham, William Woodman 5
Green Lake 59

Habeler, Peter 285
Hardie, Norman 163-281, 295
Harrison, Ginette 286
Hartmann, Hans. 120, 123, 126, 127, 131, 135, 136
Henderson, Jill 150, 171, 179, 192, 265, 275,

Index

Herbert, Edwin 169, 185
Herzog, Maurice 145-146, 180, 198,
Hillary, Ed 31, 146, 154-156, 157, 159, 163, 166,
　198, 199, 229, 235, 238, 244, 247, 250, 253, 259,
　267, 271, 281, 295,
Hoerlin, Hermann 83, 86, 88, 105- 107, 111
Hooker, Joseph 5
Hunt, John 149-156, 159, 160, 169, 178

Jackson, John 163-281, 295
Jackson, Peter 274
Jackson, Ron 150, 153,
Jacot-Guillarmod, Jules 13-44, 56,57, 63, 87, 91,
　128, 147, 190, 196, 204, 289, 290
Jonsong Peak 112

K2 3, 4, 16-26, 28, 42, 43, 78, 115, 146, 173, 255,
　256, 258-259, 268, 276, 284, 286, 289, 290, 293

Kamthang 112
Keddar 70, 72, 73
Kempe, John 148-156, 171, 185, 189, 193, 194, 195,
　201
Knowles, Guy 17
Kraus, Karl Von 55, 64, 67-73, 120
Kukuczka, Jerzy 286
Kumar, Narinder 285

La, Laden 56
Lachen 57- 59, 74, 121, 123
Lachenal, Louis 145-146
Lear, Edward 3
Lewis, Gilmour 147- 148, 150-154,
Lobsang (1929-1930) 79, 80, 81, 91,
Lobsang (1945) 79

Mackinnon, Tom 163-281, 285
Makalu 9, 150, 198-200, 211, 214, 224, 238, 246,
　248, 251, 259, 261, 270, 271, 272, 275

Mather, Neil 163-281, 265
Matterhorn 51
McFarlane, Jim 155
Messner, Reinhold 285
Mont Blanc 6
Monte Rosa 51
Morin, Denise 294
Muller, Gustav 47
Mummery, A.F. 7, 163, 213

Nanga Parbat 7, 32, 54, 139, 140, 141, 146,
Nansen, Fridtjof 147
Norgay, Tenzing 148, 157, 171, 180, 275, 276
Nursang 57

Old Man of Hoy 298

Pache, Alexis 23, 34, 35-40
Pamirs, The 52
Pasang (1929) 70, 72, 73
Pasang (1931) 126-128, 130, 137
Pasang II (1931) 132-133
Pugh, Griffith 167

Ramzana 21, 36
Reymond, Charles Aldolphe 23, 30, 34, 35-40
Rungneet 150, 171, 175, 179, 192, 275
Ruskin, John 3
Rustomji 174
Rutkiewicz, Wanda 286

Salama 21, 33
Schaller, Hermann 120, 126- 130, 137, 247, 284
Schneider, Erwin 84, 88, 105- 110
Scott, Doug 285-286
Sella, Vittorio 6, 16
Shebbeare, Edward 66, 68
Siniolchu 60, 63, 71, 141
Smythe, Frank 84-140, 151, 285

Index

Streather, 163-281, 295-296
Strutt, Edward
Subhana, 21
Schlagintweits 5, 51

Talung Peak. 60, 153, 193, 252
Tasker, Joe 286
Tenzing, Dawa 156 – 281, 295
Terray, Lionel 200, 214
Thoenes, Alexander 70, 73, 74
Thondup 179, 182, 207, 265, 273,
Tilman, Bill 162, 201
Tobin, Lt-Col Harry 56, 66, 84, 89, 90, 100, 104, 105
Tseram 27

Urkien 272

Whillans, Don 164-165
Wieland, Uli 83, 88, 105, 107, 110, 111
Wielicki, Krysztof 286
Wien, Karl 126, 127, 130, 135-136
Winthrop Young, Geoffrey 298

Younghusband, Francis 113,

www.ingramcontent.com/pod-product-compliance
Lightning Source LLC
Chambersburg PA
CBHW070039230426
43661CB00034B/1438/J